Royal Racing

Royal Racing

The Queen and Queen Mother's Sporting Life

SEAN SMITH

First published in 2001 by BBC Worldwide Limited
80 Wood Lane
London W12 0TT
Copyright © Sean Smith 2001
The moral right of the author has been asserted

ISBN 0 563 53807 4

Commissioning Editor: Ben Dunn
Project Editor: Rachel Copus
Copy Editor: Tessa Clark
Designer: Paul Vater
Picture Researcher: Susannah Parker

Set in Garamond and Helvetica
Printed and bound by Imprimerie Pollina s.a. - n° L 81741
Colour separations by Kestrel Digital Colour, Chelmsford
Jacket printed by Imprimerie Pollina s.a.

Author's note: Her Majesty Queen Elizabeth the Queen Mother is officially called
Queen Elizabeth by those who work with her and by the world of racing. I have followed that courtesy.

Contents

❧ Introduction

The Epsom Downs, bathed in brilliant sunshine, were a kaleidoscope of colour. There is no sight in racing, perhaps in all of sport, to match the view to Tattenham Corner on Derby Day. Looking past the bookies' boards, the funfairs and the open-top buses full of merry day-trippers you strain your eyes to pick out the colours of 'your' horse as the whole field merges into one giant canvas thundering towards the straight. It was 1979, the 200th Derby and, back then, held on a Wednesday. The colours I was searching for were the most famous in the game – purple, scarlet sleeves, black cap with a gold fringe. Lester Piggott was wearing them on the Queen's well-fancied colt Milford. It all happened so quickly. One moment the royal silks were well to the fore and then this magnificent horse stormed down the centre of the course and all eyes were turned to watch Troy, stable companion of Milford and the chosen mount of Willie Carson, win by seven lengths. Milford was nowhere.

Researching *Royal Racing* brought it all back. How stupid of me to go against the selected mount of Willie Carson. He was, after all, the stable jockey and was not going to pass up his first Derby winner for reasons of sentiment. When I mentioned to him that I had backed Milford in that particular Derby, I had the distinct impression he thought me an idiot. It was a lesson well learnt. Horses do not run any faster because of the colours they are wearing and there is absolutely no room for sentiment when it comes to backing them. My theory was that the Queen winning the 200th Derby was such a good story that I could imagine the headlines in the newspapers the following morning: 'A Right Royal Victory – Lester wins Derby for the Queen' … 'Majestic Milford. Well done Ma'am.' It is a curious fact of journalism that normally talented and sensible writers dust off their copies of the Ladybird Book of Clichés to find all manner of obsequious phrases for use in royal stories. I was determined not to follow suit with *Royal Racing*. There has always been quite enough flunkyism in the sport without me adding to it.

In 1999, when I first began investigating the racing careers of the Queen and Queen Elizabeth the Queen Mother, I had absolutely no idea that it was all of 50 years since they had begun by co-owning a steeplechaser called Monaveen. That brave horse became their first winner and then, alas, the first of many disappointments when he was killed in a fall. Monaveen provided both the elation and despair that everyone involved with racing feels at some time or another. As I uncovered the triumphs and disasters of half a century of racing, I became more aware that this is not just a sport, it is a way of life. A racing stable is not a place of work, it is a community. We are not talking here of 90 frenetic minutes on a Saturday afternoon followed by a lengthy session in the bar. It is a round-the-clock commitment.

Between them the Queen and the Queen Mother have had more than 1000 winners since Monaveen. I quickly abandoned plans to run through them race by race. There is nothing more boring than a chronicle of victories. It became clear to me early on that this was a story full of the most wonderful characters, human and equine, and that by using the royal involvement as my point of reference I could build up a portrait that reflected racing as a whole through the majority of the twentieth century. This book, therefore, is, I hope, not an account of what the two famous royal owners have given racing. It is a tribute to racing itself and what it has given them.

Part One, Traditional Values, sets the scene and reveals how her family's involvement in racing led to the sport becoming the Queen's principal diversion in life. I decided to begin with Persimmon, Derby winner of 1896 for the Prince of Wales, later Edward VII. I was much taken with the statue of the great horse which stands outside the entrance to the Royal Stud at Sandringham in Norfolk. It is a tranquil, rural setting where one can imagine time standing still. Persimmon was homebred and the most important aspect of the Royal Family's involvement in racing is the emphasis on breeding their own winners. The Queen's devotion to horses from an early age has led to an expertise in all areas of the sport, but particularly in breeding. Ian Balding, her trainer for 35 years, says she is a complete natural where horses are concerned and unquestionably could herself have been a trainer.

In Part Two, Fairlawne, I describe the remarkable world of Queen Elizabeth's first trainer, Major Peter Cazalet. The saga of this country house in Kent would have made a fascinating book on its own. I felt as if I had stumbled on some sort of *Upstairs, Downstairs* epic in which luminaries such as Elizabeth Taylor, Noel Coward and Winston Churchill drifted in and out of the story. Most fascinating of all was the discovery that Peter Cazalet's first wife was Leonora Wodehouse, stepdaughter of the novelist P.G. Wodehouse. Their son Edward is a great Wodehouse enthusiast, something he shares with the Queen Mother.

In the halcyon days of the Fairlawne stable during the Fifties, the world of National Hunt racing was far less competitive than it is today and to a great extent the royal patronage helped bring the sport to public attention. The story of the horses is just as colourful as that of the people involved. Everyone knows about Devon Loch's famous Grand National disaster but I was particularly intrigued by the doping of Laffy, another of Queen Elizabeth's excellent steeplechasers. It is an absorbing tale of skulduggery.

If life at Fairlawne paints a picture of a bygone age then so, in person, does Captain Cecil Boyd-Rochfort, trainer to both George VI and the Queen. According to his stepson, the champion trainer Henry Cecil, the Captain was very much an Edwardian gentleman. His story and that of his famous yard, Freemason Lodge, is told in Part Three, A Golden Age. At 6 feet 4 inches tall the Captain loomed large over the world of racing for most of the twentieth century. He trained Aureole to finish second in the royal colours in the Coronation year Derby of 1953, the nearest the Queen has ever come to winning the greatest classic. Like Major Cazalet, he could be very fierce on occasion but inspired tremendous loyalty in his staff. Henry Cecil told me some marvellously entertaining stories of the eccentric and chaotic life at Freemason Lodge. I particularly enjoyed his account of how he had to tell the Captain at breakfast one morning that on the previous night he had driven the family limousine into the front room of someone's cottage. The Captain, apparently, took it very well.

After the death of Peter Cazalet, Queen Elizabeth transferred her horses to the Lambourn stables of Fulke Walwyn, who many consider the finest ever trainer of steeplechasers. These were the years of the Queen Mother's most notable successes including the unforgettable victories of Special Cargo in the Whitbread Gold Cup and Tammuz in the Schweppes Gold Trophy. The story of these great races comes to life in Part Four, A Special Place. It also recounts the death of Game Spirit, her favourite horse, when he collapsed and died following a race at Newbury. On a lighter note, the tale of Special Cargo and the boot polish is one of the best racing stories I have come across.

The story of *Royal Racing* manages to stir almost every emotion. That is clearly in evidence in Part Five, Celebrations and Controversy, which records the joyful classic successes of Highclere and Dunfermline, the tragic accidents of Magna Carta and Special Leave, and the anger stirred by the controversial sacking of Major Dick Hern as royal trainer. The Major gave me a lovely lunch at his home

Opposite: Troy [Willie Carson] routs the Derby field, including the Queen's Milford, at Epsom, 6 June 1979.

Royal Racing

in West Ilsley in Berkshire but when I asked him about the circumstances of the end of his contract he diplomatically told me, 'I need prior notice of that question.' Fortunately Ian Balding, Willie Carson and Lord Oaksey were willing to share their recollections and opinions on the most controversial episode in the whole of *Royal Racing*. The story speaks for itself and does not require any further comment from me.

Part Six, A Thousand Winners, brings the story up to date with the celebrations for Queen Elizabeth's 400th winner, an otherwise undistinguished animal called Nearco Bay. In the last two or three years the fortunes of the Queen seem to have taken a marked turn for the better. Her best horses are now with Sir Michael Stoute, back at Freemason Lodge. Bruce Hobbs, the distinguished trainer and former assistant to Captain Boyd-Rochfort, believes she is enjoying greater success again because her horses are not being aimed too high. At the end of the book I offer some reflections on the racing careers of the Queen and her mother and what their patronage means for the sport. I hope my conclusions are thought-provoking.

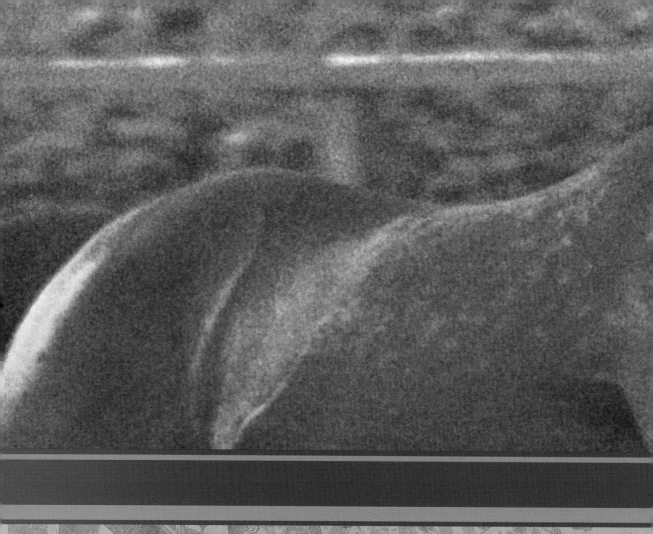

✺ Part One

Traditional Values

On her first visit to a racing stables Princess Elizabeth joined her mother and father to cast an eye over the royal horses at the famous Beckhampton stables of Fred Darling. The 16-year-old Princess was allowed to run her hand over the powerful frame of Big Game, recent winner of the 2000 Guineas. She later confessed to not washing her hands for the rest of the day, so awe-inspiring was the occasion.

❦ Persimmon and the Social Whirl

Across the road from the big house stands a statue of the great Persimmon, Derby winner of 1896 and proud custodian of the entrance to the Royal Stud at Sandringham in Norfolk. The statue was presented by the Jockey Club to Edward VII in honour of his favourite colt. Sadly, it all too soon became a memorial after the Stud's greatest foal slipped in his box, aged 15, and fractured his pelvis. All subsequent efforts to save him, which included suspending him in slings, failed and eventually and inevitably he was put down. Nevertheless, Persimmon standing imperiously on a manicured lawn remains a symbol of royal success in racing. More than that, he shows how one good horse and a famous victory can transform years of disappointments almost at a stroke. And yet the spectre of unexpected death is one all racing owners have to bear, and one which the Queen and Queen Elizabeth the Queen Mother met with their very first horse, Monaveen.

In 1864, more than 30 years before Persimmon's Derby, the then Prince of Wales was elected to the Jockey Club even though at the time he had yet to start owning thoroughbreds himself. His mother, Queen Victoria, had re-established a Royal Stud at Hampton Court and achieved enormous success. Like our present queen, she was a more than able rider and a sound judge of a horse. She loved a day at the races in the happy times when Prince Albert was alive, and was not afraid to register her excitement at a close finish. While watching the New Stakes at Ascot in 1861 she famously failed to notice that a window previously open had been shut and broke the glass with her head. After the death of her beloved Albert in December of that year Victoria, condemned to a lifetime of mourning, never set foot on a racecourse again.

During his long apprenticeship as heir to the throne the Prince of Wales enjoyed the traditional trappings of a royal heritage, a world of garden parties, banquets and balls, and the Turf. His biographer, Sir Sidney Lee, observed, 'He loved a good race meeting, a good dinner and a good game of bridge.' After his election to the Jockey Club at the age of 22 the Prince was unswerving in his support of racing. Newmarket, Epsom, Doncaster, Ascot and Goodwood would always receive an annual royal visit. He also patronized smaller racecourses including Sandown Park, then a minor track holding regimental races, a tradition followed by Queen Elizabeth who still regards the Grand Military Meeting at the Esher course in early March as her favourite racing occasion

Opposite: The statue of the great Persimmon guards the entrance to the Royal Stud at Sandringham.

of the year. The Prince of Wales provided ample evidence of how easy it was to build a life around the world of racing. In those late Victorian days it was not a case of just dropping in for an afternoon's entertainment. Each big race would involve a week of grand socializing. The Prince would stay with Lord Stafford for the St Leger at Doncaster, with Lord Sefton for the Grand National, the Duke of Richmond for Goodwood, with Leopold de Rothschild at Newmarket and with the Duke of Westminster at Eaton Hall for the Chester Races. 'Bertie' was immensely popular.

This was a life of social whirl. Some of the Prince's annual jaunts, August yachting at Cowes for example, remain popular with today's Royal Family. Others, like three weeks on the Riviera in spring or visits to Wiesbaden spa in autumn, have not found subsequent favour. He wholeheartedly embraced the racing milieu, treating it like a large gentlemen's club of which he was honorary chairman. In fact, he founded his own establishment, the Marlborough Club, at 52 Pall Mall in protest at the restrictions on smoking imposed on him by White's Club.

His racing cronies were much to the fore in the membership of the Marlborough. Among them was Henry Chaplin, who won the Derby in 1867 with Hermit but who is much better remembered for his involvement in one of the greatest of Victorian love scandals. His fiancée, Lady Florence Paget, the 'pocket Venus', eloped with the rakish aristocrat the Marquis of Hastings just a few days before

Mares and foals in the paddocks at the Royal Stud, Sandringham.

the wedding. The ill-fated Hastings subsequently lost £120,000 in bets on Hermit's Derby, a ruinous form of comeuppance. He died the following year, crippled by debt, a puppet of unscrupulous Victorian bookmakers. Shortly before he died, aged 26, he reputedly declared, 'Hermit's Derby broke my heart. But I didn't show it.' The more popular and socially acceptable Chaplin received a great deal of public sympathy, became Minister of Agriculture, a steward of the Jockey Club and, in 1916, a peer of the realm. Hermit, the instrument of his revenge,

ironically died at the same age as Hastings. Chaplin sent a hoof as a memento to his friend the Prince of Wales who used it as a much treasured inkstand.

Bringing in the mares and foals in late afternoon.

The Prince became increasingly absorbed with racing in middle age, rather like Queen Elizabeth the Queen Mother. He was won over by what he himself so memorably described as the 'glorious uncertainty' of the sport. Triumph and despair, the two essential ingredients for a lifetime's addiction to racing, were ever present. He took the plunge into ownership registering the royal colours, so familiar now, of purple, gold braid, scarlet sleeves, black velvet cap with a gold fringe in 1875. They were first seen at the Newmarket July meeting in 1877, when his Arab horse Alep raced in a match over four miles against another Arab – the grey, Avowal – owned by Lord Strathnairn. Starting at the prohibitive odds of 4/9 on, the Prince's charge finished second, beaten by a resounding 30 lengths. It was an early signal that royal runners are always apt to carry far too much of the public's money. The Prince himself was never averse to a bet even when money was tight.

Despite an association with the legendary trainer John Porter at Kingsclere, the Hampshire stables from where Ian Balding has dispatched so many royal

John Porter, legendary
master of Kingsclere.

runners in recent years, and advice from his friend Lord Marcus Beresford, the Prince's early forays were disappointing. Lord Marcus, however, was instrumental in persuading him to establish a stud at Sandringham in 1887. Although John Porter had achieved little success as a trainer for the Prince, it was he who bought the mare Perdita II for £900. Edward was later to calculate that purchasing her brought him a return of a quarter of a million pounds within a 20-year period. The matching of Perdita with the sire St Simon proved outstanding and in six glorious years, between 1891 and 1897, she produced Florizel II, the great Persimmon and the almost equally splendid Diamond Jubilee, foaled 60 years after the Prince's mother had ascended to the throne in 1837.

In many years of racing the Prince had displayed one of the great attributes of both the present Queen and the Queen Mother, namely the quality of patience. He wrote to his friend Henry Chaplin in 1890, 'I still hope with patience to win one or more of the classic races with a horse bred by myself.' A change of trainers coincided with much-longed-for success. Porter, despite his legendary status, had managed to win just 18 races in six seasons for the Prince and the string was transferred to the stables of Richard Marsh in Newmarket in 1892. It was not entirely with Porter's wholehearted agreement. He later described the incident as an 'old sore'. The late Arthur Fitzgerald, historian of the Royal Studs, lays the blame firmly on a personality clash between the solemn and steady Porter and the more extrovert Lord Marcus, who enjoyed the title of 'racing manager'. Fitzgerald believes Porter, the greatest trainer of his day, would not have wished to take high-handed orders from the autocratic peer. It is a clash eerily prescient of the greatest controversy of the Queen's racing career – the sacking of trainer Dick Hern and the role played in it by her racing manager, Lord Carnarvon. For Lord Marcus Beresford's part, not one of the brood mares he bought for Sandringham produced a classic winner.

Royal Racing

Marsh was an altogether more stylish character than Porter. His Egerton House stables spared no expense in catering for the thoroughbreds of royalty and the aristocracy. The charming and courteous Marsh liked to do things on a grand scale, which probably explains why he left an estate worth just £383 when he died. Florizel II started the ball rolling in style, winning good-class staying races including the Goodwood Cup and the Gold Vase at Royal Ascot, as a four-year-old. When he was retired at five to take up stallion duties at Sandringham, Persimmon was ready to fly the royal flag.

From the beginning Persimmon was earmarked to be a star. Richard Marsh wrote, 'I must say I have never set eyes on a more beautiful foal.' After the horse's first serious gallop as a two-year-old Lord Marcus remarked, 'This is the first time, and it may be the only time, we shall have a chance of a Derby horse.' And so it was to prove, with the royal colours prevailing at Epsom by a hard-fought neck from 2000 Guineas winner St Frusquin. Jockey Jack Watts brought Persimmon through to lead in the last 100 yards amid a crescendo of cheers and hats thrown into the air. It was an early indication that a royal victory was somehow a shared victory and everyone present could take some pleasure from the occasion.

Persimmon went from strength to strength and after cantering away with the St Leger he emerged the next season as an imposing four-year-old and romped home in the Gold Cup at Ascot by eight lengths. Just as important as his racecourse successes was his impact as the top stallion at Sandringham. He was champion sire four times before his untimely death. Perhaps his best-known progeny was the magnificent filly Sceptre, who won four classics in 1902. The Queen's talented colt Doutelle, who excelled himself to beat the champion colt Ballymoss at Chester in 1958, was a direct descendant of the great sire and proved himself a chip off the old block as a stallion until he too met with an untimely fatal accident.

Lord Marcus's opinion that Persimmon might be the Prince's only chance of Derby glory was wide of the mark for in Diamond Jubilee, an ill-tempered colt who once bit the thumb off the lad saddling him, Edward had a horse who would win the much coveted and rarely achieved Triple Crown of 2000 Guineas, Derby and St Leger. Amazingly, in the same year of 1900, he had already watched his horse Ambush II take the Grand National. Thanks to Diamond Jubilee, the Prince was leading owner for the first time with winnings

Part One ❧ Traditional Values

Hats off for a royal winner! The Prince of Wales (Edward VII) leads in Persimmon [Jack Watts] after his triumph in the 1896 Derby.

of £19,585. It was a dream year that no owner has enjoyed since. Sentiment, however, was put aside when he sold Diamond Jubilee for the very fine sum of £31,500 to an Argentine horse-dealer.

As is typical of racing, the exploits of Persimmon and Diamond Jubilee proved the gateway to several years of disappointment and failure. The famous patience Edward had exercised as Prince of Wales was needed just as much when he was King. In 1905 he even took the step of writing to his trainer, 'We have a number of bad horses, Marsh. I consider it my duty as your first master, to get rid of these animals to save your reputation of trainer.' Fortunately this initiative coincided with the King leasing six horses from Colonel William Hall Walker's Tully Stud which was the forerunner of the National Stud. They included Minoru, leased as a yearling in 1907.

No reigning sovereign had ever owned a Derby winner. But in 1909, thanks in no small part to the skill of jockey Herbert Jones, the King's colt prevailed by the shortest of short heads. In the days before the photo finish it would have been a very brave judge indeed who called a verdict against a royal

Minoru [Herbert Jones], the 1909 Derby winner, is inspected (from right to left) by Edward VII, Lord Marcus Beresford and trainer Richard Marsh.

Derby winner. Amid unprecedented scenes of joy, the King led in Minoru while the crowd struck up cries of 'Good old Teddy' and many well-wishers slapped him on the back. Once again it was a victory shared and one reflecting the popularity of the King. If fortune ever smiled on the Queen and she achieved her ambition of owning the Derby winner one cannot imagine cries of 'Good old Lizzie' from the Silver Ring.

The King died the following May after receiving news that his two-year-old Witch of the Air had won the Spring Plate at Kempton Park. 'I am very glad,' he said, before lapsing into a coma from which he never awoke.

Edward VII set many of the standards and traditions which royal racing followed throughout the twentieth century. A sense of the fun of it all, patience through lean times, generosity in both victory and defeat. The Royal Studs at Sandringham and nearby Wolferton, which have been so important in the racing activities of both the Queen and Queen Elizabeth the Queen Mother, began to flourish under his patronage. With such a rock-solid family foundation, the devotion to racing of subsequent royal generations is more easily understood.

Taking the Limelight

After lunch on Sundays, George V would walk over to the stables at Sandringham and have a word and an encouraging pat for the many yearlings and mares at the stud. On occasions he would indulge his favourite granddaughter, the future Elizabeth II but now merely 'sweet little Lilibet', and allow her to accompany him. Past the inspiring statue of Persimmon, the young Princess would be introduced to the foals, perhaps to the stallion Limelight and certainly to the mare Scuttle, who was always afforded a certain gravitas as the one and only classic winner for the King. In 25 years at the helm of the royal racing empire George V had just the 1000 Guineas of 1928 to show for all his classic endeavours. He was a singularly luckless owner.

Despite some initial concerns that he might not follow his father's devotion to the Turf, George V proved an enthusiastic follower and in the eyes of many experts, including the royal trainer Richard Marsh, a far greater judge of horseflesh than Edward VII. He was not, however, such a good judge of a wager. On his 20th birthday Queen Victoria sent him a stern warning, 'As for betting or anything of that kind, no end of young and older men have been ruined, parents' hearts broken and great names and titles dragged in the dirt.' Perhaps heeding that advice, George V was a desultory punter who, according to biographer Kenneth Rose, 'clung to the comforting illusion that his winnings were copious enough to subsidise his stamp collection'. Buoyed by the success of Scuttle in the Guineas, he had a sizeable bet on her in the Oaks at Epsom but she was comprehensively outstayed by Lord Derby's Toboggan. The King wrote in his diary, 'It was a great disappointment to me, there was no excuse; perhaps she didn't like coming down the hill. We returned wiser but certainly poorer.' He was not, however, as poor as his brother-in-law Prince Francis of Teck who lost £10,000 on a single race at the Curragh in Ireland and had to be bailed out by the King.

For the cover of his biography of George V, Kenneth Rose was given permission by Queen Elizabeth the Queen Mother to reproduce a painting by Walter Sickert of the King and his racing manager, Major Fetherstonhaugh, watching the 1927 Grand National. They cut a pair of glum bowler-hatted figures. 'You can tell they didn't back the winner,' Queen Elizabeth observed to Rose.

The exploits of Persimmon and Diamond Jubilee meant that the new King inherited a financially very healthy racing business. He cherished the Sandringham estate, which his father had bought for £220,000 in 1862 and subsequently renovated and restored. In particular, he loved shooting, perhaps even more than racing which must have tried his patience. In 1913 he attended the Derby at Epsom and witnessed the tragedy when the young suffragette Emily Davison dashed on to the course as the field thundered round Tattenham Corner and brought down, perhaps deliberately, his horse Anmer, a 50/1 outsider. She suffered a fractured skull and died in hospital a few days later. Amazingly the horse was unhurt and the jockey, Herbert Jones, escaped with a severe shaking. In his diary the King described it as 'a most disastrous Derby'. The incident was captured on an early newsreel and remains a poignant reminder of the powerful feelings evoked by women's suffrage. Some racing historians have literally got on their high horse to describe the dead woman as a 'misguided' soul who knew nothing of racing. It is typical of a certain insular arrogance in horse-racing which, fortunately, the sport's royal patrons have always eschewed. Perhaps it is in the breeding. Intriguingly, Queen Elizabeth the Queen Mother was friendly as a young girl with Thelma Cazalet, sister of Peter Cazalet who would train her horses for more than 20 years. Thelma would subsequently champion feminist causes as a Member of Parliament.

Just like his father, George V was a generous winner. On the morning of Scuttle's triumph in the Guineas he was riding on Newmarket Heath and sent for his big-race jockey, Joe Childs, to canvass his opinion on the filly's chances. The King had with him a cane ornamented with red and blue enamel. He told Childs, 'If you win the race for me I will present you with this cane.' The jockey earned his gift, not least by persuading the excitable Scuttle to jump off only a length or two behind the rest of the field. She came through strongly to win by half a length. Afterwards an exhausted Childs admitted, 'It was the toughest race I ever experienced. The strain was severe. It was not so much the actual race but the terribly anxious time I had at the starting gate that took a tremendous lot out of me.' The King made his own way to the weighing room to congratulate his jockey. 'It was a fine race. Thank you,' he said, shaking Childs's hand. The cane was dispatched as promised and became the jockey's most cherished memento. In his diary that evening the King wrote, 'I am very proud to win my first Classic and that I bred her at Sandringham. She is certainly a game little filly.' The extra ingredient in the triumph is undoubtedly the fact that Scuttle was homebred. The great family pride in the

Royal Stud was an early and powerful influence on the racing ambitions of George V's granddaughter.

Despite his comparative lack of big-race success, the King was a keen devotee of the social element of the sport. He followed his father's tradition of giving a Derby Day dinner at Buckingham Palace for members of the Jockey Club. For Royal Ascot there would be a house party at Windsor. If he had a winner during the week each lady at dinner would receive a brooch bearing the royal colours of purple, scarlet and gold. Victories at Ascot have always given the greatest pleasure to the Royal Family and continue to do so for the present Queen. The colt Limelight's thrilling victory in the 1933 Hardwicke Stakes under another patient ride from Joe Childs was, after Scuttle, the finest victory of George V's reign. Queen Mary was quite overcome. After the race and the congratulations Childs was summoned to the royal box where she told him, 'Do you know it was I who patted you on the back in the enclosure. I could not help it. I was so excited!' The delighted jockey replied, 'It was the greatest honour I ever had in my life.' It would be quite wrong to assume that royal owners remain unmoved by the thrills of racing, even though they do usually tend to keep their delight under control. Edward VII once admonished a racehorse owner who was bending the royal ear with tales of equine misfortune: 'To be neither unduly elated by success nor dismayed by reverses has always been considered the first attribute of a good sportsman.'

The mare Scuttle failed to produce a legacy for future generations at Sandringham to enjoy. She died giving birth to her fourth foal. The most important new arrival at the stud during the stewardship of George V was the mare Feola, purchased at the Newmarket July Sales of 1934 by the King's racing manager, Brigadier Henry 'Mouse' Tomkinson. It was 3000 guineas well spent. She was to become the grand dam of the Queen's fine colt Aureole, and founding mare of influential dynasties all over the world.

George V had an enormous influence on his favourite granddaughter's lifelong passion for horses, not just communicating the thrill of racing but also instilling the virtues of patience and expertise that have so marked her attitude towards the sport. She would sit next to him in a highchair at breakfast and listen most attentively while he talked very seriously about horses and sportsmanship. He was always happy to indulge her. On one famous

Opposite: Only the weather changes at Royal Ascot. *Above* George V and Queen Mary enjoy the sun in 1925, while *below* the Queen and Queen Mother keep smiling in the rain during the carriage parade down the course in 1997.

occasion the Archbishop of Canterbury arrived for an audience with the monarch only to find him on all fours, snorting and neighing in a passable imitation of a horse, while his little granddaughter led him along by his beard. In 1928 George V had decided to name a foal Lilibet after the Princess, then two years old, but the filly was not very good and failed to win a race. Of more significance was a diminutive Shetland pony called Peggy, which he gave her on her fourth birthday.

◑ A Natural Horsewoman

Young Princess Elizabeth lived with her parents, the then Duke and Duchess of York, at 145 Piccadilly, London. Here, on the top floor, were arranged her collection of toy horses, a childhood obsession which, according to her nanny Miss Crawford, 'lasted unbroken until real horses became important'. 'Crawfie', like the King, frequently found herself playing a horse in the nursery. From the moment the Princess was lifted into the saddle of her beloved Peggy she was able to move on from fantasy to the real thing. Horses have remained her principal recreation and diversion from duty ever since. To begin with she was taught the rudiments of riding by her parents. Within a short period of time she was sufficiently confident to be led on horseback by her mother to a meet of the Pytchley Hunt in Northamptonshire that was honouring the retirement of a famous huntsman, Frank Freeman.

At this point Henry Owen, the stud groom from Windsor, took over the riding tuition of the young Princess. He was considered omniscient by the little girl and for many years quoted as an oracle on all manner of subjects. So much so, in fact, that her father was once heard to tell his daughter, half-jokingly, 'Don't ask me, ask Owen. Who am I to make suggestions?'

A more serious approach to riding lessons began when the Princess was 12 and both she and her sister, Princess Margaret, were taught by the famed royal riding master Horace Smith. By this time, the summer of 1938, the family, including the collection of toy horses, were settled at Buckingham Palace and Smith would present himself twice a week at the Royal Riding School to put the girls through their paces. He taught many society figures, including the leading racehorse owner Dorothy Paget and actresses Gladys Cooper and Evelyn Laye, at his own school in Cadogan Place. Smith also had a successful hunting stables

Opposite: Princess Elizabeth poses with her pony Greylight at Windsor on her 13th birthday.

at Holyport near Maidenhead in Berkshire where his manager for many years was Vincent Francis, the father of royal jockey and world-famous author Dick Francis. The young novelist-to-be gained many of his riding skills at the yard, particularly on ponies which would later be dispatched to London for the royal pupils. He later wrote, 'It was a great source of pleasure to me then, and it still is, to reflect that I helped to train several of the ponies which the two Princesses rode when they were children.' It is further evidence, should any be needed, of the small-world nature of racing and of royal racing in particular.

Smith began from scratch, teaching Princess Elizabeth the correct way to hold the reins and adjust stirrup leathers. He was soon impressed by her progress: 'She was very conscientious and anxious to improve her horsemanship. She was just as interested in the care of horses as she was in riding them, and she asked me numerous questions about feeding, stable management and methods of training. She was always very fond of her ponies and never forgot to give carrots to her mount when the lesson was over. I think that in those days, when she was 12, her chief interest in life was horses. She confessed to me once that, had she not been who she was, she would like best to be a lady living in the country with lots of horses and ponies.'

From time to time George VI and Queen Elizabeth came to watch their daughter's progress which, according to Smith, a hard taskmaster, was exemplary. During the Second World War when she was resident at Windsor Castle the Princess took up carriage-driving and won her private driving class at the Royal Windsor Horse Show. Now a teenager and an accomplished young horsewoman, she would go to Holyport twice a week, accompanied by Miss Crawford, for instruction on riding side-saddle. A few years later Smith presented her with the side-saddle on which she had taken her lessons, to use in the first Trooping the Colour ceremony in which she took part. He also gave her an engraved riding whip which she punctiliously brought with her to Holyport.

Recalling her devotion to horses Smith observed, 'The Queen is not, and never has been, a person who takes up interests lightly, only to drop them just as easily a short time later.' He was also greatly impressed during the war years by her knowledge of racing form and breeding, which was not limited to the horses that belonged to her father. The sport remains her principal diversion in life and the great names of racing in the past 50 years have commented on the level of expertise she continues to display. Ian Balding, her trainer for 35 years, acknowledges, 'The Queen is an absolute natural with horses in every way. Once we were watching some yearlings in a field when six or seven started galloping at us. The Queen knew to stand absolutely stock-still and not bolt for the gate. I stood with her and the horses pulled up. And if you go round the stables with her, she wants to look at all the horses, not just her own. There are some horses where I would advise an owner not to stand too near because they could kick. In her case, I don't have to say it. She just understands straight away.'

The Hirelings: Big Game and Sun Chariot

Sandringham's future looked bleak when Edward VIII succeeded George V in 1936. The estate had been left to him by his father. One of his first decisions was to order that the clocks at Sandringham be set to the same time as those in the rest of England. The eccentric 'Sandringham Mean Time' had been devised by Edward VII when, as Prince of Wales, he had put all the estate clocks back by half an hour to allow extra shooting time in winter and to counteract his wife's notorious lack of punctuality. His grandson put the estate up for sale following his abdication and had found a buyer by the end of the year, prior to leaving the country for exile in France. The new king, George VI, had to step in and buy it back from his brother and take steps to assure the racing community that it would be business as usual for the royal racing interests. He wrote to Brigadier Tomkinson, 'I shall certainly take a great interest in racing, but of course at the moment I know nothing about breeding or anything else so you must teach me.'

The new King quickly learnt the frustration of ownership. In 1937 he had 21 horses in training with Willie Jarvis, who had taken over in 1924 from Richard Marsh at Egerton House. Just four of those 21 managed to win a total of six races that season. In 1938 the grand total was two victories and the following year it was a paltry five. Something had to be done. Brigadier Tomkinson had died suddenly in 1937 and the new racing manager, Captain Charles Moore, was to have a profound influence on royal fortunes until his retirement 26 years later. A hero of the First World War, he was the proud recipient of the Military

Cross and the *Croix de Guerre*. He had many years bloodstock experience with his own home stud in County Tipperary.

Captain Moore arranged for the King to lease some yearlings from the National Stud, as Lord Marcus Beresford had done 30 years before. Lord Marcus had been lucky with Minoru and Captain Moore was to be equally fortunate with the great filly Sun Chariot and the formidable colt Big Game. They were put into training with the leading trainer of the day, Fred Darling at Beckhampton, forming an association with those famous Wiltshire gallops outside Marlborough that continues today with Roger Charlton. While the Royal Stud itself was going through a period of transition, the National Stud imports, nicknamed 'the hirelings' by Captain Moore, gave the King his best ever season in 1942, winning four of the five classics between them. Sun Chariot was such a madam that at one stage it was decided to ship her back to stud in Ireland. She left Beckhampton and was transported to Swindon railway station where it was discovered that she did not have the correct papers, which was highly embarrassing and resulted in her being returned to Fred Darling.

Both Big Game and Sun Chariot were the champion two-year-olds of their sex so expectations for a Guineas double to offer some wartime cheer were very high. Big Game was an imposing 16.1 hands, a powerhouse who trounced his rivals at Newmarket winning by four lengths under a confident Gordon Richards, stable jockey at Beckhampton. The smaller Sun Chariot sauntered home in the fillies' equivalent by the same margin – not without a degree of anxiety, however. She had put in a mulish display to finish third in her opening race of the season at Salisbury, the only defeat of her career. Fortunately the skill of Gordon Richards managed to get her racing in the 1000 Guineas. During the early stages of the war both Princess Elizabeth and Princess Margaret were not allowed to be seen in public, their exact whereabouts kept secret for security reasons. They missed the Guineas but, after much pestering, King George and Queen Elizabeth decided to take them to Beckhampton to watch the classic winners at work. It was to have a great effect on Princess Elizabeth.

Sun Chariot was on her worst behaviour. Gordon Richards later told racing writer Bill Curling, 'I could not get her to start and, at one stage, she took me straight into a ploughed field, got down on her knees and roared like a bull. It was most unpleasant.' Fortunately Big Game was more amenable and worked well. The 26-times champion jockey recalled how Princess Elizabeth, now 16, took everything in and remembered all the horses, 'Fred Darling was highly impressed and remarked that Princess Elizabeth must have a natural eye for a horse.' It was at the end of this exhilarating day that the Princess was allowed to run her hand over the massive frame of Big Game who, at the time, appeared destined for greatness. That was not to be and, in the final analysis, it was Sun Chariot who far outstripped his achievements and was awarded the accolade by Gordon Richards of the best filly he rode. She is remembered in October each year in the Sun Chariot Stakes at Newmarket.

During the war both the Oaks and Derby were held at Newmarket and the King and Queen travelled to the heart of racing to see their filly attempt the first leg of what was hoped would be a famous double. Sun Chariot was a hardly generous 1/4 to capture the Oaks, a price that looked even skinnier when she ruined three attempts to get the runners away. Now, in the days of starting stalls, she would more than likely have been abandoned by the stalls' handlers. Gordon Richards managed to cajole her away, having given the rest of the field an improbable start. As her opponents galloped past the first furlong marker, she had covered about 50 yards. She then proceeded to run wide into the straight but, despite all this, Richards remained motionless and the filly began to run on and whizzed up the straight. It was one of those occasions when all the other runners appeared to be moving in slow motion. She made the winning post a length in front and was led in by her delighted owner, who was wearing a smart RAF uniform.

The following day Big Game was also odds-on for the Derby. The price of 4/6 was slightly better than the filly's because there remained a slight doubt about the colt's stamina. The doubt was to prove well founded. In the paddock beforehand Big Game looked magnificent, carrying a frame more like a four-year-old's than a Derby candidate's. But in the race itself he refused to settle and, despite leading two furlongs out, was a spent force in the final furlong and faded to finish a disappointing sixth. The winner, Watling Street in the famous Lord Derby colours of black with a white cap, had finished behind the King's colt on three previous occasions including the Guineas. The race was a triumph for Harry Wragg, the 'head waiter', who had no faith in Big Game's stamina and rode his mount to pounce late.

Dropped back in trip to the mile-and-a-quarter Champion Stakes again at Newmarket in the autumn, Big Game was able to partially redeem his reputation with a fluent victory before retiring to stud. Sun Chariot, meanwhile, went from strength to strength and fully avenged the royal honour when she easily brushed Watling Street aside to win the St Leger, also held at Newmarket that year. Gordon Richards provided a fitting postscript to her career when he observed, 'I have no doubt at all that had Sun Chariot run in the Derby, she would have won that just as easily as the St Leger.'

Looking dapper in his RAF uniform, George VI proudly leads in Sun Chariot [Gordon Richards] after her spectacular victory in the Oaks at Newmarket, 12 June 1942.

∾ A Rising Light

Rising Light was the apple of Princess Elizabeth's eye. She had first seen him when she paid a visit to look over the mares and foals at the Hampton Court Stud. They had been moved there from Sandringham after the death of her grandfather and, during the war, it was convenient for her to travel from Windsor and spend time wandering around the paddocks. It helped that Captain Moore had a grace-and-favour home at Hampton Court and was able to give the Princess the benefit of his experience and knowledge. She paid her first visit soon after her trip to Beckhampton and perhaps that had inspired her to seek closer contact with the royal horses. Armed with a camera she quickly picked out the newly foaled Rising Light as her favourite among the equine residents and proceeded to photograph the young bay colt through all the stages of his early life.

The King also developed a soft spot for Rising Light, who helped to revive the fortunes of the royal homebreds after the drought of the early part of his reign. The colt was by the 1933 Derby winner Hyperion out of a mare called Bread Card which Captain Moore had bought from Lord Astor in 1938. Hyperion had been the smallest Derby winner for nearly a century, standing little more than 15 hands, but he proved to be a giant at stud. He was champion sire six times, including in 1954 when his son Aureole proved himself an outstanding colt. He also sired the unforgettable Sun Chariot. In Rising Light the King was able to experience the thrill of watching a horse he had bred win a race. It is a special excitement which, early on, proved an inspiration for his daughter.

Princess Elizabeth had to wait until Rising Light was a big, backward two-year-old before she was allowed to see her favourite horse in training at the Newmarket stables of the new royal trainer, Captain Cecil Boyd-Rochfort. This was 1944, the war was still raging and the visit had to be carried out amid great secrecy. She had not yet been to a race meeting. That changed a year later in June 1945 when she was taken by her parents to the Derby, still held at Newmarket. Epsom was not yet ready to hold a day at the races. Troops were encamped at Tattenham Corner and many of the buildings had suffered bomb damage. It could hardly host a grand occasion. Rising Light ran a stout race to finish fifth to the northern raider Dante. Although many of the Newmarket crowd would have loved to see a royal winner, Dante was also a very popular horse. Princess Elizabeth followed her mother's example and they both appeared positively cheerful after the disappointment of Rising Light. It was an early display of the correct way to behave in defeat or disaster. Dressed in her khaki ATS uniform the Princess joined her parents in the unsaddling enclosure to congratulate the winning connections. She had the consolation of being cheered with her parents all the way to their car as they left the course.

Two months later, on a sunny August afternoon, Princess Elizabeth accompanied the King and Queen, who was celebrating her birthday, to Ascot for the first time. Rising Light was once again the star attraction but on the day Gordon Richards hogged all the attention, winning five races out of seven. Rising Light, however, proved himself a hero in the eyes of the Princess, scrambling home by a head. The King had spent the morning discussing the implications of the atomic bomb with President Truman who would sanction the destruction of Hiroshima two days later. Yet he still felt moved to write in his diary of Rising Light's victory, 'It was thrilling for me as I had never seen one of my own horses win before.' That illuminating comment reveals that, despite leading in a classic winner, the King did not regard the horses leased from the National Stud as entirely his own, and demonstrates once more the unique thrill of breeding a winner. Rising Light did his best to provide a homebred classic success in the St Leger but was beaten two lengths into second place by Chamossaire, ironically a product of the National Stud.

It was time for the Princess to make a trip to the races on her own, or at least as much on her own as a royal visitor can ever be at a racetrack. In reality a royal racing party descended on Newmarket to watch the up-and-coming star of the royal stable, the bay filly Hypericum, contest the Dewhurst Stakes for the best two-year-olds of the year. Among the friends who joined the Princess was Lord Porchester, who was to become the single most influential figure in her racing world and would eventually become the Queen's racing manager in 1970. At this time he was a lieutenant in the Royal Horse Guards. His father, the 6th Earl of Carnarvon, had bred the 1930 Derby winner, Blenheim, and owned Highclere Stud near Newbury.

Like Rising Light and Sun Chariot before, Hypericum was by Hyperion and she inherited the contrary nature of many of the stallion's stock. Boyd-Rochfort was always of the opinion that the best of the Hyperions were difficult. She threw her stable jockey, Doug Smith, to such effect on the gallops that the Captain banned him from riding her in normal work for safety reasons. Hypericum's dam was Feola who was at the time the most important brood mare at the Royal Stud, producing five good winners in six years.

Hypericum was the best of them, though she had started inauspiciously by imitating Sun Chariot and dawdling away from the start at Newmarket on her debut

Princess Elizabeth flanked by the two captains, racing manager Charles Moore (on her right) and Cecil Boyd-Rochfort (on her left), gazes approvingly at Hypericum after the filly's victory in the 1000 Guineas at Newmarket, 3 May 1946.

Royal Racing

and losing narrowly. She also ran second when she returned there to take on some top two-year-old colts in the Middle Park Stakes. The prospects for the Dewhurst were good and she was made odds-on favourite in a field of 10. For once everything went according to plan and she won by an easy two lengths from Airborne, the grey colt who would win the following year's Derby. Initial optimism that Hypericum would carry all before her as a three-year-old was quickly dashed at Hurst Park, a popular track near Hampton Court, on Easter Saturday when Princess Elizabeth joined her parents to watch her seasonal debut. Hypericum was brushed aside by the champion two-year-old filly Neolight and prospects for the 1000 Guineas looked bleak. The King and Queen would not be at Newmarket for the classic so it would be left to the Princess to represent royal interests.

She watched nervously from the stands as Hypericum proceeded to disgrace herself. As the runners lined up at the start, Hypericum, drawn one, made a mad dash at the tapes, deposited Doug Smith on the ground and cantered riderless down the course. She disappeared behind the stands before eventually being caught by the car park and gingerly returned to meet her jockey, who had been given a lift down the course in an ambulance. Bookmakers promptly pushed the price of the royal filly out to 100/6 but the escapade had not harmed her chances. No less a judge than the trainer Jack Jarvis, who himself had two runners in the field, nipped down to the ring to back Hypericum at the now generous price. He reasoned, quite correctly, that the filly would be nicely warmed up while her opponents, waiting some 14 minutes at the start, would be cold and miserable. Whether they would have waited 14 minutes to start a classic if any horse other than one owned by the King had been involved is a question to ponder.

Eventually the race began 16 minutes late. Needless to say Hypericum jumped off like a crab, moving sideways while the rest of the field was galloping forward. Doug Smith quickly made up the ground, however, and had the King's filly tucked in behind the pacesetters on the stand side. The favourite, Neolight under Gordon Richards, challenged strongly on the outside but Hypericum outstayed her by a length and a half. She was the first homebred classic success for the Royal Stud since Scuttle's victory in the same race in 1928. Princess Elizabeth, just turned 20, was elated. Bill Curling, who that year took on the mantle of 'Hotspur', racing correspondent of the *Daily Telegraph*, observed, 'I can see her now standing in the unsaddling enclosure, the only woman amongst a sea of men. Captain Charles Moore, 6 feet 3 inches tall on her right, Captain Cecil Boyd-Rochfort, 6 feet 4 inches tall on her left.' The whole family subsequently watched Hypericum finish a disappointing fourth in the 1946 Oaks. Her finest moment was behind her and, after another lacklustre effort at Royal Ascot, she was retired to the Royal Stud.

In the days when the King was still in good health Princess Elizabeth was able to indulge her passion for horses and racing to the full. Although it would remain her principal diversion in life, she would never again be able to make it the number one priority. She even missed the dramatic triumph by Dunfermline in the Silver Jubilee Year Oaks of 1977. By then roles had been reversed and it was the Queen Mother who had the pleasure of greeting a royal classic winner. Jockey Willie Carson still recalls how the 76-year-old was so consumed with delight she was 'like a young schoolgirl. It was great to see.'

❧ The Gift Horse

The Aga Khan meant well. As a wedding gift to Princess Elizabeth he presented her with her very first racehorse. Although she had adopted Rising Light as very nearly her own, this was a landmark in her career of racing ownership. A filly bred at the Aga Khan's Sheshoon Stud at the Curragh was chosen. The sire was Turkhan and the dam Hastra. The Princess, who would always name her horses especially well, called her Astrakhan and waited with great expectation for her to grow old enough to travel across the Irish Sea to Captain Boyd-Rochfort's stable. Eventually the filly arrived at Freemason Lodge, a weak, small chestnut.

The Captain was faced with the old training dilemma of having to tell an enthusiastic owner that their precious horse was useless. It was an opinion doubly difficult to express to a royal owner. Astrakhan was a sickly filly with weak forelegs and a kneecap that slipped. Eventually, Boyd-Rochfort admitted to the racing manager, Charles Moore, that he did not think Astrakhan would ever make it to a racetrack. The Princess was determined that every effort should be made as a mark of courtesy to the Aga Khan's generosity.

It was decided that Astrakhan should be taken out of training and instead undergo an electrotherapy course at the stables of William Smyth, private trainer to the Duke of Norfolk, at Arundel in Sussex. The filly was treated not by a

vet but by a physiotherapist called Charles Strong who specialized in treating rheumatism. The treatment consisted of attaching electrodes to Astrakhan's troublesome kneecap and charging them with current from the physio's car battery. It was a bit hit-and-miss but it worked and, against the odds, Astrakhan began to respond. Meanwhile the genial Aga Khan had heard that his gift was turning into a nightmare and offered the Princess a substitute. She chose a brown filly by his stallion Stardust. The filly was called Marsa and was scheduled to go into training at Freemason Lodge the following year, 1950. The Princess registered her own racing colours for the first time. They were scarlet with purple hooped sleeves and black cap, a variation on the famous royal colours. There now seemed every prospect that Astrakhan might reach the racetrack after all. By a twist of fate, however, the filly was not, after all, destined to be the first to win a race under the new colours. That honour would befall an honest old steeplechaser called Monaveen.

Princess Elizabeth's racing colours were seen for the first time when Astrakhan [Tommy Burn] contested the Sandwich Stakes at Ascot, 7 October 1949.

Part One ❧ **Traditional Values**

The King's failing health meant there was much less time for the Princess to devote to going to races so in 1949 it was a happy family that was able to go together to Royal Ascot. The visit was a successful one and King George was greatly cheered to see his filly Avila take the Coronation Stakes by three lengths. At a celebratory dinner at Windsor Queen Elizabeth found herself seated next to the charming and persuasive Lord Mildmay, who suggested that she and her daughter should consider owning a steeplechaser together. Perhaps moved by her daughter's disappointments with Astrakhan, Queen Elizabeth enthusiastically agreed that a suitable horse should be found and put into training with Peter Cazalet whom she had known as a family friend for many years. Coincidentally, Cazalet bought Monaveen on behalf of the royal partnership the same day that Marsa was transferred to the Princess. At the very least Monaveen would be a diversion from the troubles of Astrakhan.

Both horses were entered for their first run in the Princess's colours at the beginning of October, Astrakhan in the Sandwich Stakes at Ascot and Monaveen in a twopenny-ha'penny race at picturesque Fontwell Park near Arundel. The Princess's plans to fly down from Balmoral to see her filly race were ruined because of fog. Stranded in Scotland, she had to hear news of the race by telephone. Astrakhan managed a creditable second place and earned her excited owner the princessly sum of £81 12s in prize money. Three days later Monaveen sauntered home, earning the immortal accolade of being the first winner for both mother and daughter.

Astrakhan continued to battle on, finishing third at Windsor before tackling a field of 13 in the Merry Maidens Stakes at Hurst Park. Ridden by the Australian jockey Tommy Burn, she took up the running fully three furlongs from home and stuck her brave neck out all the way to the line for a deserved victory. All the patience and hard work invested in restoring a virtual equine cripple to health was worth it in the end. The Princess, flushed with her filly's success, entertained fleeting thoughts of a run in the following year's Oaks but a poor effort in a trial race brought everyone to their senses and the filly was retired. There must be a moral here involving gift horses and mouths, but the final irony involves the replacement gift horse Marsa. She really was useless and finished nearer last than first on her only two outings.

During his time at the helm of royal racing interests George VI was a good deal luckier than his father, even if he did come to appreciate the sport quite late in life. At least racing knew royal patronage would be enthusiastically continued by his daughter and wife. He liked to maintain a firm business hand on his sport, something which rubbed off on the future Queen. This careful strategy, though prudent, may have actually led to thwarted ambitions for the Queen. She has never allowed herself to buy success.

The King enjoyed his last big win when the staying filly Above Board, a daughter of Feola, won the 1950 Cesarewitch. It revealed quite a lot about the man and his attitudes to fair play. Above Board's six-length victory was a good old-fashioned coup orchestrated with consummate skill by Captain Boyd-Rochfort. The filly won the Yorkshire Oaks at York in the manner of an improving horse. She clearly had a turn of foot although she was yet unproven over a true staying distance. The handicapper allotted her the generous mark of 7 stone 10 lbs and Boyd-Rochfort booked Eph Smith, deaf as a post but one of the strongest of jockeys. Captain Moore, who regularly fell out with the trainer, was not in favour of Above Board running more than two miles in the Cesarewitch, worried that it might adversely affect her future. But Boyd-Rochfort managed to talk both him and the King round to his way of thinking.

Above Board had two reasonably undistinguished warm-up races on unsuitable soft going and was a massive price for the Newmarket race. Boyd-Rochfort had a very substantial ante-post punt and even persuaded Captain Moore, a very occasional punter, to have £30 on at 40/1. On the day, the filly started at the still generous price of 18/1 and according to Eph Smith, with masterful understatement, won 'quite easily'. The rest of the field would have had to start an hour earlier to have beaten her. The King was not at Newmarket but made sure his jockey received a pair of cuff links in appreciation. The two captains, Boyd-Rochfort and Moore, were at ease with the world until the King summoned his trainer for a private audience. He was alarmed because controversial rumours had reached him that a stroke had been pulled with a royal horse. He asked for reassurance from Boyd-Rochfort that everything was indeed 'Above Board'. The Captain who, according to his stepson, the champion trainer Henry Cecil, most certainly was not a liar, explained that the filly had not been 'right' for her last run. The King accepted it. Henry Cecil recalls that they had an old wind-up gramophone recording of the race which was so popular at Freemason Lodge that they wore it out.

Above Board [Eph Smith] casts doubt on his name by winning with embarrassing ease the Cesarewitch at Newmarket, 11 October 1950.

Part Two

Fairlawne

Noel Coward was a popular guest at Fairlawne during the weekends when a house party had been arranged for Queen Elizabeth. One early morning, to everyone's amazement, he was persuaded to watch the horses work. On his return he announced that it would be the last occasion he indulged in such equestrian pursuits. On being asked why, he declared 'Too cold' and retired to his room until luncheon.

❧ Brothers in Arms

Anthony Mildmay is a legend of racing. His untimely death engraved his image as 'the last of the Corinthians' on the hearts and minds of the racing community and the nation. In the aftermath of the Second World War his bravura in the saddle and his great charm brought him the kind of fame that in these professional-obsessed times would almost certainly relegate him, despite his skill, to the status of an amusing sideshow, an eccentric postscript to the sporting rat race. His celebrity meant he overshadowed his great friend and mentor Peter Cazalet, but in many ways Cazalet was the stronger character and one who should not be underestimated.

The two friends first met at Eton where they were both in the same house, although they had little to do with one another because Cazalet was two years the elder. Mildmay in those days bore no relation to the sporting gladiator of the future being small and useless at games, while Cazalet was an outstanding sportsman excelling at tennis, racquets and, in particular, cricket. He scored a century for Eton against Harrow at Lord's, won a blue at Oxford in 1927 and made 150 for Kent against his old university sharing in a partnership of 178 with the incomparable Frank Woolley. On being invited to captain the Kent county cricket side he had to choose between willow and saddler's leather and committed himself to the Turf.

After Cambridge Mildmay embarked on a career in the City of London with Baring Brothers, finding time whenever he could to indulge a passion for horses. At the time Cazalet was making a name for himself as an accomplished amateur rider and taking an interest in training horses at Fairlawne, his imposing estate near Tonbridge in Kent. The Mildmay family's country home of Shoreham was only a few miles away and Mildmay hit upon the idea of keeping a horse at Fairlawne so that that he could ride out before travelling the 30 miles to work in London. By this time he had grown into a tall, gangly young man, always apparently undernourished, but fiercely determined to succeed as an amateur rider. Cazalet gave him an old selling chaser called Phibisher to ride, which clearly delighted the young man because he promptly told his father, Lord Mildmay, the good news. His father, a sceptic where racing was concerned, informed his son that there must be something wrong with the horse and was greatly amused when a mere fortnight later he was told that Phibisher had dropped down dead.

Opposite: Princess Margaret accompanied by the dashing Lord Mildmay.

Peter Cazalet, on his grey hack, inspects his team at morning exercise, led by Monaveen with Lord Mildmay's chaser Cromwell following.

Within a couple of years Mildmay and Cazalet were almost a racing partnership, seeking out cheap horses to lease or buy and competing against each other on the tracks around Britain. In the 1932/3 season Mildmay had five winners from just 19 rides and rode Cazalet's horse Youtell in his first try at the Grand National. It was a cavalry charge over the first fence with just one faller: Youtell. Anthony Mildmay was left sitting in the grass nursing a broken nose. He was still combining riding with his duties in the City. Peter Cazalet's mother, Mollie, called Mildmay the 'boiled egg boy' because he would ride out in the morning and then eat just a single egg before hurrying off to catch the 8.15 train up to London.

Peter Cazalet never enjoyed the limelight and was happy that the charismatic Mildmay attracted the attention of press and public as the fortunes of Fairlawne prospered. Their success has to be measured against the fact that National Hunt racing was very small beer before the Second World War, with only the Grand National commanding much public interest. In 1933 Peter Cazalet married Leonora Wodehouse, stepdaughter of P.G. Wodehouse. Even though the Cazalet family was prosperous and well connected, the newspapers of the day reported the occasion as 'P.G. Wodehouse's daughter weds'. The great writer was very fond of Leonora, whom he addresses in countless letters as 'Darling Snorky'. The letters form an important part of the Wodehouse biographical archive. On hearing of the engagement he wrote to Leonora declaring, 'You know me on the subject of Peter. Thumbs up, old boy. Not only a sound egg but probably the only sound egg left in this beastly era of young Bloomsbury novelists.'

When Peter Cazalet's father died, death duties forced the newlyweds to move temporarily into a house called The Grange on the Fairlawne estate. Mildmay would often drive over from Shoreham for dinner and one evening he was invited to stay overnight. He never returned home and became the Cazalets' permanent guest during the winter months. P.G. Wodehouse wrote to Snorky, 'I'm glad Anthony has moved in. The Grange never seems the same without him.'

Plum, as the author was known, always liked the odd punt and the family connection was cemented when, on several occasions, Cazalet's advice enabled him to bring his betting account out of the red and into the black.

It was a family connection that delighted Queen Elizabeth who regards Wodehouse as one of her favourite authors. She has always much enjoyed talking about the many and varied characters in his books with Peter and Leonora's son Edward, now a retired High Court judge and one of Britain's leading authorities on the great writer. Edward remembers her saying, 'If the cares of the world come upon you and you cannot sleep, the best way of drifting off is to move into the world of Blandings Castle or the Drones Club. When you go to sleep you have the most wonderful smile on your face.' As a gesture of friendship and appreciation, Queen Elizabeth unveiled a blue plaque in 1988, honouring the author at 17 Dunraven Street near Park Lane, his London address in the 1920s.

Anthony Mildmay's love affair with the great British public was cemented in the 1936 Grand National. Riding his father's Davy Jones, an unconsidered 100/1 shot, he was going easily in the lead two fences from home, well clear of the previous year's winner, Reynoldstown. He jumped the second-last fence but, disastrously, the reins broke which left him with no steering. He tried to guide Davy Jones to the last fence with his whip but the horse ran out left leaving Reynoldstown to coast home. The winning rider was none other than Fulke Walwyn, then an amateur rider with the 9th Lancers, later to be only the second principal trainer for Queen Elizabeth. Racing is a very small world. Peter Cazalet would not have realized it then but the National was to prove a

The author P.G. Wodehouse, father-in-law of Peter Cazalet and occasional punter.

total jinx for both Fairlawne and his royal patron. There is nothing the British public likes better than a gallant loser and Anthony Mildmay was transformed overnight from plucky amateur to heroic horseman.

After a bad fall at Sandown, in which he broke his wrist, Peter Cazalet gave up race riding in 1937. P.G. Wodehouse wrote to him, 'Rotten luck getting crocked like that.' Anthony Mildmay was now effectively the stable jockey and in the following season he shared the amateur riders' title with 21 wins. These were the days when amateur riders were a breed apart. In a race confined to amateurs, like the Grand Military at

Sandown Park, it was customary for each rider to introduce himself formally to the senior amateur riding. Perhaps because of Mildmay's influence amateurs received special rank at Fairlawne throughout Peter Cazalet's tenure. They were always afforded a polite 'Mister' and invited for meals at the house, something mere professional jockeys were never allowed. Lord Oaksey well remembers riding out at Fairlawne and being treated differently in this respect to professionals like Arthur Freeman and David Mould. This social position did not cut much ice with Mould, who told Oaksey (then the Hon. John Lawrence), 'The only thing I say to amateurs is "Get out of the f***ing way".'

Peter and Anthony both served in the Welsh Guards in a Second World War blighted by tragedy. Just two weeks before they were due to leave for France in 1944 Leonora Cazalet was in a London clinic for a routine operation. During the night she suffered a haemorrhage but the hospital was a sea of confusion because of a bombing raid which had left many children injured. No one was aware that she needed treatment and she died through loss of blood.

In the last days of the war, and while still under enemy fire, Cazalet and Mildmay decided that if they made it home they would endeavour to transform Fairlawne into one of Britain's best training establishments. That ambition paid almost instant dividends with Mildmay becoming leading amateur again in the 1946/7 season with 32 winners, the first of four consecutive titles. The racing public adopted a familiar cry of 'C'mon milord' or 'C'mon Lordy' after he inherited the peerage from his father in 1947.

That autumn, a very moderate horse with the sinister name of Fatal Rock gave Mildmay an appalling fall at Folkestone, permanently damaging the muscles in his neck. From then on he was subject to paralysing neck cramps, the most famous one coming on his excellent chaser Cromwell at the Canal Turn in the 1948 Grand National. He could not offer the horse any assistance from the saddle throughout the final mile, and for the last two fences could not raise his head at all. Cromwell finished third, just seven lengths behind Sheila's Cottage, the second monstrous piece of fortune in the race for Peter Cazalet. Devon Loch was to famously prove that bad luck comes in threes.

On the eve of Royal Ascot in 1949 Peter Cazalet married his second wife, Zara Strutt. It was while they were on their honeymoon that Anthony Mildmay, now Lord Mildmay, sat beside Queen Elizabeth at dinner at Windsor and persuaded her to share a horse with her daughter. Both she and Princess Elizabeth were bowled over by his unbridled enthusiasm for the sport. When Cazalet returned, Mildmay told him the good news and the trainer found Monaveen for the royal owners. It was an enormous boost for both Fairlawne and for National Hunt racing. The royal venture guaranteed maximum publicity for the sport. Lord Mildmay was officially appointed to manage the royal jumpers, or jumper as it then was.

The future for the Mildmay-Cazalet team was extremely bright. By now the Cazalets were back in the big house and Zara was more than happy for Anthony to continue staying at Fairlawne. She set about returning the house, which had become akin to Victorian bachelor quarters since the death of Leonora, to its former style and elegance. In the early summer of 1950 Mildmay was staying at his family estate at Mothecombe in south Devon when, as was his custom, he went for an early morning swim. He was a very strong swimmer and would swim a great distance out to sea. This time he never came back, almost certainly stricken by an agonizing and fatal cramp.

At the end of the war Peter Cazalet and Anthony Mildmay had planned to establish Fairlawne as one of the most successful stables in the land within five years. Cruelly, fate had taken a hand just when their ambition had been realized. In a leader in *The Times* Peter Fleming, renowned travel writer and brother of the novelist Ian Fleming, wrote of Anthony Mildmay, 'There never was a harder rider, a better loser or a more popular winner; and although he always valued the race more than the victory, and the victory more than the prize, he would not perhaps have disdained the reward he has won – which is a kind of immortality among the English.' In her 50 years as an owner Queen Elizabeth has continued to personify many of the values that Anthony Mildmay brought to the sport.

❧ Monaveen: First of the Many

Peter Cazalet's experienced eye for a horse was first taken by Monaveen during the Grand National of 1949, not least because Fairlawne's stable jockey, Tony Grantham, had the ride. He had been 'only cantering' in the lead when he ejected Grantham at the 19th fence, another Aintree 'if only' story. Monaveen proved his toughness by turning out in May to outclass a small field at Folkestone, beating the unattractively named Cazalet-trained runner The Frog into second place. At the end of that season he had won three, and been placed twice more, from eight runs.

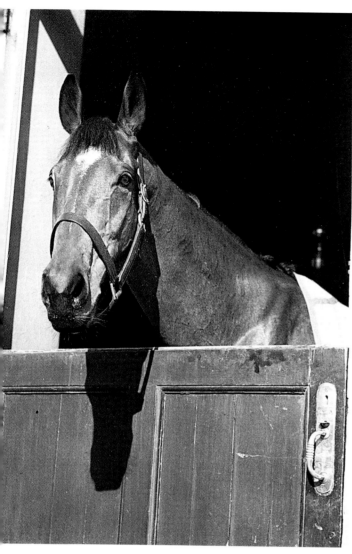

Monaveen looks out from his box at Fairlawne.

As the first purchase for Queen Elizabeth and her daughter, Monaveen attracted Cazalet for several reasons. He was tough and game, liked to lead and liked to win. He was the sort of animal who would give a new owner fun and a chance. The Fairlawne record of royal runners describes Monaveen as a 'bold jumper and a courageous horse when in front or disputing the lead'. He was a medium-sized, light-framed bay horse, who did not take much getting fit and would be ready to run on the firm summer ground which he obviously relished. The owner was a Mr Dal Hawkesley, a West Ham greyhound trainer, who had picked the animal up for just £35 and was persuaded to part with it for £1000, a nice profit but, as it turned out, a bargain for the new royal owners.

Monaveen arrived at Fairlawne on 22 July 1949. The eight-year-old gelding had come a long way since his early days in Ireland when he had pulled a milk float delivering a daily pinta to the good folk of Navan. It was an old Irish trick to try and calm a horse's spirit. Cazalet decided to waste no time in which to allow royal enthusiasm for their new purchase to cool, so selected a moderate chase at delightful Fontwell Park on 10 October. Fontwell, in a leafy part of the Sussex Downs near Arundel, is a peculiar figure-of-eight course which some horses take to and some do not. Monaveen had already won around the track. Princess Elizabeth was there to see her colours carried for the first time over jumps, and there was a great feeling of expectation because the race appeared to be there for Monaveen's taking if he put in a clear round.

Wearing a pair of black blinkers, often favoured by Cazalet to help his horses concentrate, Monaveen had just two rivals, Random Knight and Martin M, who led at a sensible pace until Tony Grantham took over at the 12th fence. Although the race was still open as the trio turned into the straight for the final time, Monaveen pulled steadily clear to win by 15 lengths. It was the perfect beginning and Monaveen collected the tidy sum of £204 for hardly breaking sweat. Author and trainer Ivor Herbert put it succinctly when writing of Queen Elizabeth's racing ownership: 'Had Monaveen run half a dozen dreary races round sad tracks I doubt whether this tale would have come to be written.'

Peter Cazalet shrewdly and expertly realized that the thrill of winning was the most important thing, especially because the Royal Family were deeply concerned at the King's failing health. Any ray of sunshine was a welcome diversion and Monaveen provided it. His next stop was Aintree and a creditable second place over the National fences in the Grand Sefton Chase. Only Freebooter, who would win the next Grand National, finished ahead of the royal runner. Victory at Sandown, the first of Queen Elizabeth's 75 winners at the Esher track, followed before Cazalet took the bold step of entering Monaveen for the prestigious Queen Elizabeth Chase at Hurst Park, named after the horse's part-owner. It would be too much of a fairy tale for her first horse to win her race. And it was New Year's Eve.

Hurst Park was near the river at Hampton Court and a rowing boat used to take enthusiasts from one side of the Thames to the course. It closed, regrettably, in 1962 and is now a housing estate. Monaveen started at 10/1 against a field of seasoned chasers of the day including Roimond, Wot No Sun and Freebooter. Tony Grantham started briskly and, with a fine leap at the first, Monaveen was away. He led almost from start to finish coasting in by six lengths. The prize of £2328 was a bonus. Monaveen had won three times his purchase price in three months. Racing, it would seem, was an easy game for the new owners.

Monaveen became their first Grand National runner the next March and attracted a great deal of sentimental money. It is a fact of racing life that a royal runner invariably starts at a shorter price than it merits, something which Queen Elizabeth is very aware of and one reason why she only likes her horses to run with a clear chance. Monaveen was 100/7, one of those delightful old prices for which a degree in mathematics would help the punter. He ran a gallant race and earned full marks for entertainment value. First and foremost, he jumped safely round which 42 of the 49 starters failed to do. More than that, he gave his royal audience the thrill of leading for the first circuit before making a ghastly blunder at the fence before The Chair and dropping right back. After that Tony Grantham concentrated on getting him home, a distance behind Freebooter. In a letter to her trainer Queen Elizabeth wrote, 'I had steeled myself for anything, for falling at the first fence, being knocked down, almost any disaster but I must say the race was far more thrilling than I could have imagined.'

The untimely death of Anthony Mildmay cast a long shadow over Fairlawne at the beginning of the next season. Monaveen made a slow start running down the field in two outings before attempting to redeem himself by trying to win the Queen Elizabeth Chase for the second time. Some of the vigour of his first royal season seemed lost. Queen Elizabeth travelled from Sandringham to Hurst Park for the race and, as expected, Monaveen dashed off into the lead. At the water jump second time round, out of sight of the royal audience watching in the stand, he stood far too far back, slid on landing and crashed to the ground, a leg broken. Tony Grantham was given a fair old kicking as the rest of the field piled through, leaving him with broken ribs and keeping him out of action for two months. In those days the racecourse vet rode a cob horse, a less speedy form of transport than today's ambulances and Land Rovers. On arrival at the scene, however, he needed only a moment before putting the horse down. It was a salutary reminder for the royal owners that death is the lowering sky hanging over every jump race. Afterwards Queen Elizabeth said, 'This has been a very sad day.' Sir Michael Oswald, her racing manager since 1970, observes, 'If you are a proper owner you have to take disaster and disappointment in your stride. Nobody can do it better than Queen Elizabeth.'

Monaveen was buried near the winning post at Hurst Park. In the space of little more than a year he had encapsulated all the joys and all the gloom of steeplechasing. It twists at the emotions like no other sport. After defeat there is another day. After death there is not. After the demise of Gloria Victis in the 2000 Cheltenham Gold Cup, Alastair Down eloquently wrote in the *Racing Post*, 'To love racing is to enter into a devil's pact in which we accept that the price of the immortality of champions is the fatality of the horse.'

❧ The Blue and Buff

Monaveen was not the start of a great royal partnership in racing. He remains the only horse to be shared by mother and daughter. The decision to go their separate ways was made well before his tragic death at Hurst Park. In his will Lord Mildmay had left all his horses to Peter Cazalet, who offered Manicou for sale to Queen Elizabeth. She, already finding racing a wonderful new excitement in her life, was eager to expand her interests. Princess Elizabeth was invited to join her in a second partnership but decided against it.

The Monaveen adventure had been fun, but the Princess was mindful that she would in time take over the responsibilities of the Royal Stud and there would be no way she would have the time to indulge in steeplechasing as well. In any case, she had been absorbed with the breeding side of racing from an early age. By history and tradition that would be primarily a flat-racing operation. In future years any royal flat horses thought suitable for jump racing would be leased to Queen Elizabeth, an arrangement that allowed Tammuz and Insular to be two of the most successful horses to carry her colours.

While the Princess liked nothing better than to cast a professional eye over the mares and yearlings at Sandringham, Queen Elizabeth has always loved what the Irish racing fraternity would call the 'craic'. Sir Michael Oswald observes, 'She prefers steeplechasing because it's not commercialized and arguably involves a more colourful lot of people. They are a bit more fun.' Edward Cazalet remembers quite clearly the afternoon he realized the immense enjoyment Queen Elizabeth derived from her racing. He was saddling the horses at Lingfield one sunny afternoon when his father was too ill to travel. He recalls, 'I suddenly became aware that she got a terrific kick out of it. She loves it.' It is a sentiment echoed by Sir Michael: 'Some people win a race and you think they have just come from a funeral. She shows great and obvious joy.'

Manicou was a horse to put a spring in any owner's step. The Fairlawne record describes him as 'robust and strong'. He was a handsome dark bay with a white star on his forehead and two flashy white socks. Like Monaveen, he was already a proven winner. He began his career winning four flat races for the great French trainer François Mathet, who would later send both Phil Drake and Relko across the Channel to capture the Derby at Epsom. Manicou proved an instant jumping hit for Lord Mildmay. He won two hurdle races and four novice chases in succession, culminating in a Cheltenham Festival success in the Broadway Novices Chase, then the top three-mile event for novices. He was also an 'entire' horse but was, according to Peter Cazalet, 'a particularly kind and likeable horse'.

As a solo owner Queen Elizabeth had the task of registering her racing colours. She chose the now famous blue, buff stripes, blue sleeves, black cap with a gold tassel. They had been in her family for many generations, originally worn by Lord Strathmore, her great-uncle, who rode in four Grand Nationals between 1847 and 1850. Manicou carried the colours for the first time in 1950, at Fontwell Park in a hurdle race on heavy going, although his new owner was not there to see it, prevented by the court protocol of mourning for Gustav V of Sweden. Basically Manicou needed a run to get himself into top condition, so this little race was nothing more than a good blow-out. He raced up with the pace for a long way before weakening in the heavy ground, which he did not particularly favour.

The race did him a power of good and when he lined up for the Wimbledon Handicap Chase

On safari at Cheltenham in 1953. Queen Elizabeth leads an expedition to watch her horse, M'as-tu-vu, in close-up action.

at Kempton Park three weeks later he was primed for action. Tony Grantham tucked him in and moved him steadily into contention four fences out. At the last he jumped upsides the Duchess of Norfolk's useful chaser Possible and sprinted up the run-in to win by eight lengths. This was clearly a serious racehorse. Fortune had favoured Queen Elizabeth again. The first time she saw her colours she was greeting them in the winners' enclosure. She was not entirely impressed with their appearance and told Grantham, 'The colour is not quite a royal blue. They were copied from a set about 50 years old and the blue has faded. I intend to have a new set.'

Eight days later Monaveen was fatally injured at Hurst Park. Two winners and one fatality from her first two horses demonstrated how fickle racing can be with the emotions. It makes no allowance for royal ownership. As if to make the point that she was not discouraged by Monaveen's fate, Queen Elizabeth travelled to Sandown the next month to watch Manicou attempt to carry 12 stone to victory in a three-mile five-furlong marathon. With Tony Grantham injured after his fall from Monaveen, the superlative jockey Bryan Marshall was in the saddle. Sir Michael Oswald describes him as a 'very great jockey'. Marshall always sported an excellent set of dentures which he would take out before a race and then, if in the presence of royalty, put surreptitiously back in when he dismounted in the winners' enclosure. On one famous occasion, after guiding Devon Loch to victory, the stable lad guarding the false teeth forgot to return them and both Queen Elizabeth and the Queen collapsed with laughter at the sight of the toothless jockey, all gums, attempting to talk them through the triumph.

Marshall had no worries on Manicou. Starting as odds-on favourite, he took it up on the second circuit and was clear of his field four fences from home. Manicou stayed on very well and next stop would be the King George VI Chase, the mid-season jumping highlight at Kempton Park. Queen Elizabeth had already won the race named after her at Hurst Park with Monaveen and was now attempting a marital double with the race in honour of her husband, the King. Pitching a horse just out of the novice stage against seasoned chasers was a bold move by Peter Cazalet but, as current champion trainer Martin Pipe has proved with recent imports, French jumpers mature younger. Marshall gave Manicou a determined ride, keeping up with the pace throughout and outstaying the top-class chaser Silver Fame on the run-in to win by three lengths. Manicou was arguably the best young staying chaser in the country and the Cheltenham Gold Cup could be approached with optimism – but, alas, perhaps the King George did come too soon in the horse's career. He never regained that level of form and failed to win another race. Typically, the Gold Cup was won by

Top: Queen Elizabeth's racing colours are seen on a racecourse for the first time. Manicou [Tony Grantham] (right) is challenged by Sailor's Knot [Tommy Isaac] (left) and Baire [Andy Jarvis] (centre) in the Petworth Hurdle at Fontwell, 2 November 1950.

Above: In the unsaddling enclosure at Hurst Park, 5 February 1955. Queen Elizabeth is about to notice that jockey Bryan Marshall has forgotten to put back his false teeth.

Silver Fame, a popular old warrior of a chaser who, at the age of 12, was able to see off the young pretenders.

Manicou was sore after the race and began to be plagued by leg trouble, an all too familiar story for Queen Elizabeth's horses over the years. He was on and off the track for three years, mainly off, before good sense saw him retired. He was still an entire horse and proved a useful sire of jumpers. Among the progeny he sired was The Rip, one of Queen Elizabeth's favourites.

❧ Life at Fairlawne

Fairlawne was the epicentre of Queen Elizabeth's racing world for 24 years. It was a home from home for the royal owner who had visited the house as a teenager when she was friendly with Thelma Cazalet, the elder sister of trainer Peter Cazalet. Thelma was one of the more outspoken political figures between the two world wars. She was elected as Conservative MP for Islington in London in 1931 and as Thelma Cazalet-Keir she was a strong advocate of women's rights and a sharp thorn in the government's side. In 1944 she helped to engineer Churchill's wartime government's only defeat in Parliament, over the issue of equal pay for women. After the Second World War she became a junior education minister before she, like many others, lost her seat in the Labour victory of 1945.

Although the privileges of Fairlawne had always sat uneasily with Thelma, particularly as a young woman, she remained a good friend of Queen Elizabeth who would visit her at her flat in Eaton Square. They were both born in 1900 and when Thelma died in 1989 Queen Elizabeth wrote to Edward Cazalet, 'I was so fond of her and used to enjoy my visits to her flat. She was a real friend.' The bond between the Cazalet family and their royal patron over many years is a significant factor in Queen Elizabeth's long connection with racing. Thelma may even have had some influence on the 'Queen Mum's' inimitable rapport with everyone, regardless of their class or standing.

The Cazalets came to Fairlawne in 1871 when the estate was purchased for £100,000. Originally a French Huguenot family, they had fled France for England at the beginning of the eighteenth century. A hundred years and more later, the family fortune was made in Russia through various businesses including a brewery, a candle and soap works – the Cazalet candles lit the imperial palaces – and a sewing-machine agency. Fairlawne was the local manor house and with its purchase Peter Cazalet's grandfather, Edward, became the squire of the village of Shipbourne. He owned the estate, the farms and most of the village, which he transformed by introducing many new buildings and replacing the church. He also extended the existing house, adding a covered real tennis court and a large swimming pool. More significantly, he built a number of very fine stables in the Queen Anne style, which were to form the basis for the Cazalet stables after the Second World War.

Although Fairlawne enjoys a splendid hilltop position and was the 'big house' of Shipbourne, the Cazalets were not aloof from the local community. Frank Chapman, in his chronicle of the house, observes, 'In an age where many of his contemporaries were surrounding their properties with high walls, sometimes topped with broken glass against incursion from the rougher element without, Edward Cazalet made Fairlawne an open park to be shared by all who wished to enjoy it.'

Peter Cazalet's father, William, and his mother, Mollie, became respected society hosts. As well as Fairlawne they could call on a London town house in Whitehall Gardens and a large family villa on the French Riviera. Queen Victoria, no less, was a welcome guest and allowed herself to be photographed with the family. She even wore a white shawl for the picture, believing her customary all-black dress to be too glum. She enjoyed the company of Mollie

During the Second World War Fairlawne was converted into a hospital school. Here, children from Plumstead are taking lessons in March 1940.

Part Two ❧ Fairlawne

Elizabeth Taylor, *top*, and Noel Coward were among the guests at glittering parties at Fairlawne throughout the 1950s.

Cazalet although there is no record of whether she approved of Mrs Cazalet's support for women's suffrage or her commitment to Christian Science. She agreed to be godmother to the Cazalets' second son, Victor. In England an invitation to Fairlawne was much prized by people in any walk of life. The future Edward VII once attended a dance in his honour when he was Prince of Wales and waltzed with Mrs Cazalet. Rudyard Kipling would frequently travel over from his home in Sussex.

The elegant world into which Peter Cazalet was born in 1907 played host to tragedy when his eldest brother, Edward, was killed on the Western Front in 1916. The Cazalets' second son, Victor, performed heroic deeds in the war and won the Military Cross. He was elected Conservative MP for Chippenham in Wiltshire in 1924 and represented that constituency until he became the family's second victim of war 20 years later. By then he was military attaché to the Polish leader, General Sikorski, and died with him in a mysterious air crash off Gibraltar in 1943.

Between the wars a parade of the most famous in the land came to Fairlawne, including David Lloyd George, Winston Churchill (later to be an owner in Peter Cazalet's yard) and the painter Augustus John, who completed a canvas of Thelma while at the house. It was a world of the great and good in which Queen Elizabeth always felt comfortable, providing a happy social backdrop to the principal business of racing which Peter's father had begun in a small way, although he was more interested in bloodstock. After the First World War he had horses with Alec Taylor at Manton in Wiltshire, now the headquarters of the Robert Sangster racing empire. From there Taylor sent out the all too aptly named Air Raid to win the 1918 Cesarewitch in the Cazalet colours of canary and blue.

When his father died in 1932 Peter Cazalet inherited the horses and, with Anthony Mildmay, gradually expanded Fairlawne into a proper racing stables. Because of her obvious affinity with all things Fairlawne, racing fitted very easily into Queen Elizabeth's world and provided an oasis of fun, first in her early days of widowhood and then as it became her number one diversion in life. Peter Cazalet and his second wife, Zara, re-created some of the grand occasions of old. They always held a large weekend house party for the Lingfield races in December when Queen Elizabeth would have a number of runners carrying her colours, and guests like Noel Coward and Elizabeth

Taylor would enliven proceedings. Peter Cazalet had become great friends with the film star when her father, the art expert and dealer Francis Taylor, acted as picture-buying adviser to Mollie Cazalet. He proved an excellent judge, championing the works of Augustus John, several of which found their way to Fairlawne, when they were not very fashionable.

❧ The Great Races

Devon Loch: The Grand National, Aintree, 24 March 1956

'The date,' said Peter Cazalet 10 years later, 'is engraved on my heart.' It is the most astonishing and painful race in the whole history of racing. Queen Elizabeth never talks of it. In 1987, when she agreed that Central Television could make a film of her racing life, there was one overriding condition: 'We could not mention Devon Loch,' recalls producer Gary Newbon. Sir Michael Oswald confirms, 'She doesn't like to be reminded of it. It is not a popular subject. If Dick Francis had put it in one of his novels you wouldn't have believed it.' It was Francis himself who, less than 50 yards from the finishing line, was inexplicably robbed of riding a Grand National winner for Queen Elizabeth.

Devon Loch, a strongly built, brown horse bought in Ireland after winning a bumper, had matured steadily over four seasons at Fairlawne and had won four chases before lining up at Liverpool in March 1956. He was 100/7 in the betting but hopes were high at Fairlawne that the 10-year-old was a true National sort. The Queen and Princess Margaret joined their mother for the race. They discussed the prospects with Dick Francis, then stable jockey at Fairlawne, in the paddock beforehand and everyone agreed that Devon Loch was nicely handicapped with 11 stone 4 lbs on his back. 'There was a good deal of excitement in the air,' said Francis.

The race went like a dream for Francis and Devon Loch who took to the demanding National fences right from the start and gained lengths in the air over the early obstacles. A relatively small field of 29 allowed the jockey to pick and choose his position early and Devon Loch had the pace to lie handy without taking too much out of himself. Although the horse is described in the Fairlawne record of royal runners as having a 'bold disposition' which helped him at Aintree, he also had the priceless asset of intelligence. He thought about what he was doing fence to fence. In describing the race afterwards Francis

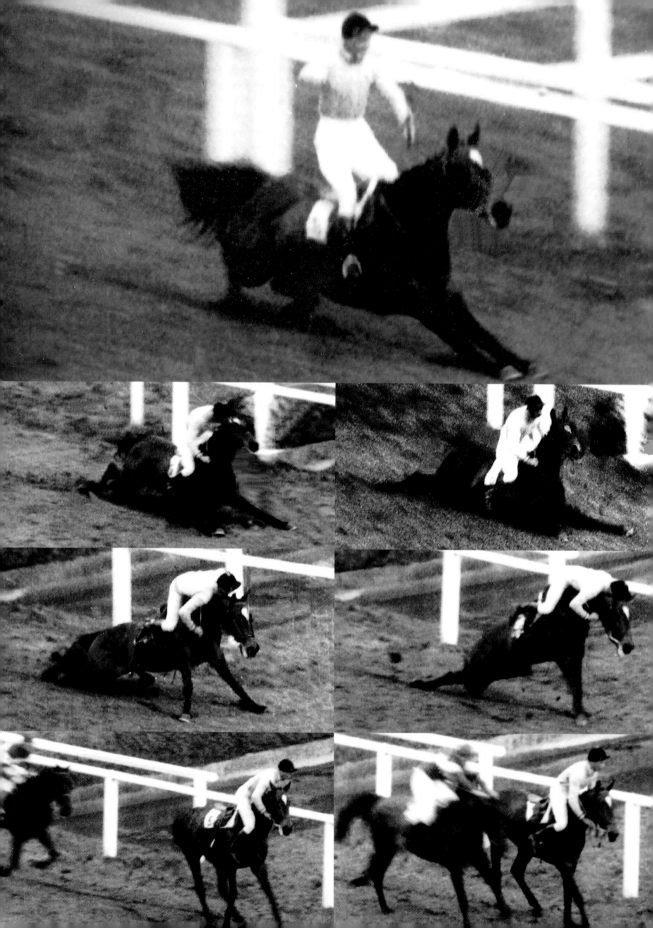

admitted to just one anxious moment when a horse called Domata fell in front of him. Devon Loch simply changed his direction in mid-jump and neatly missed Domata's sprawling legs.

In the stands the excitement was growing as Devon Loch, with his large white star on his forehead, easily improved his position until, by the Canal Turn on the second circuit, he had moved into second place behind Armorial III. Dick Francis eased off: 'Never before in the National had I held back a horse and said, "Steady boy". Never had I felt such power in reserve, such confidence in my mount, such calm in my mind.' E.S.B., ridden by Dave Dick, was still upsides going to the last fence but Francis was clearly going the better. Devon Loch landed nimbly over the fence and set off for the elbow and the run-in to the line. Francis, like an old-fashioned huntsman, was doing little more than ease his mount ahead. Dave Dick and E.S.B. gradually fell further back, fully 10 lengths down as the winning post loomed larger in Devon Loch's eyes. Dick Francis later recalled, 'I have never experienced a greater joy than the knowledge that I was going to win the National.' Ten long, easy strides to go and Devon Loch was still running fresh, straight and powerfully. From the stands the crescendo of cheers rose in a wall of sound similar to the one that greeted the England team in the World Cup Final of 1966. The roar was deafening. The royal party on top of the stand were in a frenzy of excitement. Sir Martin Gilliat's hat was raised in the air. The Queen herself was shouting her mother's horse home. Princess Margaret was cheering and Peter Cazalet was hoarse and gripping his bowler as if he were about to explode. Queen Elizabeth's face was etched with tension as she willed her gallant horse home those last final few yards.

The calamity was unexpected, inexplicable and total. Devon Loch pricked his ears, his back legs stiffened, refused to function and the great horse was down, legs splayed all over the place. He struggled up. The world was for a moment held in slow motion. He could still win if Francis could galvanize him forward but the horse was paralysed and a weary E.S.B. went past. In the stands there was disbelief and hushed horror. A million voices had died in a moment. Peter Cazalet went down to the course to see his stricken horse who, to everyone's relief, was led away to the racecourse stables, apparently sound.

Dick Francis was inconsolable and was taken by Cazalet up to the Royal Box. There, Queen Elizabeth demonstrated what Sir Michael Oswald has called

Opposite: The drama unfolds. Dick Francis is powerless to help as Devon Loch flounders yards from the post. In the last frame E.S.B. is about to claim the race.

the ability to deal with disaster and disappointment. Whatever her private thoughts, she managed to offer sympathy and kindness to a much admired jockey. She told him resignedly, 'That's racing I suppose,' but Francis noted that 'Both she and the Queen were obviously sorrowful and upset by what had happened.'

The postmortems began immediately and have never stopped in 45 years. There are four principal theories. Dick Francis feels that the wall of noise frightened the horse and that he was literally paralysed with fear for a moment, like a rabbit trapped in the glare of a car's headlights. Lord Oaksey, who has discussed the race with Queen Elizabeth, believes she slightly favours this theory. Fulke Walwyn thought Devon Loch had tried to jump a nonexistent fence – he was nearly level with a water jump on the other side of the rail – and this shadow jump theory is the one favoured by Sir Michael Oswald and Lord Oaksey. Bryan Marshall reported that on three occasions when he rode the horse he felt him falter, as if he had some sort of medical weakness. The fourth conjecture is that he suffered a severe bout of cramp. It may be one or none of these. It may even be a combination. Devon Loch may have become disorientated by the noise *and* tried to jump an imaginary fence. We shall never know.

Happier times for Devon Loch and Dick Francis, enjoying a gallop at Fairlawne.

Devon Loch was not finished and later the same year in the King George VI Chase he ran a superb second place to Rose Park, also Fairlawne trained, and part-owned by Queen Elizabeth's great friend Dick Wilkins. He was injured a few months later and retired. Queen Elizabeth gave him to Noel Murless, one of the Queen's trainers, to use as a hack. He and Murless did not hit it off so the old horse was ridden out every day by the trainer's teenage daughter, Julie, until 1963 when he was put down aged 17. He never went back to Aintree. Dick Francis was persuaded by Lord Abergavenny, who looked after Queen Elizabeth's racing affairs at the time, to retire at the top and he too never took on the National fences again.

Royal Racing

The reason for Devon Loch's sprawl has never been important, other than as a topic for racing discussion for countless years. The race can never be rerun. Defeat has a contrary nature in sport and Devon Loch is assured an immortal place in racing's history, a far more famous one than if he had actually won the Grand National. Queen Elizabeth was quite wrong when she said, 'That's racing'. What happened to Devon Loch was a million-zillion to one shot and will surely never happen again. It will always be unfathomable.

∾ The Feast of Lingfield

It quickly became a tradition for Queen Elizabeth to spend a long weekend at Fairlawne in early December to coincide with an agreeable two-day meeting at Lingfield, then a most picturesque Surrey jumping track. The local vicar of Shipbourne, Archdeacon Edward Maples-Earle, gave the annual jaunt the grand title 'The Feast of Lingfield'. Feast was an appropriate term because for many years the chef at Fairlawne was Albert Roux, whose restaurant Le Gavroche is now one of the most applauded in Britain. The routine on a typical Saturday would be to watch the horses work, travel the dozen miles to Lingfield races for the afternoon and then return for a dinner prepared by Monsieur Roux and a little light entertainment afterwards from Noel Coward who was happy to oblige with a song. On the Sunday Queen Elizabeth would go to St Giles Church for the morning service. She would invariably walk down the main aisle to leave, and pause outside for a chat should anyone wish to take a photograph.

The villagers and the Fairlawne staff all appreciated her interest in them. Edward Cazalet recalls, 'She loved to chitchat, especially with the local characters like Bunny Dunn, the Fairlawne blacksmith. He was a huge hulk of a man, a village smith in the best tradition of that bygone breed. Then there was Joe Hills, the gallops' man. He was always out on his tractor and she would stop to speak to him. He took over as captain of the village cricket team when my father retired from the role. Queen Elizabeth loves genuine people but is always very quick to spot a poseur. At Fairlawne we always appreciated her sense of fun.'

Peter Cazalet would always make sure there were four or five royal runners at the Lingfield meeting and many of Queen Elizabeth's favourite horses won there, Double Star, The Rip, Laffy, Makaldar and Escalus among them.

Of these, Double Star was a great favourite and a standing dish at The Feast of Lingfield where he won the Ashdown Handicap Chase three times. He was a grand servant to the stables winning 17 times in 50 outings. He also won at least once every season from 1956 to 1963, eight consecutive years. Double Star was a product of an Irish connection set up by Cazalet to find suitable horses for Queen Elizabeth. He was spotted by Judge Wylie after winning a Leopardstown bumper in Ireland and Queen Elizabeth immediately appreciated that he was a very good-looking horse, rangy and nearly black with a small white star and three white socks. Ivor Herbert, a very good judge, described him as a 'beautiful horse'.

The cost of bringing the elegant Double Star to Fairlawne in 1956 was not far short of £4000 but, like Monaveen and Manicou before him, he proved an almost instant success winning three out of seven novice hurdles and earning an accolade from *The Sporting Life* as, 'the most promising steeplechasing prospect we have seen for many seasons'. After limbering up with a hurdles win at Cheltenham the following season, he set about proving *The Sporting Life* right with a chasing win at Sandown on his second attempt over fences. Sir Martin Gilliat, Queen Elizabeth's private secretary and keeper of the royal racing notebook, wrote, 'His jumping was a joy to behold.' Even better was his next outing in the inaugural Tote Investors Cup at Newbury, the most important novice chase before Christmas. Arthur Freeman, new stable jockey at Fairlawne, only had to push him out for a victory that presented officials with a protocol problem. Queen Elizabeth was due to present the trophy to the winning owner. She was spared having to present the trophy to herself by the sponsors' chairman, Jim Phillips. It was her very first trophy. She enthusiastically told Peter Cazalet, 'Didn't he jump the last fence beautifully!'

A little headstrong in his early career, Double Star was settling better and beginning to shape as if *The Sporting Life*'s glowing praise might not be too wide of the mark. He contributed to another royal first as one-half of Queen Elizabeth's first winning double as an owner when he won at Hurst Park on 8 January 1959. He actually was a 'Double Star'. During a comparatively lean period for his owner – she had 30 consecutive losers in 1959 – he was the only decent horse. The trainer's son, Edward Cazalet, a more than useful amateur rider, took the mount at Hurst Park just before Christmas that year when Freeman was injured. Double Star was a horse that took a little knowing.

'He was as fast a two-miler as there was,' recalls Edward, 'but I didn't realize that he didn't like the open ditch. If you sat still he would measure it himself, but he did not appreciate being kicked into it. I booted him into the fence and he belted it, which knocked the stuffing out of him.' Even so Double Star only just failed to give more than two stone to Certain Justice.

The turning point in the horse's career came when he tried to break Queen Elizabeth's Cheltenham Festival hoodoo in the 1960 Champion Chase over two miles. Freeman was back in the saddle and the horse was going like a winner when he tried to uproot the fifth fence from home. It was a miracle that Freeman stayed on, but their chance was gone. It knocked the horse's confidence and he rarely showed the same élan again, although his beloved Lingfield still brought out the best in him. Arthur Freeman, who rode Double Star to victory 10 times, will forever be associated with the horse but he was riding in his last Cheltenham before he retired on medical advice. Freeman was a very tough jockey but took more than his fair share of falls. He also had weight problems and lived on a diet of 'pee pills' as the jockeys call them. It did his health no good at all and the Injured Jockeys Fund later had to help him through a bout of alcoholism. David Mould, then a junior jockey at Fairlawne, remembers Arthur Freeman with regard: 'He was a tough guy. He wasn't a stylist, being more of an old huntsman but if he'd had a few quid on, you couldn't beat him.'

Double Star would win four more times at Lingfield, twice at the 'Festival'. On 9 December 1961 he was again part of a history-making day when he was the second leg of the first royal treble. He was ridden by Bill Rees, the new stable jockey. David Mould wanted the job but Cazalet thought he needed someone more experienced at that stage. French import Laffy took the Oxted Novices Chase Div.II at 1.30, Double Star his favourite Ashdown Handicap Chase at

The handsome Double Star [Edward Cazalet] at Hurst Park before the Westminster Chase, 18 December 1959.

The Rip [Bill Rees] jumps the last fence upsides the incomparable Mandarin [Fred Winter] in the Walter Hyde Chase at Kempton, 25 January 1962.

2 o'clock and half an hour later the treble was sealed by The Rip in the Eridge Handicap Chase. Queen Elizabeth was there and it remains one of her favourite racing days. A specially commissioned painting by the artist Peter Biegel depicts all three horses together under the trees at Fairlawne and was later used as a Christmas card by their proud owner.

Legend has it that The Rip was discovered by Queen Elizabeth in a field behind the Red Cat pub in Wootton Marshes not far from Sandringham but, like all good stories, it's not strictly true. The colt was domiciled next to the pub but Queen Elizabeth had known all about him since he was foaled. He was by her good horse Manicou out of a mare called Easy Virtue, which the landlord's son, Jack Irwin, had bought for 41 guineas as a prospective hunter. Easy Virtue proved unridable so he decided to breed from her. Queen Elizabeth was kept appraised of the progress of the colt – called Spoilt Union – who had grown into something of an ugly duckling. Eventually she went to the Red Cat with Major Eldred Wilson, who broke in her horses, to see for herself. Captain Charles Moore, manager of the Royal Studs, sealed the deal with Mr Irwin for 400 guineas, a considerable bargain as it turned out.

Spoilt Union was promptly renamed The Rip and sent to Major Wilson's farm to be prepared for his racing career. Wilson was a key figure in Queen Elizabeth's racing activities for many years, and one of the great characters to whom she always took a shine. She once said that he had 'a touch of Irish in him'. He had a special system of ropes, arranged so that he could lower himself into the saddle from above an unsuspecting young horse. If it took exception and started to do an impersonation of a bucking bronco, the good major could speedily shin back up the rope to safety. In his younger days Major

Wilson was an excellent point-to-point rider, managing to survive the customary selection of falls with nothing more than a broken collarbone. His secret was many an afternoon spent on the tennis court practising his tumbles. He would run to the net at speed, leap over and then fall on purpose, taking care not to injure himself.

The Rip, a big bay horse, was a kindly but clumsy soul who displayed a lack of grace that he took with him into the chasing game. At the now defunct Birmingham course he started at 1/4 for his second chase, and only made it to the second fence before catapulting Bill Rees out of the saddle with a jump which Ivor Herbert described as that of a 'stiff-legged cat on to a table'. At the end of the season he turned out in a better-class race at Folkestone and started as a friendless 20/1 'rag'. He was deserted by Rees who rode his stable companion and hot favourite Blue Dolphin. David Mould had the leg up on The Rip, who now sported black blinkers to liven him up, and who blasted on at the eighth fence and was never headed again. The victory was Mould's first in a steeplechase for Queen Elizabeth. He recalls, 'The Rip was a bit cumbersome but I knew I was going to win on him. I built his confidence as we went along. Every time he jumped a fence I would pat him down the neck and pull his ears and say, "You've cracked it son. You've made it."' Not too many royal winners start at 20/1. Queen Elizabeth received the news of the win by telegram while on a train journey in the White Highlands in Kenya.

Next season The Rip was even better. He won four races in a row, including his part in the Lingfield treble, before running the great Mandarin to half a length at Kempton Park. He had jumped the last fence upsides the horse who would win the Cheltenham Gold Cup that March. The Rip took his place in the Gold Cup but was outclassed, probably not staying up the famous Cheltenham hill. But for a 400 guinea horse who started life behind a pub The Rip's rise to join racing's elite was nothing less than a wonderful fairy story, and his best ever run was yet to come.

In the 1964 Hennessy Gold Cup at Newbury The Rip was placed third in a field of nine. Twelve lengths in front was the useful Ferry Boat. Ten lengths clear of Ferry Boat was the immortal Arkle. Admittedly the greatest chaser of all time was conceding 33 lbs to The Rip but, even so, it remains one of the best races ever run by one of Queen Elizabeth's horses. It was always important to find a good home for a retired racehorse and, on Edward Cazalet's recommendation, The Rip went to a young barrister called Richard Scott for point-to-point races and some hunting. The up-and-coming barrister is now Lord Scott, well known for the 'Arms to Iraq' Inquiry.

✎ The Doping of Laffy

Laffy, inexplicably named, had a touch of class and in his best season of 1962 was beaten by just three lengths by the legendary Mill House. He was discovered by Colonel Wladyslaw Bobinski, the Fairlawne French connection, who knew the Cazalets through Victor's association with General Sikorski. In the relatively early days of Queen Elizabeth's racing ownership French horses did not command the huge prices of today. In any case she would not pay enormous sums. Bobinski, who had an expert eye for a horse, had been specifically asked to look out for a steeplechaser and recommended Laffy, who had reasonable hurdles form and the stamp of a chaser. 'He had big feet,' observed Bobinski. Laffy was described in Fairlawne's royal record as a 'strongly made bay with plenty of class. A very safe jumper.' Bill Rees, however, quickly noticed that the horse had a dislike for the water jump, which may in part account for all but three of his 12 wins coming at Lingfield where the water jump was taken only once in a three-mile chase.

After settling in at Fairlawne and taking his novice chase comfortably at the Festival of Lingfield, Laffy lined up at Hurst Park against Mill House in the New Century Chase. Fortunately on this occasion the giant chaser tipped up at halfway, leaving the way clear for Laffy to take the lead two out and notch up his second royal victory. Hurst Park was soon to be closed to make way for a housing estate so a plan was hatched for Laffy to go for the Monaveen Chase, named in honour of the first royal chaser, at the track's very last jumping meeting in mid-March. He would never make it to the start. He was the only one of Queen Elizabeth's horses to be involved in a doping scandal, which was hushed up at the time. It had all the trimmings of a Dick Francis story.

Racing is often awash with rumours of doping rings and in this particular season the key figure was thought to be a glamorous, well-dressed young woman who arrived at stables posing as a prospective owner. She would case the joint, carefully noting the security of the equine residents. Sure enough,

The riderless Laffy had already deposited jockey Bill Rees at the first fence in the Cheltenham Handicap Chase at Cheltenham, 16 November 1962. He kept going, however, keeping Limonali [David Nicholson] (centre) and Generous Star [Josh Gifford] (right) company.

a chauffeur-driven limousine containing just such a lady pulled up to the gates of Fairlawne one afternoon while Peter Cazalet was away at Newbury races and the yard was in the care of head lad Jim Fairgrieve. She was not expected. Fairgrieve, before he died, revealed the whole story to Bill Curling: 'She told me she was sending two horses to be trained at Fairlawne and they were on their way from France. She also said she had spoken to the guv'nor the previous evening and made arrangements with him to look around the stables. She spoke with an accent and said, "I expect he forgot to tell you", which didn't sound like the guv'nor to me. He never forgot things like that.'

Such a deceit would be impossible today in the age of mobile phones. A simple call could have ascertained the truth, but on this occasion Fairgrieve thought it best not to upset a prospective patron. He escorted her and the chauffeur, who took copious notes, around the yard and boxes. No one really noticed the chauffeur because the *femme fatale* was so charming. 'She said she would look forward to seeing me again,' remembered Fairgrieve. 'The whole staff felt they would look forward to seeing her again!'

Peter Cazalet hit the roof when he found out, although admitted he should have warned his staff about rumours of a beautiful horse-doper. Security was tightened at Fairlawne as a result and Laffy was put in one of five alarmed security boxes to await his run in the Monaveen Chase. On the morning of the race Jim Fairgrieve unlocked the stables and turned off the alarms at 5.15 to feed

Part Two ❧ Fairlawne

the horses before the stable lads started work. He didn't lock up again as he could hear some of the lads up and about, and went for a cup of tea. Fairgrieve and Cazalet went out with the first lot while the day's runners were prepared for travelling. On their return they were called urgently to look at Laffy. They quickly realized he had been got at: 'We called the vet and he thought the same as we did. He took a saliva and blood sample and signed the horse off as unfit to run and told me to let him rest. The blood sample showed he was full of dope.'

It was a significant event to dope a royal horse. Detectives turned over every stone at Fairlawne and grilled each member of the stable staff but the culprit remained undiscovered. Whoever did it was, in effect, foiled by the new stable security. He or she had been forced to wait until Jim Fairgrieve switched off the alarms at 5.15 a.m. so the doping had been easily discovered, forcing Laffy's withdrawal. If he had been doped in the middle of the night the obvious signs would have worn off by morning. His condition might well have gone undetected and he would have raced with disastrous consequences for both horse and punters. As it was, Laffy recovered quickly and won a chase at Lingfield five days later. The racing public never knew what drama had unfolded behind the scenes.

Six months later a gang of five horse-dopers was brought to trial at Lewes Assizes in Sussex. They had travelled throughout the country doping more than 40 horses in the process. Among the defendants was a former au pair, Micheline Lugeon, the stunning daughter of a Swiss cemetery superintendent. Three stable lads from Fairlawne had been able to identify her, not from her face but from her excellent legs and slim calves. Prosecuting, Mr Owen Stable, later Judge Stable, told the court that, 'A young and attractive Swiss beautician, working in league with the horse-doping gang, exploited her good looks and got into 23 stables in different parts of the country.' Jim Fairgrieve and the stable lads at Fairlawne were evidently not the only heads to be turned by Mademoiselle Lugeon. Mr Justice Melford Stevenson gave the gang varying sentences of between one and two years. This was quite lenient considering that some horses had actually run while doped, which was highly dangerous for the jockeys. Peter Cazalet was far from amused at being kept waiting for more than a day to be called by the court as it kept him away from the important business of racing.

Meanwhile Laffy, showing no ill effects, travelled across the Irish Sea for The Ulster Harp National at Downpatrick in Northern Ireland. It was a wonderfully colourful experience, rather in the manner of the BBC television series *Ballykissangel*. Laffy was sent over a week in advance with Fairlawne's travelling head lad, Bill Braddon, to acclimatize before the race. Braddon would exercise him every day along the sands at Tyrella, a few miles from the course. One morning Laffy as he had a habit of doing, dropped his shoulder, deposited Braddon on the sand and scampered joyfully along the beach. Fortunately three men attending to their lobster pots saw the riderless animal and managed to catch him. Peter Cazalet never knew of the adventure, although there was more to come when he travelled over with Queen Elizabeth and her enthusiastic private secretary Sir Martin Gilliat.

Much to the chagrin of Bill Rees, it was thought politic to engage an Irish jockey for the race and so Willie Robinson, the rider of Mill House and other Fulke Walwyn horses, was engaged. During the second race on the card, Robinson took a heavy fall at the final flight of hurdles and was promptly given a fearful kicking by a horse behind. He clearly did not know what day it was afterwards and would not have been allowed to continue riding today. The problem was that there was no replacement available. The royal party had severe misgivings. Sir Martin Gilliat observed, 'We need not have worried. He rode a super race.' Even though he could barely stand, Robinson knew every blade of the idiosyncratic switchback course with its twists and turns uphill and down, and rode a finely judged race on automatic pilot coming through two out to win cosily. The Fairlawne record showed that 'despite his comparative lack of experience Laffy is a most accomplished and versatile performer. Robinson rode a perfect race.'

The finish of the race was a glorious mixture of triumph and confusion as Laffy was actually second past the post. The problem was that an Irish horse called Connkeheley had rejoined the race after being pulled up earlier for running out at a fence. It appeared to be a tremendous duel for the line with the Irish nag running on strongly to beat Laffy by a neck. At least that's what most of the crowd, who had missed the earlier mishap, thought. Connkeheley was like the cross-country runner who hides in the bushes while the field charge round a muddy course only to join in again, fresh as paint, when they reappear near home. No wonder he finished full of running. Fortunately, the officials knew what had transpired and the course commentator helpfully announced, 'The first horse is the second if you see what I mean.'

Afterwards it seemed that every member of a bumper crowd wanted a memento from poor old Laffy's mane. The entire course was like a giant Victorian fairground. Queen Elizabeth gleefully stayed with the horse while the well-wishers patted and stroked their hero. One woman approached her and asked her to bless her twins. Laffy had started 3/1 favourite in a field of 15, so more than a few pints of stout were drunk in his honour in Downpatrick that night. It was a memorable day for everyone except Willie Robinson. He did not remember a thing.

❧ Gay Record – A Problem Solved

Gay Record and the gently eccentric Irishman Jack O'Donoghue were a perfect match. Gay Record was a bit of a nutcase at Fairlawne. David Mould remembers that on one occasion they put a sheep in his box to try and calm him down but he tried to bite the unfortunate animal's ears off. The experiment of sending Gay Record to O'Donoghue's farm in rural Surrey suited the cranky horse, who never enjoyed the disciplined regime of Fairlawne. On the farm he had the run of the place.

In 1959 the Irish-bred bay gelding was in disgrace – winless, labelled impossible at Fairlawne and sent back to Sandringham for the summer. He had always been thought to have potential as a chaser from the time Major Eldred Wilson broke him in, but he was now seven. It was Major Wilson who suggested to Queen Elizabeth that she might try sending the renegade to O'Donoghue's Priory Stables near Reigate, from where the Irishman had sent out 40/1 shot Nickel Coin to win the notorious 1951 Grand National when 12 fell at the first fence and only three out of 36 runners completed the course. O'Donoghue also had a reputation for being good with problem horses. Gay Record was certainly that.

Queen Elizabeth gave O'Donoghue two pieces of advice when he came to Sandringham to collect the beast. She thought Gay Record would prefer an open box so that he could see what was going on in the yard. She also thought his aversion to travelling in a horsebox might be cured by taking him to the racecourse several times without running him. O'Donoghue, who died in 1998, told Bill Curling, 'They were good pieces of advice and I followed them.' Certainly Gay Record would never have seen any sights similar to those at

Priory Stables. Sir Michael Oswald observes, 'Jack had a great affinity with animals. If you went to see him, he had donkeys and geese and exotic chickens. Jack himself was a very quiet, very Irish and rather lovable chap.' From his box, Gay Record had a good view of the canaries and golden pheasants in the stable aviary and enjoyed the companionship of O'Donoghue's homebred donkeys and a diet augmented by liberal dollops of home-made honey.

Collis Montgomery, a friend of O'Donoghue's from his old Irish point-to-point days, was persuaded to come over from Ireland and help look after Gay Record. He decided to take the horse hunting. At first Gay Record was very excitable, but Montgomery would make sure they hacked 10 miles on the roads before the meet and 10 miles home again. Gradually the horse's resolve to

Gay Record [Bobby Beasley] flies the last fence on his way to winning the Sevenoaks Chase at Folkestone, 20 October 1964. It was Queen Elizabeth's 100th victory as owner.

be a nuisance was softened. After four months, Gay Record was ready for a race at Fontwell and finished second to the Fairlawne-trained chaser Cupid's Charge. It was a more than promising effort after nearly a year away from the track. That progress was confirmed at the start of the new season when Gay Record returned to the Sussex track and led all the way to land his first novices chase. It was his only win of 1960/61 but it was a start.

Following the horses for courses theory, O'Donoghue reasoned that if Gay Record liked Fontwell he might well enjoy the figure-of-eight track at Windsor, one of Queen Elizabeth's favourite courses and practically at the bottom of her garden. He was correct. This time ridden by Gene Kelly, Gay Record galloped all the way from the front, jumped immaculately and smashed the course record, his best-ever performance. Afterwards O'Donoghue discovered the horse had twisted a plate during the race, and so removed it and stuck it

Gay Record and
small friend at
Jack O'Donoghue's
Priory Stables.

in his pocket. When Queen Elizabeth came up to say goodbye for the day and shake his hand, he inadvertently shoved the plate into her outstretched hand, much to her amusement.

While Gay Record soldiered on as an honest handicapper, O'Donoghue found a strapping horse called Sunbridge for Queen Elizabeth in Ireland. He was thought good enough to run in the 1964 renewal of the National Hunt Chase, a slog for amateur riders at Cheltenham. John Lawrence (now Lord Oaksey) was engaged to ride and still believes he should have won on the 33/1 shot. He recalls, 'I rode an absolute berk of a race. In those days the course was different and you went off behind the stands in the National Hunt Chase and back on to the racecourse for your last circuit. I was about eighth when we came back on to the racecourse for the second circuit. But the first two fences on the racecourse he "pinged". He passed about four horses at the first and five at the second and I was bloody well in front. Half a mile too soon, which was tragic! They went by him from the second last. Sunbridge never won a race and I never rode a winner for Queen Elizabeth.'

In the autumn of 1964 attention at Fairlawne was turned to sending out Queen Elizabeth's 100th winner, a great milestone for any owner. Both the novice hurdler Arch Point and the useful Super Fox narrowly missed the glory when, almost unnoticed, Jack O'Donoghue entered old Gay Record, rising 13, for an undistinguished contest at Folkestone. Ironically, it was called the Sevenoaks Handicap Chase, named after the town close to Fairlawne. The old boy had been coughing but O'Donoghue, after consulting Sir Martin Gilliat, decided to take a chance. Gay Record's regular pilot, Gene Kelly, was injured so his place was taken by Bobby Beasley, one of the few riders to accomplish the treble of Grand National, Gold Cup and Champion Hurdle.

O'Donoghue, feeling the pressure, told Beasley to bowl along in front. He only had two runners to beat, and one of those fell, leaving Gay Record just needing to be pushed out for a three-length win. The 100th winner caught Queen Elizabeth a little by surprise – she was in Scotland when it happened.

Gay Record continued to battle on for a couple more seasons and even won a race at the age of 14 at the old course at Wye in Kent. It was the only royal winner for Michael Scudamore, father of the champion jockey Peter Scudamore, and his last winner over fences before a horrible fall at Wolverhampton the following week left him severely injured. In the spring of 1967 Gay Record finally called it a day and was retired at 15. Since his banishment from Fairlawne the old horse had run 59 times, won nine races and been placed a further 23 times. He was as game a front runner as you could hope to find. Queen Elizabeth gave him to Jack O'Donoghue and he pottered about with the donkeys at Priory Stables until he was finally put down at the grand age of 22.

Queen Elizabeth much enjoyed the company of Jack O'Donoghue, one of the great characters of the sport. She would motor down from London with a chauffeur and a detective and spend an hour feeding apples to the horses and chatting to Jack. On her very first visit, he stationed a man outside the pub at the end of the road to make sure the royal car took the right turning. As it pulled into the stables O'Donoghue was astonished to see the Queen as well as the Queen Mother. 'The Queen has come with me,' said Queen Elizabeth easily. 'She had a slack afternoon.'

❧ Breaking the Mould

David Mould's leg stank. The normally chirpy royal jockey was in the depths of despair, feeling as if he was 'being eaten alive'. He had broken his right leg in four places when taking a fall at Folkestone. He had been tangled up in a sea of legs and kicked around like a ball on the beach. The leg had practically disintegrated and Mould, just 24, was dispatched to a Harley Street surgeon to be put back together again, the habitual lot of a jump jockey. The surgeon inserted two steel plates and enough screws to assemble a small car into the injured leg while the young jockey fretted about when he would be able to resume riding. It was November 1964, with more than six months left of a season in which Arkle, the greatest ever steeplechaser, was in his prime. Mould's anxiety about

David Mould in classic riding pose aboard Escalus in the parade before the Champion Hurdle at Cheltenham, 18 March 1970.

when he might return to the saddle soon gave way to concerns that he might never ride again when the leg became infected and started oozing pus.

His surgeon was abroad and Mould, confronted by medical etiquette, could find no one else to treat him. In desperation he approached Queen Elizabeth and told her, 'Ma'am, I'm going to lose this leg, I know I am. Can you help me?' He had asked the right person. Queen Elizabeth has always had great admiration for the bravery of the jockeys who carry her colours. She arranged for Mould to see her personal surgeon, Sir Henry Osmond-Clarke, who agreed to operate, with the warning that the jockey might wake up minus one leg. Thankfully that proved not to be the case and Mould, in plaster from hip to toe, waited with a deal more patience than before for his leg to heal. It was worth the wait because he would eventually ride 104 winners for the Queen Mother, many more than any other jockey.

While he was convalescing in hospital the next February he received an invitation to a dinner-dance at the Savoy Hotel in London to celebrate Queen Elizabeth's 100th winner, the aptly named Gay Record. The party was organized by one of her great racing chums, Dick Wilkins, a man for whom the sobriquet

Royal Racing

'larger than life' might have been devised. He was a successful stockjobber in the City and a shortish man of ample proportions. He was one of the most popular owners in racing, always twinkly, always the life and soul of the party. In his later years he lived in an exquisite apartment in the Savoy with breathtaking views of the Thames.

The party, or the 'big night' as Gay Record's trainer Jack O'Donoghue ingenuously called it, was a glittering affair befitting those Fairlawne days when racing folk brushed shoulders with famous stars. Elizabeth Taylor, violet-eyed and beautiful, took most of the admiring looks, although the star of the show was David Mould. Refusing to let a little thing like a plaster cast stop him, he had cajoled the nurses at his Kent hospital to dress him and let him loose for a night out in London. He drove himself: 'I had a Ford Zephyr which I thought was the cat's whiskers. You changed gear on the steering wheel so all I had to do was drop my leg on the accelerator. It was a bit hairy. I couldn't use the brake.'

The doorman at the Savoy solemnly opened the car door when Mould drew up outside and looked astonished when crutches and plaster cast appeared. 'Park it,' said Mould cheerfully. 'Park it?' replied the doorman, 'I'll ruddy hide it! You can't drive home in that.' Once inside, a stool was found for Mould to rest his injured leg on but Queen Elizabeth was not about to let him languish. She suggested a dance even though he warned her that if he trod on her he might break her leg and never know it. Undaunted, they enjoyed one of the most famous of royal dances, a sight that none of those present will ever forget.

Mould was not yet the first jockey at Fairlawne. When Arthur Freeman packed it in Peter Cazalet thought he needed someone of greater experience than the lad from Ashford. He went for the likeable Bill Rees and between them they shared a golden age of winners for Queen Elizabeth. Mould, whose father was a horse-dealer, began as an apprentice on the flat with Epsom trainer Staff Ingham, who in his riding days had won the 1923 Royal Hunt Cup at Ascot for George V. Ingham enjoyed a reputation for producing good, hardworking jockeys so when the 17-year-old apprentice grew too heavy for the flat he decided to sell Mould's indentures to a National Hunt trainer. He took him and a horse down to Fairlawne but Peter Cazalet chose to buy just the jockey, and so one dark Sunday evening Mould found himself travelling down with his father to the grandeur of Fairlawne. He recalls, 'No one was about.

It was dark and I went upstairs above the stables where the single staff lived and there was a pokey little room which was mine, I thought, bloody hell, what's this? It was so hard. There were about 12 of us kids starting work at five in the morning. But I wasn't going to give in and decided that I was going to crack it. After all, this was the cream, a royal yard.'

In those days it was certainly a case of work hard and play hard. Mould's partner in crime was the popular Dave Dick, who had ridden E.S.B. in Devon Loch's Grand National. Tall for a jockey, with an eye for the good life, the clubbable Dick would have to waste to manage 11 stone 7 lbs. At the start of one Grand National he spotted a banner bearing the words 'Repent or your sins will find you out'. 'Well if that's the case,' said Dave, 'I won't get as far as the first fence.'

On one occasion Mould drove the two of them to Birmingham races on a Monday. It was foggy and after struggling up the motorway they found that racing was abandoned. So they went back to London to sample the delights of a cocktail bar in the newly opened Hilton Hotel. The chosen drink was a coconut and rum concoction graphically called 'Suffering Bastards'. Mould, who was not much of a drinker, quickly developed a taste for the sugary mixture and downed several before getting up to leave. He promptly fell on the floor where he was joined by Dick who vainly tried to help his friend up. The two royal jockeys – Dick had ridden Queen Elizabeth's only Cheltenham Festival winner – were to be seen struggling up the stairs from the bar on their hands and knees. And they still had to get home to Epsom, where they were living.

It was very foggy. Mould was at the wheel and Dick was riding shotgun. After a while Mould declared, 'We've hit something, get out and have a look.' Dick returned and spoke the immortal words, 'We're in a bus.' They had driven up the open rear platform of a double-decker. The fearless twosome took the only action available to them. They did a runner. On arriving home at Epsom Mould reported the car stolen. And he got away with it.

Professionally, David Mould was determined to be a winner, something which didn't go down too well with the authorities in November 1969. The scene of his nemesis was again Folkestone. It is quite extraordinary how often this minor track played host to great drama. This time Mould lost his temper with an amateur called Peter Upson who, according to Mould, continued to take his ground on the inside, something that senior jockeys hate above all else.

They are unlikely to accept it from a fellow professional, let alone an amateur. It was just a novice hurdle and Mould was on an undistinguished sort called Master Daniel. Even so, he warned Mr Upson not to take his ground again – which, of course, Upson promptly did. Mould responded by giving the amateur the sort of wallop with his whip that he normally reserved for the gallant hurdler Makaldar. The Jockey Club were unimpressed and gave Mould a four-week holiday, which might have been less but for his belligerent attitude towards authority. While Mould was out of action, Richard Dennard stepped in for the ride on Master Daniel at Worcester and galloped to a comfortable victory giving Queen Elizabeth a landmark 200th winner – a much harder punishment for Mould than anything meted out by the stewards. The only consolation was that his suspension gave him some honeymoon time with his new wife, the Olympic show-jumper Marion Coakes.

Marion, a delightful blonde, did wonders for Mould's status at Fairlawne. While they were searching for a house to buy near the stables he asked Peter Cazalet if she could come and ride out. Cazalet readily agreed and took her under his wing when she arrived with the stable jockey. Normally Cazalet decreed that there was no talking during riding out but on this particular morning he continued to engage Mrs Mould in cheerful conversation. Marion, who had won an Olympic silver medal on the popular pony-sized show-jumper Stroller, impressed the trainer with her expertise and, at the end of work, he invited her up to the house for breakfast. Mould, who had never been asked to breakfast in more than 10 years at Fairlawne, piped up, 'Does that include me sir?' to which Cazalet had no choice other than to declare testily that of course it did.

Mould is perhaps a surprising royal jockey. He was a bit of a geezer, far removed from Dick Francis, the country parson of racing. His results did the talking for him and there was no one more determined to ride winners for Queen Elizabeth. Racing historian George Ennor observes that, 'In terms of excitement, David Mould was a terrific jockey.' He rode his last royal winner on the big grey horse Inch Arran in the Topham Trophy at Liverpool in March 1973. It was a famous victory and was also Peter Cazalet's 262nd and final royal winner. According to Queen Elizabeth's racing manager, Sir Michael Oswald, 'Inch Arran didn't always bother to take off properly on a park course. But in the Topham he never touched a twig.' There had been more

The dashing grey Inch Arran [Richard Dennard] is in hot pursuit of Charlie Potheen [Barry Brogan] during the Kencot Handicap Chase at Newbury, 25 March 1972. Unfortunately he fell, handing Charlie victory.

drama before the race. Mould was nowhere to be seen as the 3.05 start time approached. Unbeknown to the connections, he had missed the exit on the M6 and was driving like a madman to try and make the race. Meanwhile, John Lawrence was standing by in the weighing room wearing the royal colours. With barely a minute to go before Lawrence would have to mount up, Mould dashed in and literally tore the colours off him. As he ran out Mould took the opportunity to shout over his shoulder to the future Lord Oaksey, 'He'd have run away with you.' Typically, Mould and Inch Arran broke the course record.

Makaldar: Old Lop-Ears

Queen Elizabeth has always hated her horses being punished with the whip. Makaldar, her most successful hurdler, was a contrary individual who would be galvanized for battle by the stick but never seemed to be soured by this. He formed a special bond with David Mould who won 12 races on him, not one without a struggle. The jockey confessed to Queen Elizabeth that he had to be hard on the horse or he would never win. She replied, 'Well, try not to be too hard.'

Makaldar was found for Fairlawne by the French connection. Colonel Wladyslaw Bobinski spotted him running well in a hurdle race at Auteuil and recommended him to Peter Cazalet. The imposing chestnut, fully 17 hands with his big donkey's ears, arrived at Fairlawne in the spring of 1963 a gauche, inexperienced colt, and was promptly gelded by Cazalet who decided to run him in his own colours until a suitable owner could be found. That suitable owner was watching on television when Makaldar, ridden by Mould, made his debut in a good-quality novice, the Hedge Hoppers' Hurdle at Newbury, at the end of October. Kirriemuir, later to win the Champion Hurdle at

Cheltenham, made all the running but Makaldar stayed on well to take the runner-up spot. Mould learnt the secret of the horse that day: he was lazy. He recalls going to see him after that first defeat and telling him, 'You lazy git, you should have won today.' Makaldar looked at the jockey laughingly as if to say, 'You weren't tough enough today.'

After the race Queen Elizabeth telephoned Cazalet and bought the Gallic giant. It quickly proved an inspired choice. He won six races off the reel, four of them in the space of just seven weeks. The most exciting victory came at Sandown in the Village Hurdle. Although just a four-year-old, Makaldar was clearly a man. He was soon off the bit, with Mould apparently riding for his life. Practically tailed off as they passed the stands for the first time, Mould was 'peeling him two or three off', which is nothing to do with preparing an apple but polite jockey talk for 'leathering' a horse with the whip. Another jockey called over to Mould to leave the horse alone. 'Why don't you mind your f***ing business,' shouted the royal jockey. Makaldar resolutely plugged on. Having made up a huge amount of ground he almost threw it away by ploughing through the second last hurdle. A smaller, less robust, horse would have downed tools but Makaldar was made of sterner stuff, shrugged it off and charged up the hill to win going away by four lengths.

Afterwards Mould was approached by the jockey with whom he had exchanged words in the country. 'Who won?' the latter inquired. 'I did,' said the jubilant Mould. His also-ran rival could not believe it until Mould drew his attention to the winning numbers on the board. Queen Elizabeth was in the unsaddling enclosure to greet the victorious combination. 'He's never made a mistake before,' she observed ruefully.

Soon afterwards Queen Elizabeth was rushed to hospital for an emergency appendix operation. Makaldar was one of several horses in the yard to send flowers to her: a bouquet of baby roses. Double Star and The Rip also sent bouquets and the royal patient wrote to Peter and Zara Cazalet thanking her horses for their good taste. Makaldar also cheered her recovery by taking the Victor Ludorum Hurdle at Haydock in March 1964. It was now a familiar Makaldar story. He was 20 lengths off a good pace at halfway but Mould was confident and the horse came through to win comfortably. That would be enough for his novice season. Makaldar appeared to be something special and there was the whiff of expectation at Fairlawne that one day this might be the yard's best ever chaser.

David Mould was languishing in hospital when Makaldar won again the next December in truly unimpressive fashion. This time it was Bill Rees who learnt that the big chestnut would never do anything the easy way, flattening several hurdles and needing to be stoked up to win a small race at Windsor. John Lawrence came out with the memorable description, 'Makaldar would make a race of it with a donkey.' He too was of the opinion that the horse's future lay over fences. He too would be wrong. Rees kept the ride to win the Stroud Green Hurdle at Newbury before he was injured leaving Dave Dick to take the reins for the County Hurdle at Cheltenham. At this stage of his career Makaldar was not thought speedy enough to try for the Champion Hurdle, certainly not on the fast ground prevailing that year. He put in a lacklustre effort in the conditions.

Makaldar clearly relished the return of his regular pilot at the start of the 1965/6 season. David Mould drove him home by a head in an egg-and-spoon race at Folkestone after he had made his customary 'crucial' error in the latter stages. Mould hogged the inside route all the way round which probably made the difference on the run-in. Makaldar's next outing was the Mackeson Handicap Hurdle at Cheltenham where, after the brilliant but ill-fated Dunkirk had won the Mackeson Gold Cup, he provided the Fairlawne stable with the second half of a rare double at the home of steeplechasing.

Mould powered him up the Cheltenham hill to beat old rival Kirriemuir, who was trying to concede 10 lbs. Makaldar was an unusual horse in that he shaped like a stayer, appeared to win his races at two miles thanks to his stamina but, in reality, did not stay a yard further. His courage saw him through. Back at Cheltenham a month later he resumed hostilities against Kirriemuir but this time was outrun up the hill by another pretender to the hurdling crown, Salmon Spray. Unlike today, when the best horses seem to dance around avoiding each other, it was a treat during this golden age to see the best horses renewing rivalries every few weeks. The modern trend is to gear everything towards one mighty clash at the Cheltenham Festival in March.

Makaldar became the first of Queen Elizabeth's horses to win two races at Cheltenham when he took the TWW Hurdle from Salmon Spray the following October. During the winter the Queen Mother underwent a serious abdominal operation and her first visit to the races for several months saw Makaldar have his warm-up race for the Champion Hurdle in the Eastleigh Handicap Hurdle at Newbury. It was a breathtaking effort and he revelled

Makaldar [David Mould] is at the top of his form winning the Eastleigh Handicap Hurdle at Newbury, 3 March 1967.

in his preferred soft ground. For once, Mould was going so well he allowed himself a look behind fully three flights from home. He needed only to give his mount one powerful hurry-up before he streaked away to win by four lengths. It was probably Makaldar's easiest ever victory and he found himself favourite for the Champion Hurdle.

In 1967 the Champion Hurdle was held on the second day of the March Festival, which was to Makaldar's considerable disadvantage. The going was soft on day one, but much less testing on day two when 23 contested the hurdles' crown. The admirable Worcran was Makaldar's pacemaker and he set a scorching pace out into the country. Makaldar was among the immediate chasers along with old rival Kirriemuir, the Irish challengers Talgo Abbess and Interosian, and Saucy Kit, trained in Yorkshire by Peter Easterby. Held up behind was perhaps the most interesting runner – the talented but wayward

Aurelius who had won the 1961 St Leger for the Noel Murless and Lester Piggott combination. He had proved a flop at stud so was gelded and returned to try his luck over timber. At the top of the hill Saucy Kit and Talgo Abbess moved clear with Makaldar, who had typically just failed to quicken at this stage, giving chase with Aurelius. Jumping the last, Saucy Kit was just in front of the Irish raider with Makaldar and Aurelius three lengths behind.

David Mould is convinced he had Saucy Kit 'covered', but as he prepared for a last surge up the hill the temperamental Aurelius hung badly left carrying Makaldar across the track. 'This Aurelius bastard ran me out,' recalls the still aggrieved Mould. The chance was gone. Saucy Kit beat Aurelius by four lengths with the gallant Makaldar a further length behind. It was no consolation that the stewards threw out Aurelius, placing the royal horse second, the closest Queen Elizabeth would ever get to a Champion Hurdle victory. Mould, never short of a word for his colleagues, addressed Dessie Briscoe, the jockey on Aurelius, as they pulled up: 'You bastard, I'll kill you!'

It was to be Makaldar's last hurrah as a hurdler. Peter Cazalet and Queen Elizabeth had long entertained thoughts that here was a young horse with all the ingredients to make a top-class chaser. Both his royal owner and Cazalet very much represented the old school who thought hurdling was just the hors d'oeuvre before the main course of steeplechasing. The outspoken Mould was convinced the stable star still had a Champion Hurdle in him. He was, after all, still only a seven-year-old. He was also concerned that Makaldar, despite his size, was not a true chasing type. A schooling session and a novice chase at Sandown convinced him. Mould spent a circuit of the Esher course 'eating bracken' as Makaldar finished down the field. After the race Cazalet asked his jockey what had gone wrong. 'This isn't his game,' reported Mould. 'He didn't jump.'

Makaldar did manage one important chasing win, in the Black and White Gold Cup at Ascot when two of his main rivals fell. He plugged away for three seasons with nothing to show for it. Richard Dennard was convinced the horse would have won the 1968 Mackeson Gold Cup but for a heart-stopping mistake when he went straight through the last fence. Makaldar was not clever enough on his feet to put himself right at an obstacle. The old horse began to feel he had done enough and, by the time he lined up for the Londesborough Chase at Sandown on a wintry January afternoon in 1970, he was running in a hood to keep him interested. It was a case of *déjà vu* as

Makaldar ran on strongly up the hill to win the day close home. It was his 15th and last victory in the royal colours in 48 races.

Clearly Makaldar was far superior as a hurdler than as a chaser. But that is not to say he would have continued to enjoy such a magnificent run of success over the smaller obstacles if he had been kept to those. Young pretenders have a habit of improving past the old stagers. And Persian War, one of the all-time greats, was lurking when Makaldar switched to fences. His best chance at Cheltenham was almost certainly in Saucy Kit's race. Softer ground and better fortune might have seen him home but, in any case, like many Fairlawne inmates he was probably a better horse before Christmas. Cazalet never trained him specifically for March at Cheltenham. Although not such a favourite of Queen Elizabeth as The Rip or Game Spirit, Makaldar would be her most successful hurdler. He remains in the memory as David Mould's favourite horse and was, in the jockey's own words, 'an old gent'.

To Say Goodbye

History tends to underestimate Peter Cazalet's achievements. His critics point to the relative absence of big-race winners, certainly in comparison to his contemporaries Fulke Walwyn and Fred Winter. He was cruelly deprived of the Grand National on three occasions and never won the Cheltenham Gold Cup or Champion Hurdle. His biggest race winner was Dunkirk in the two-mile Champion Chase, although he also won the King George VI Chase at Kempton Park four times in the 1950s. He never particularly trained a horse to win a big race. His son Edward Cazalet observes, 'He didn't put a horse away. He would get as much pleasure out of a moderate horse running third in a novice hurdle at Wincanton as in training the winner of a big race.'

Cazalet trained at Fairlawne for 41 years from 1932 until his death in 1973, although for the first six years the training licence was held in the name of Harry Whiteman whom he employed. He was champion trainer three times and in the 1964/65 season he sent out a then record of 82 winners. He cast his net wide to Ireland and France to buy horses to win races.

Queen Elizabeth and her trainer Peter Cazalet at Lingfield Park where they enjoyed so many successful days.

And when they arrived at Fairlawne they were introduced to interval training up a short, steep, three-furlong gallop. It would, he said, 'get their lungs open'. He would send out a fleet of horses to mop up the early season races in the southwest of England. All these Cazalet strategies have proved phenomenally successful for Martin Pipe.

Behind the scenes Cazalet worked hard to clean up racing. 'He was determined to put racing on the straight and narrow,' recalls Edward Cazalet. His efforts to improve the image of the sport were helped first by Anthony Mildmay and later, and more importantly, by Queen Elizabeth. Cazalet trained her horses for 24 years and, from Monaveen at Fontwell Park in 1949 to Inch Arran at Aintree in 1973, he tried to win as many races as possible for her. He deserves considerable credit for keeping her interest alive through the good times and the bad. Although he seldom 'saved' his horses he managed to keep them going through many seasons: Double Star 1956–63, The Rip 1960–66, Laffy 1961–67, Makaldar 1963–70 and the game and popular grey, Chaou II 1967–72. Chaou's career was nearly cut short after his horsebox was involved in a crash near Hampton Court. Poor Chaou was hurled through the partition into the cabin, almost flattening the driver. It must have been a peculiar sight to see a horsebox apparently driven by a large grey horse.

Fairlawne was run very much on military lines with Cazalet as the commander-in-chief. He could be quite aloof, but was loyal to his staff and in return enjoyed great loyalty from them. He could be particularly stern if he discovered anyone smoking in the yard. Sir Michael Oswald remembers watching him give a very attractive lady owner the most 'almighty rocket' when her groom lit up in the yard: 'For about 10 seconds there was an incredible explosion. But when it was over, it completely blew over and he returned to his normal, charming and happy self. But that chap would never light up a cigarette in the yard again.'

David Mould remembers the 'old man', as he called him, finding a cigarette butt on the floor of the yard one morning and instigating an inquisition to discover the culprit. Cazalet banged his riding stick on the desk in the tack room and threatened to sack the lot of them unless someone owned up. The incident has been much embellished over the years, but after administering severe reprimands all round Cazalet discovered that the offender was in fact the Fairlawne postman.

Cazalet never smoked and kept himself very fit, a legacy from his competitive sporting days. On one occasion he was unhappy with the ride David Mould had given a horse and told his jockey back at the stables, 'You're not fit. Get down on the floor and do some press-ups.' Mould obliged and reeled off eight or nine whereupon Cazalet, in his 50s, got down and did 30.

By the time he ran in the Sussex Handicap Chase at Lingfield in March 1973, the grey Chaou II [David Mould] had won 17 races in the royal colours. He did not add to that record here, eventually pulling up.

'Don't tell me you're fit!' was his closing remark.

The thirst for winners at Fairlawne did not diminish in the late Sixties, and nor did the search for good horses. Escalus was found in the border country between England and Scotland and, after Makaldar, was Fairlawne's best royal hurdler. Much of the credit for making the horse went to the second jockey, Richard Dennard, who was very involved in breaking in young horses. He also seized many opportunities when the injury-prone Mould was off games. Escalus was immensely promising, showing class and speed throughout his novice season, and won at the Festival of Lingfield in 1968. A year later he had the chance to show what he was made of when he took on the reigning champion hurdler Persian War at Sandown. Although Persian War needed the race, Escalus charged away from him up the hill to win by an impressive five lengths on the quick going he preferred. At Fairlawne they were hoping that the rains would keep away from Cheltenham in March.

Typically the going was yielding for the Champion Hurdle, and Persian War outstayed his field. Escalus ran a very creditable third. Mould held him up and brought him through to have every chance two out. The horse could have done no more. Escalus was still only five, and the best years looked to be ahead of him. Before he had the chance to prove this he was taken ill, probably with a twisted gut, in the following season and died during an operation to save him.

The sad demise of Escalus occurred in 1970, Sir Michael Oswald's first year as Queen Elizabeth's racing manager. He has looked after her affairs ever

The mud-splattered excitement of National Hunt: King of the Isle [Arthur Freeman] challenges Belgrano [Derek Ancil] at the last flight of the Newtown Hurdle at Newbury, 10 January 1958, but was just run out of it at the line.

since and, despite the obvious disappointment over Escalus, he still looks back on Black Magic as the 'one that got away'. The young chaser was a striking individual, described by Bob McCreery as a 'marvellous young horse'. McCreery, a great racing friend of Queen Elizabeth, was one of the finest postwar amateur riders and would have taken high rank as a professional, as Cazalet himself hoped, had injuries not taken their toll. He broke in Black Magic at his stud in Warwickshire. He described the horse as '17 hands, magnificent limbs, light on his feet, well balanced and a terrific jumper'.

Sir Michael would agree. He enthuses, 'I thought he was a brilliant two-mile chaser. He won a race at Sandown beating Crisp in a faster time than the winner of the hurdle race the same afternoon which contained several Champion Hurdle candidates. I think that takes some doing. He got foot trouble and was never able to fulfil what I considered to be a great potential. He would have gone on to great things.' The Sandown Park Pattern Chase was Black Magic's seventh and final victory in the royal colours.

Queen Elizabeth's favourite racehorse, Game Spirit, joined Fairlawne and had already won 11 races by March 1973 when Peter Cazalet was dying from cancer. The trainer was too ill to travel to Liverpool to watch Fairlawne's last big triumph, Inch Arran in the Topham Trophy. He died two months later aged 66. Afterwards Queen Elizabeth made two last visits to Fairlawne, to say goodbye first to the family and second to all the stable lads. Each one saw her privately with no one else present. It was the end of an era because Edward Cazalet had already decided not to follow his father into a racing career.

Royal Racing

He was already a successful barrister, a profession in which his father had greatly encouraged him. Looking back he says, 'I have no regrets about not taking over the stables.' Queen Elizabeth's own enthusiasm was undimmed despite fears that, with her 73rd birthday approaching, she might give up racing. Fairlawne still has some racing connection: it is now the palatial residence of Prince Khalid bin Abdullah who bought the estate in 1980.

Of the Fairlawne years, Sir Michael Oswald says, 'It was a different age that doesn't really exist now. Competition was less intense. It wasn't the least bit commercialized and everybody knew everybody. It was a smaller world and a very nice one.' After Peter Cazalet's death his name was added to that of Anthony Mildmay, to honour both men's contribution to racing, in the Anthony Mildmay/Peter Cazalet Memorial Handicap Steeplechase at Sandown, one of the best staying chases of the year.

Black Magic [Richard Dennard] leads future Aintree hero Crisp [Richard Pitman] over the last fence in the Sandown Park Pattern Chase at Sandown, 6 November 1971.

A Golden Age

After viewing the horses on the Newmarket gallops the Queen
would return to Freemason Lodge and join Captain Boyd-
Rochfort for a lunch prepared by his eccentric continental
domestic staff. On one occasion the caramelized topping on
a crème brûlée was so hard that the Queen took off her high-
heeled shoe and, to everyone's astonishment, cracked it open
with the heel.

❧ The Captain's Progress

When George VI died, his trainer Captain Cecil Boyd-Rochfort was already 65 and a tangible link with another racing age. He was an Edwardian, described by his stepson, the leading trainer Henry Cecil, as an 'old-fashioned gentleman'. He had been a fixture in the royal racing operation since 1943, but there was no question of retirement when Princess Elizabeth became Queen. His most successful days were still ahead of him although he would never have recognized the game pursued today by his stepson. Boyd-Rochfort was the champion trainer five times but seldom had more than 60 horses, while Henry Cecil routinely has more than 200 in his care. It was a different world.

Despite in some respects appearing to be the quintessential English gentleman, well dressed, courteous and a touch bombastic, the Captain was in fact from County Westmeath in Ireland where his father, Major Hamilton Boyd-Rochfort, was one of the largest landowners. The name Boyd-Rochfort came about when the Captain's great-grandfather, Abraham Boyd married the widow of the Earl of Belvedere whose family name was Rochfort. Cecil's father died of rheumatic fever when he was just six months old leaving his mother to bring up seven children in the magnificent family mansion, Middleton Park. The Boyd-Rochforts were landed gentry and the young Cecil grew up in an environment where hunting and shooting were more important than lessons from the governess. He became a most accomplished shot.

An early interest in horses blossomed into a fascination with the Turf when he travelled across the Irish Sea to Eton. There, at the age of 13, he had a winning bet on a 100/9 shot in the Liverpool Autumn Cup. It was not a schoolboy whim but a careful wager, based on information indirectly received from the owner. Cecil would cycle over to Windsor racecourse to try and elicit information from any trainers or jockeys with whom he built up a passing acquaintance. This was the way he would conduct his betting affairs throughout his life. Henry Cecil remembers that he kept a small black book for betting purposes and would have just one or two bets a season. The horses invariably won. The Eton schoolboy thus found little time for work and a priceless report from his classics master read, 'There has been a good deal of mental nourishment about: but he has not acquired a plate for himself or even a spoonful.'

By the time he left Eton, Boyd-Rochfort was intent on a career in racing. His elder brother, Arthur, was establishing a successful stud at the family

Opposite: Captain Boyd-Rochfort joins Queen Elizabeth and the Queen in the winners' enclosure after Aureole's success in the Hardwicke Stakes at Royal Ascot, 18 June 1954.

estate but Cecil looked to England to make his way and was taken on by fellow Irishman Atty Persse, who had just begun training. From Atty he was to learn the art of a well-organized coup. A two-year-old called Sir Archibald was showing the new team plenty on the gallops at their Park Gate stables at Grateley, a village on the border of Hampshire and Wiltshire. The seeds of the coup were carefully sown. Persse was hardly a household name, the colt's owner was from Cornwall and not well known in racing circles, the jockey engaged was an anonymous American called Lucienne Lyne. They were the connections of a 20/1 outsider, which was exactly the starting price for Sir Archibald in the Liverpool Autumn Cup. In those days betting could be done by telegram and the organizers of the coup arranged for a host of small bets to be dispatched from minor post offices all over Britain to various bookmakers, timed to arrive after the race had been run. Sir Archibald won by a length from an odds-on favourite. Bill Curling, friend and biographer of Boyd-Rochfort, believed the Persse stable had £1000 on their horse, a very large amount in those days. In his next race Sir Archibald comfortably won the New Stakes at Royal Ascot. Boyd-Rochfort, aged 19, fully appreciated the lesson. No wonder a coup like Above Board in the 1950 Cesarewitch was carried out so adroitly.

Boyd-Rochfort soon moved on to Newmarket where he would remain for the next 60 years. It was 1909, the year Minoru won the Derby for Edward VII, and although it would be more than 30 years before he would train a royal winner he was already moving in the right social circles. Boyd-Rochfort was still learning the craft of training, this time as assistant to another Irishman, Captain Bob Dewhurst, a patient trainer of good-class handicappers. In a world of jockeys and stable lads, Boyd-Rochfort, 6 feet 4 inches, handsome and eligible, was bound to stand out. He joined Dewhurst for dinner at Regal Lodge, the home outside Newmarket of Lily Langtry, the famous Jersey Lily and former mistress of the Prince of Wales. She was now Lady de Bathe, a successful racehorse owner and a leading society hostess. He also met the millionaire philanthropist Sir Ernest Cassel, who owned Moulton Paddocks where Edward VII, a close friend, would stay when attending Newmarket races.

In 1911 Boyd-Rochfort was appointed Cassel's racing manager and promptly impressed him with his judgement of a young horse by buying Hapsburg for 3200 guineas, a price that looked a bargain when in 1914 his purchase won both the Eclipse Stakes, then the most valuable race of the year worth £10,000, and the Champion Stakes. His knowledge of breeding would be a great benefit to the Queen in future years. Commissioned into the Scots Guards, Boyd-Rochfort was subsequently wounded at the Somme and awarded the *Croix de Guerre*. His brothers, Harold and Arthur, had an even more distinguished war. Harold won the DSO and MC and was mentioned in dispatches four times while Arthur won the Victoria Cross. He had picked up a German mortar bomb and hurled it out of a trench, thereby saving countless lives. Cecil saw out the war in comparative safety as a staff captain. But his best friend from Eton, Percy Wyndham, who had shared his betting coup on the Liverpool Autumn Cup, was not so lucky and was killed on the Aisne shortly after the war began. Percy's photograph always stood on the mantelpiece in Boyd-Rochfort's study.

After the war Boyd-Rochfort returned to Newmarket where he took on the additional role of managing the horses of a young American millionaire, an old Etonian called Marshall Field III. Cassel died in 1921 and his estate was sold, so when Field offered to help him set up on his own a couple of years later, Boyd-Rochfort, then 36, jumped at the chance. He borrowed £6000 from Field and a similar amount from his mother to buy Freemason Lodge, the stables on the Bury Road, from 'Flash Alf' Sadler. The Captain, as he was now familiarly known around Newmarket, built up an impressive list of owners embracing British aristocracy and American millionaires. His ability to mix socially with them was an enormous advantage, allowing him to train better horses and climb the ladder of classic success.

Much of the credit for Boyd-Rochfort's early success goes to Joe Childs, a tall, doleful but very skilful jockey who agreed to ride the Freemason Lodge horses back in 1923. In 1918 Childs had ridden a Triple Crown on Gainsborough, who would be the top sire of the 1930s. In 1925 he became first jockey to George V, for whom he won the 1000 Guineas on Scuttle three years later. He would ride Boyd-Rochfort's first English classic winner, Brown Betty, owned by New York Jockey Club chairman William Woodward, to win the same race in 1933. Childs was a master of riding a waiting race, always preferring to settle a horse and come through late. He was particularly adept at riding stayers, and a great influence on Boyd-Rochfort's success in long-distance races. The trainer would always prefer his horses to be ridden patiently.

When Childs retired in 1935 Boyd-Rochfort took on Rufus Beasley, so called because of his red hair. A member of a famous Irish racing family, Rufus forgot

Captain Boyd-Rochfort and his glamorous wife Rohays, his son Arthur (left) and stepson James Cecil, wait at Waterloo station for a trip to the United States in January 1960.

to take his cap off when he arrived to ride on his first morning working for the Captain. Boyd-Rochfort gave him a rocket: 'Take your cap off when you meet me on the gallops,' he bellowed. Beasley never omitted to do so again. Together they forged a successful partnership that led to Boyd-Rochfort topping the trainers' lists for the first time in 1937 and again the following year. There was still time for a coup, however. The Captain picked out a maiden two-year-old called Longriggan as a likely prospect to pay for the summer corn. At the Newmarket July meeting of 1937 he told Beasley, 'Give this horse a nice race but don't let Stephenson see.' Willie Stephenson was the Freemason Lodge chief work rider and would later be a very successful trainer, winning a Derby with Arctic Prince before the Captain won the Epsom classic.

On this occasion, Boyd-Rochfort was adopting a careful 'need to know' policy about Longriggan in order to bring off a quiet gamble at Glorious Goodwood a few weeks later. Beasley had the horse so far out with the washing that they almost sent out a search party. Longriggan was, however, flying at the finish and would undoubtedly have been spotted under today's non-triers rule. He duly won at Goodwood by a neck, much to Beasley's delight although nobody watching would have realized this. In the unsaddling enclosure afterwards the Captain solemnly said, 'That was a surprise Rufus!' Equally solemnly the jockey replied, 'Yes Captain, he has improved.'

When George VI was looking for a new trainer in late 1942 Boyd-Rochfort was in pole position. He had achieved a considerable reputation in the 1930s, he was upper class with all the right social connections and he was an old acquaintance of fellow Irish captain Charles Moore, the King's racing manager. It was Moore who rang to tell him to expect half a dozen royal horses for the next season. Moore, just an inch shorter than Boyd-Rochfort, had also won the *Croix de Guerre* in the First World War and was equally indomitable, and the two formed a formidable – if at times uneasy – partnership. Bruce Hobbs, the Captain's trusted lieutenant at Freemason Lodge, recalls, 'They were not best friends and did not see eye to eye. I think Captain Boyd-Rochfort did not like having to play second fiddle to anyone.' On the occasions when

Captain Moore took breakfast at Freemason Lodge he would always assume the privilege of carving the ham because he knew it would annoy the trainer. It always did.

Meanwhile Boyd-Rochfort formed a more equable alliance when he started wooing a beautiful red-haired widow who lived at Gesyns Farm, Wickhambrook, about 12 miles from Newmarket. It was a '*Brief Encounter*' that turned into something more after they met at Newmarket station, having both travelled from London on the same train. Mrs Rohays Cecil had been left with four children including the twins Henry and David when her husband had been killed by an enemy bomb while serving with the Parachute Regiment in North Africa during the Second World War. Boyd-Rochfort was 57, and considered by many a bachelor for life, when he dusted off his old bicycle – he never learnt to drive – and set off along the Clare Road to court the woman, 30 years his junior, whom he intended to be his bride. His stepson Henry Cecil observes, 'There was a lovely greengage tree in the garden at Gesyns and my stepfather was very fond of greengages. He started off more interested in them I think.' The stately trainer was such an unmistakable figure it was difficult to achieve any discretion in the courtship. He met Rohays in April and they were married by July.

From being the residence of a single man, set in his ways, Freemason Lodge became a family home for six, soon to be seven when the Captain and his bride had a son of their own.

◦◦ The Great Races

Aureole: The Derby, Epsom, 6 June 1953

Derby Day was a bright, sunny Saturday. Just five days before the world had watched the grandeur and regal pomp of the Coronation at Westminster Abbey. Now it was the chance for the young Queen to cast off the formality of that occasion and enjoy the trappings of the world's greatest race day. She had a promising contender in Aureole, a flashy, headstrong chestnut, who had shown ability as a two-year-old before reappearing in the 2000 Guineas at Newmarket and finishing a close-up fifth. There is an old adage in racing that fifth in the Guineas wins the Derby. There could no better story than the newly crowned Queen winning the Derby – or could there?

The mighty Pinza [Gordon Richards] storms to victory in the Coronation Derby, 6 June 1953. The Queen's colt Aureole [Harry Carr] is a distant second.

Gordon Richards, the greatest jockey of the first half of the twentieth century, had been knighted in the Coronation Honours List. It was a timely recognition of an astonishing career in which he had ridden more than 4700 winners and been champion jockey in all but two of the previous 27 years. The public loved him; he was a true punters' friend who enjoyed a reputation for riding fewer bad races than any other jockey before or since. He had forged a strong royal link riding the Fred Darling-trained horses leased by George VI from the National Stud. This association had brought him classic success with Sun Chariot and Big Game but, despite 27 previous attempts, he had never won the Derby. His mount in 1953 was the massive-framed Pinza, owned by Sir Victor Sassoon and trained by Norman Bertie who had been Darling's travelling head lad until the great trainer retired in 1947. Fred Darling himself had bred the horse but, sadly, he was a dying man, just able to listen to the race on the wireless.

Aureole warmed up for the big race with a workmanlike victory in the Lingfield Derby Trial. Harry Carr was confident he would handle the difficult undulations of Epsom and stay the mile and a half well. He chose to ride the Queen's colt in preference to Captain Boyd-Rochfort's other hope, Premonition, owned by Brigadier Wilfred Wyatt. On the day, Pinza and Premonition shared favouritism at 5/1 with Aureole at a reasonably generous 9/1. When Gordon Richards was walking into the paddock he was stopped by the Queen who shook his hand. He later recalled, 'She gave me that wonderful smile as she shook hands with me and said "It's all terribly exciting". She wished me luck, and I wished her luck.'

Pinza looked in awe-inspiring condition. Harry Carr had been feeling quite confident on Aureole until he saw Gordon Richards and his mount: 'When I watched this magnificent and massive colt take Sir Gordon Richards across the Downs to the start my heart sank.' Major Dick Hern, who would eventually succeed Boyd-Rochfort as principal royal trainer, was at the 1953 Derby and remembers Pinza as, 'a great big powerful horse, as big as a bull. I was surprised they got him fit for the Derby.' At the start, Pinza looked like a mature four-year-old among a host of three-year-olds. He was undoubtedly the man of the 27-strong field.

Gordon Richards had a dream run close to the inside rail throughout the race. At the top of the hill, Pinza was fifth, still tight to the rails. Aureole was a few places back, wider out and would be running towards the middle of the course in the straight. For such a massive horse, Pinza showed great courage and balance coming round Tattenham Corner when Richards took him through a narrow gap into second place about four lengths behind the Aga Khan's Shikampur: 'I gave him a little kick and he went through like a lion. Although I was still four or five lengths behind Shikampur I already knew that the race was over.' By this time Aureole had moved into sixth and was staying on nicely, but Pinza was always going to have first crack at the leader. When Richards made his move just past the two-furlong pole the big horse cruised into the lead and, in truth, won easily. Aureole ran on steadily to take second, a respectful four lengths behind. He looked as if he was slightly shying away from Carr's whip, something Dick Hern thought was ungenuine.

The crowd were ecstatic. Sir Gordon looked completely stunned and later confessed to feeling 'numbed' by the reception he and Pinza were given as they were led back. Aureole had run a very gallant race and Harry Carr believed the colt would have won many an average Derby. Pinza's reputation as one of the great Derby winners seems to have faded with time but Richards observed, 'Good horse though Aureole certainly was, he never had a chance against Pinza, who was one of the greats of all time.' Perhaps the sentimentality of the occasion has simply outshone the race itself, but Harry Carr also thought Aureole unfortunate to come up against one of the 'outstanding Derby winners'.

Afterwards the Queen, genuinely delighted for her newest knight, invited Sir Gordon to the Royal Box. The Duke of Edinburgh asked him if he was going to retire now that he had won the Derby. Before he had a chance to answer, the Queen interrupted, 'Of course not! He is going to ride for me in the Derby next year, on Landau.' There is no one more optimistic than a hopeful owner. Landau, leased from the National Stud and trained by Noel Murless,

The Queen and Prince Philip congratulate Gordon Richards after his Derby triumph on Pinza.

proved best at a mile. Gordon Richards never rode in the Derby again. His career ended the following season when an undistinguished royal two-year-old called Abergeldie reared over in the paddock at Sandown and crushed him. As a result, he was in a hospital for a month with a fractured pelvis and several dislocated ribs. He decided to retire from race riding to begin a new career as a trainer. Aureole's second to Pinza remains, nearly 50 years later, as the best placing in the Derby of any of the Queen's horses.

❧ Leading Owner

Only two horses ever carried the colours of Princess Elizabeth to victory: the disappointing Astrakhan on the flat and the ill-fated Monaveen over jumps. When her father died and she became Queen, her horses ran in the colours of the monarch and have done so ever since. It was never in doubt that she would continue the royal racing interests. Unlike her father, who admitted he had no great knowledge of the equine world when he ascended the throne, the Queen had a passion for horses. She had closely followed the exploits of Hypericum, Sun Chariot and Big Game and had always been absorbed in the nuances of breeding racehorses. When her father was ill and she had taken on so many of his duties, racing was her means of escape. Henry Cecil calls it 'her form of relaxation'.

The Queen's new racing empire consisted of 20 brood mares, seven yearlings and three two-year-old fillies at Sandringham. The Captain had two three-year-olds and four juveniles at Freemason Lodge. The fastest of the youngsters was Aureole, a moody son of the Derby winner Hyperion. He was highly strung, temperamental and needed to grow up. The royal jockey Harry Carr observed, 'He was a rare handful though he could gallop when he consented to jump off.' With his large white blaze, great splashes of white on his legs and bright chestnut colouring this was a horse that even the resourceful Boyd-Rochfort would have difficulty keeping under wraps. As a three-year-old it looked as if his temperament was going to prevent him from fully realizing his potential.

There was little he could do about Pinza, who easily beat him in both the Derby and the King George VI and Queen Elizabeth Stakes at Ascot, but when that muscular colt broke down and was scratched from the St Leger it seemed nothing could prevent the Queen's horse from capturing her first classic success.

In an effort to quieten Aureole's temperamental nature Boyd-Rochfort and Charles Moore called in Dr Charles Brook, a London neurologist who calmed his patients by laying his hands on them and releasing their nervous tension through his own body. He had graduated from people to horses and had already had some success with chargers who took part in the Coronation. Could he work some magic with Aureole? Three times a week during August he travelled from London to Newmarket for a consultation with the wayward colt. Bruce Hobbs, then assistant to the Captain, recalls, 'He was a little old man, aged about 70, with a goatee beard. He would always walk from Newmarket station to Freemason Lodge and then walk back again after he had finished. He would never accept a lift.' The doctor would put his left hand on the horse's withers, his right on his girth and rest his head on Aureole's shoulder. He would remain absolutely still and quiet for 20 minutes and, according to Harry Carr, would come out of the horse's box looking 'ashen white and completely spent'.

In the long term the administrations of Dr Brook, combined with the infinite patience of Bruce Hobbs, Harry Carr and Boyd-Rochfort, probably 'made' Aureole. The effect was not immediately clear on St Leger day when the Queen travelled from Balmoral to watch her colt start, for the first time a hot favourite for a classic. She had lunch at the course with Sir Winston and Lady Churchill who were celebrating their 45th wedding anniversary. It had all the trappings of a perfect day. Next year's classic hopeful, Landau, easily landed the Doncaster Produce Stakes to keep everyone buoyant. He was trained by Noel Murless who had taken over from Fred Darling as trainer of the royal horses leased from the National Stud. He and Boyd-Rochfort were great rivals throughout the Fifties and Sixties.

Once again the Freemason Lodge team fielded two in the final classic of the season. As in the Derby, Premonition joined Aureole. He had been disqualified, unluckily, from first place in the Irish Derby and then won the Great Voltigeur Stakes at York, a traditional trial for the Leger. Aureole was the more fancied of the two at 5/4 and was ridden by Harry Carr while Eph Smith had the ride on Premonition, a 10/1 shot. Aureole was coolness itself in the paddock but the moment he joined the pre-race parade he boiled over and the prospects looked bleak. He refused to stay in the parade and took Carr away for at least a furlong, continually fighting for his head. In the race he refused to settle and used up far too much energy in the early stages of a contest which Carr had thought would stretch his stamina in any case. Sure enough, when he came to challenge in the straight he was quickly a spent force. Aureole scraped home in third behind Premonition, much to the embarrassment of the Captain who would have preferred the accolade of a royal classic winner.

So far Aureole, despite a run of placed efforts in the top races, had won just once in his three-year-old season. In an effort to double that tally, Boyd-Rochfort sent him to Ascot for the Cumberland Lodge Stakes. Harry Carr could not do the weight so Eph Smith was asked to ride. He had a reputation for being tough on his horses, which was perhaps just what Aureole needed. He also cannily asked the trainer to try Aureole in a neckstrap so that he could put his fingers in this rather than constantly take a tug on the reins to try and control him. The horse seemed to prefer the strap and won easily. Captain Moore was much taken with the ride Eph Smith gave Aureole and Harry Carr could not get back in the saddle for the colt's four-year-old career in 1954.

An inauspicious start to that career came in the Coronation Stakes at Sandown where, in a relatively rough race, Aureole was the worst sufferer and finished second. He sauntered to victory in the Coronation Cup at Epsom making up for the disappointing effort of the non-staying Landau in the Derby. In the Hardwicke Stakes at Royal Ascot he at last showed his true battling colours. He was strongly challenged in the last furlong by the French horse Janitor ridden by the brilliant Manny Mercer. Janitor edged ahead, but Mercer had brought the horse so close to Aureole he could not use his whip without changing his whip hand and risk unbalancing his colt just yards from the line. It cost him the race. Eph Smith put Aureole under the strongest pressure and the royal colt fought back in the last few strides. The photograph of the finish showed Aureole had prevailed by a very short head. Manny Mercer thought about objecting on the grounds that Eph had interfered with the use of his whip. Smith told him, 'You were riding too close. Anyway, you can't object to the Queen.' The same afternoon Landau won the Rous Memorial Stakes over a mile to complete a first Royal Ascot double for the Queen.

The stage was set for Aureole's opportunity for greatness: the King George VI and Queen Elizabeth Stakes at Ascot in July. He was back to his old tricks again, and played up so badly in the parade that Eph Smith broke ranks and took him straight to the start. On the way there a nearby spectator put up an umbrella and he shied away, jumping a few feet into the air. Smith, caught unawares, shot up in the air and landed on the grass. The jockey was able to catch the horse and prevent him from doing a tour of Ascot Heath. When the starting gate went up Aureole mulishly dug his toes in and was left 10 lengths behind. Smith's race was saved by a slow early gallop in rain-softened ground which allowed him to catch up without ruining his chance. He moved on to the heels of the leaders at Swinley Bottom, was third turning into the straight and took up the running two furlongs out. The French challenger Vamos moved up menacingly but Eph Smith gave Aureole a hefty crack of the whip and he held on by three-quarters of a length.

Aureole [Eph Smith] gets the better of a titanic struggle with French colt Janitor [Manny Mercer] in the Hardwicke Stakes at Royal Ascot, 18 June 1953.

Part Three ∾ A Golden Age

Bill Curling recalled making his way to the unsaddling enclosure after the race: 'As I reached the back of the stand, a small figure came racing by. It was the Queen running to greet her champion. Kings and queens are not often seen running in public.' It was a fleeting glimpse of the true excitement the Queen, just like any other owner, feels at a big-race win. Aureole was the champion four-year-old of 1954 and contributed more than £30,000 towards the total prize money of nearly £41,000 that secured her the title of leading owner. The Captain won his third trainers' title. That Christmas the Queen sent him a lacquered cigarette box bearing the inscription, 'Cecil Boyd-Rochfort, leading trainer 1954 from Elizabeth R, leading winning owner 1954.'

✺ Eph, Doug and Harry

Eph Smith was almost completely deaf and was the only jockey riding with a hearing aid. Whereas Lester Piggott has always been selective in what he can and cannot hear, Eph was hard of hearing as a child and progressively more so throughout his life. After the Second World War he was almost completely deaf and could not hear a thing without his hearing-aid. Joe Mercer recalls, 'He was as deaf as a post.' He would keep the batteries for the hearing-aid in a little holster beneath his racing silks, with a wire leading up to an earpiece which he kept in place with a headband. The only trouble was that, as often happens with those who are hard of hearing, people would always speak loudly to him and he, in return, would bellow at them, oblivious to the fact that he was shouting the house down. As a result many an owner would cower as Eph Smith told them in no uncertain terms that their horse was a useless nag. It also led to considerable embarrassment for Eph when he told Lester Piggott off for causing interference in a race at Sandown. He thought he was having a quiet word along the lines of 'What the f***ing hell did you do a f***ing stupid thing like that for?' Unfortunately his quiet word had all the discretion of a town crier announcing the news, and the television microphones picked up the whole thing for general broadcast. The stewards were unamused and warned him to take care with his language in future.

The Smith brothers: Eph (above) and Doug rode the Queen's horses to some of her most important victories.

Before he rode Aureole in the Hardwicke Stakes at Royal Ascot in 1954, Eph went to the paddock to meet the Queen. A few days earlier the colt had knocked a leg but, unknown to Eph, that morning he had bumped his eye on a horsebox. 'What bad luck,' said the Queen to Smith, who immediately thought she was referring to the leg. He replied, 'Oh, he's sound enough now Ma'am.' The Queen, realizing his mistake, said, 'Oh no, I didn't mean his leg. I meant his eye. He bumped his eye coming along in the box today and he can't see out of it.' Eph, always quite cheeky, suggested, 'Well, Ma'am, we're both handicapped then. He's blind and I'm deaf. Our chances can't be too good today, can they?'

Although he enjoyed success with Aureole and when winning the Derby on Lord Rosebery's Blue Peter in 1939, Eph Smith rode, for most

Harry Carr put some disappointments in the royal colours behind him when Parthia won the Derby, 3 June 1959. The colt's owner, Sir Humphrey de Trafford, leads in the winner.

of his career, in the shadow of his younger brother, Doug, who was champion jockey five times and, according to racing historian George Ennor, 'unquestionably the better jockey'. Doug was a masterful rider of stayers, which always endeared him to Captain Boyd-Rochfort who afforded him the honour of being the only jockey he regularly called by his Christian name. 'Douglas!' he would boom across the gallops. Both Doug and Eph, sons of a sporting farmer from Shottesbrook near Maidenhead, had the misfortune to be apprenticed as boys to Major Fred Sneyd near Wantage, Berkshire. Major Sneyd was not a lovable man and it was a very hard life for a young lad. The living quarters for the apprentices was a converted wash house at the back of the main house, draughty and dank with just a single blanket each and a paraffin stove for warmth. 'You lived on a bowl of gruel and sixpence a year. I'm quite sure he was a bastard,' observes George Ennor. On one occasion Eph Smith did a passable imitation of Oliver Twist and asked the cook if they could have something different and more filling than the usual cold fried egg for breakfast. Next morning the apprentices were given cold pickled herrings. No one complained of the cold fried egg again.

Despite, or perhaps because of, the incredible Spartan regime – it also later produced Joe Mercer – the Smith brothers had great success as young riders. Eph was only 24 when he won the Derby. Doug was just 26 when he was retained by George VI and 29 when he rode Hypericum to classic success in 1946. Just when things were going so well, Doug Smith decided to quit as royal jockey at the end of that season to accept a retainer from the 17th Lord Derby, a decision that raised a number of old-school eyebrows. In Smith's defence, Lord Derby's stable was then one of the biggest in the country and Doug was almost at once able to take the ride on Alycidon, one of the finest stayers of the century and the horse Smith thought the best he rode. The perceived slight to the royal owner was in the minds of the commentators and Doug Smith still frequently donned the royal colours, most notably when he gave the Queen her only classic success with a colt in 1958 when Pall Mall won the 2000 Guineas.

In many ways Harry Carr was unlucky as the 'royal jockey'. Although he rode some great horses, not least Alcide, Meld and Parthia, for other owners he missed out on the most memorable royal victories: Doug Smith rode Pall Mall in the 2000 Guineas, Lester Piggott was on Carrozza when that Noel Murless filly took the 1957 Oaks and Eph Smith powered Aureole home to his best triumphs. Carr was from the north of England, originally from Westmorland before his father, a travelling head lad, moved to the Yorkshire training centre of Middleham. He had ridden with great success in India, but was little known in the south of England when he was plucked from relative obscurity to be Boyd-Rochfort's stable jockey, a job he held for 18 years until he retired in 1964. He was first 'interviewed' for the exalted position by Sir Humphrey de Trafford who asked him if he would be willing to move south to ride for the King. The dapper and genial Sir Humphrey, a close friend of both George VI and Queen Elizabeth, is one of the characters in the royal story who shows just what a small world racing really is. He was Boyd-Rochfort's best man when the Captain married Rohays Cecil. He was also the father of Cath Walwyn whose husband, Fulke, would become Queen Elizabeth's trainer.

Boyd-Rochfort and Captain Moore spoke to Carr about the job six weeks later at the York Ebor meeting. Even though there had been much speculation in racing about who might take over from Doug Smith the name Harry Carr was, as betting pundit John McCririck might put it, one of the 'rags', certainly a 33/1 shot. When the two 6-feet-plus Irish captains, both wearing the blue-and-red striped tie of the Brigade of Guards, met the obscure northern jockey outside the weighing room, a potential scoop was missed by the gentlemen of the racing press.

Carr had a considerable amount of misfortune in his early years at Freemason Lodge. He missed winning the 1948 St Leger on William Woodward's Black Tarquin because of a broken leg. In the 1950 Derby he was aboard the same owner's Prince Simon, a colt Boyd-Rochfort thought the best he ever trained. They were beaten by a fast-diminishing head by Galcador and would have won in another stride or two. Carr's effort was criticized in much the same way that Greville Starkey's was when he was beaten on Dancing Brave in 1986. Carr admitted he had been 'outmanoeuvred, outgeneralled and outridden' by the renowned Australian pilot Rae Johnstone. After the race one correspondent approached Boyd-Rochfort in the unsaddling enclosure and said, 'Bad luck, Captain. Your jockey threw the race away.' Boyd-Rochfort rebuked him: 'How dare you say such a thing? Don't ever speak to me again.' He then turned his considerable back on the journalist.

After Prince Simon had disappointed again at Royal Ascot a few weeks later, Queen Elizabeth was chatting with her husband the King and Boyd-Rochfort when a disconsolate Carr trudged by on his way back to the weighing room. She told him, 'You are an unlucky boy. Never mind, your luck will change.' It did not change with Aureole, the Queen's first good horse. Carr still thought him the best royal colt he had ridden. He was very annoyed at losing the St Leger ride and thought the observation in the racing press that he and Aureole did not get on was 'absolute nonsense'. Bruce Hobbs, who enjoyed a close rapport with Carr, remembers there was some unpleasantness. He observes, 'He made the blessed horse.' Carr probably would have stayed in the saddle if he had been able to do the 8 stone required for the Cumberland Lodge Stakes. He constantly fought a weight problem and continually took diuretics, colloquially known as 'pee pills', which have now been banned by racing authorities. His son-in-law Joe Mercer recalls, 'He had horrendous weight problems. In the wintertime he would be well over 10 stone.'

Choir Boy [Doug Smith] spread-eagles the field to take the Royal Hunt Cup in front of packed stands at Royal Ascot, 17 June 1953. It was the first victory for the Queen at her favourite meeting.

Harry Carr was, however, a superb stable jockey, very loyal and a diligent work rider who took the trouble to try and get to know every horse in the yard. He was also Captain Boyd-Rochfort's chauffeur. The Captain never held a driving licence but had a luxury saloon which the aptly named jockey would drive to the races. Every Sunday he would arrive at Freemason Lodge at 10 o'clock to discuss the arrangements for the following week and then give the Captain a lift to church on his way home. He was very much an old-fashioned rider. Bruce Hobbs observes, 'If the horse was good enough, then Harry would win on it. He was a very good stable jockey and admired the Captain enormously.' George Ennor, who as a young reporter on *The Sporting Life* always found the royal jockey very approachable, observes, 'His was not the 2 inches of leathers and arse in the air style of riding but he was a good, strong jockey.' Carr was perhaps the easiest to get on with of the three master jockeys who wore the royal colours in the golden age of the Captain. Eph Smith's deafness was a major stumbling block while Doug Smith was always worried about offending anyone. Ennor remarks, 'He was terribly pernickety. The most he would say would be "Nice day, but don't quote me".'

Captain Charles Moore, the Queen's influential racing manager, was probably not Harry Carr's greatest fan, preferring the riding abilities of Eph Smith. According to Eph, Moore offered him a retainer at the end of 1953 to replace Carr on all the Queen's horses but he turned it down because he was already contracted to ride for Jim Joel. That may or may not be true, but he *was* retained to ride Aureole. When Eph Smith listed his 'best jockeys' in his autobiography he included Joe Mercer, Lester Piggott and his own brother Doug but noticeably ignored Harry Carr. Boyd-Rochfort, however, stood by Carr through thick and thin. One morning, after exercising the horses, he called his jockey into his office and presented him with a fine silver rose bowl. When Harry took it home he noticed the inscription, 'To W.H. Carr in recognition of ten years' faithful service.'

All three jockeys retired in the Sixties. Harry Carr was beset with kidney problems, probably a result of abusing his frame for so many years to keep his weight down. Joe Mercer, who had married Harry's daughter Anne, remembers taking him to hospital and being told his father-in-law would be there for six weeks. Carr's body had taken a fearful battering over the years, including a famous and horrific fall from Hethersett in the 1962 Derby which knocked him out and left him with a broken shoulder. Ill health also forced Eph Smith to retire after he was told he was suffering from 'nervous exhaustion'. He did not enjoy the more commercial Sixties and found his deafness an increasing handicap. He bred and trained gun dogs, enjoyed his collection of vintage port and occasionally rode out for Noel Murless. But he also increasingly turned to drink. In August 1972 his body was found in a shallow brook near Newmarket. The inquest returned a verdict of misadventure although there is little doubt it was suicide.

Doug Smith became private trainer to Lord Rosebery in 1968 and won the 1969 Oaks with Sleeping Partner. But he and Rosebery split and leaner times forced Smith to move into bloodstock trading. He had always been very well liked, a courteous and more refined character than his brother. George Ennor makes the cogent point that Doug grew up as an old-school apprentice where the attitude towards owners and trainers was 'yessir, nossir, three bags full sir'. Ennor says of Smith's time as a trainer, 'His owners were almost too grand for him. Whereas trainers like Henry Cecil and Sir Michael Stoute today are on level terms with owners to a vast extent, Doug didn't know where he was socially. Training is not just a case of getting on a horse and riding it. I don't think he enjoyed it very much.' Racing is by no means the only sport historically riddled with class division. But it is only in the relatively modern world of sponsorship and television that the jockeys are perceived as the stars of the sport, rather in the manner of the change in status of professional footballers or rugby players. The purchase of the Queen's own stables at West Ilsley, Berkshire, by Mick Channon, a former international footballer and a man enormously popular with the general public, is perhaps a welcome indicator that the sport has moved on from the feudal, militaristic attitudes that ruled until the 1970s.

The change came too late for Doug Smith. He too had serious drink problems and spent time in hospital trying to cure his addiction. He was found dead in his swimming pool in April 1989, an eerie echo of the death of his elder brother. The inquest verdict was one of suicide.

❧ The Sickening Second

The Captain always took the major setbacks well, something the Queen and Queen Elizabeth have also been able to do through many years of disappointments. In the Central Television film, *Royal Champion*, about her racing life, Queen Elizabeth says in conversation, 'Racing must be 80 per cent disappointment, more perhaps'. It is a sentiment the Queen would echo in equal measure. Ian Balding, her trainer for 35 years, describes her as the most unlucky owner he has ever come across. Time and time again she has had to deal with misfortune and not just of the sort that saw Aureole finish as runner-up in the Derby.

Sierra Nevada was a brave and bonny three-year-old colt who finished fourth in the 1955 St James's Palace Stakes at Royal Ascot. Bruce Hobbs recalls, 'He was small and neat with a wonderful temperament, probably just short of classic standard.' The horse returned to the Berkshire course for the Queen Elizabeth Stakes named after his owner. Harry Carr was cantering on him in the straight and felt sure he would win the Queen's own race with a horse she owned and bred. In a deathly second that expectation was dashed when the jockey heard the snap of a leg breaking. He movingly described it later: 'I know of no noise in the world so sickening nor any sight so utterly heartbreaking as a magnificent horse, at the prime of his powers, standing helplessly in silent pain.' The agony was made worse by the knowledge that the Queen had been watching excitedly as her horse challenged down the middle of the course.

Of all the horses he rode for the Queen, Harry Carr described Sierra Nevada as one of his two favourites. The other was Doutelle, who would also come to a tragic end. He was by the French Derby winner Prince Chevalier out of Above Board, George VI's controversial winner of the 1950 Cesarewitch. He was bred to stay middle distances well. Breeding is not an exact science or else any old millionaire could do it. The Queen's interest and expertise was already paying off. The 1954 crop of Sandringham foals was arguably the best the stud ever produced. Four of the eight foals who went to Freemason Lodge as yearlings would win major races. Doutelle and stayer Agreement were the leading colts while Almeria and Mulberry Harbour were the best fillies. Doutelle, a dark liver chestnut with a striking white blaze, was on the small side but was full of courage. He needed to be.

He had a mixed two-year-old career ending with a close-up second to the Noel-Murless-trained Crepello in the Dewhurst Stakes at Newmarket. He was not entered in the 2000 Guineas of 1957 but won his first two races, including the Lingfield Derby Trial, and went to Epsom with a real chance. Harry Carr described that year's Derby as 'the roughest I have ever ridden in, much worse than the 1962 race when I was badly injured on Hethersett'. Little Doutelle

was swept round Tattenham Corner wedged in the middle of the field like a thin slice of ham between two thick slices of bread. 'I swear there were times when his feet never touched the ground,' said Carr, who felt sure he and Doutelle would be brought down. They eventually finished 10th to Crepello and returned to the unsaddling enclosure a bloody mess of cuts and bruises, a fetlock badly damaged. Crepello was an outstanding Derby winner but there was every reason to think that in a clean race Doutelle would have bustled him up. The Derby was becoming progressively more difficult to win for the Queen as the years passed. She is far from alone in finding the Epsom race a step too far. After Carr had finally won the Derby on Parthia in 1959 he told Joe Mercer who had finished second on Fidalgo, 'Don't worry, you've plenty of time to win.' Joe retired 26 years later never having won the race.

Amazingly, Doutelle was fit enough by the autumn of his three-year-old career to win two more races. But his finest hour came as a four-year-old on the idiosyncratic tight-turning track of Chester when he beat the great Irish champion Ballymoss. For once, scooting round the bends of the Roodeye, Doutelle's size was an advantage. He led from the start and as they turned into the short finishing straight Ballymoss was forced to pull two horses' width wide,

Harry Carr has the Queen's Colt Doutelle (white blaze and noseband, centre) handily placed early on, but was later to suffer a rough ride in the Derby won by Crepello, 5 June 1957.

Part Three ❧ A Golden Age

Doutelle [Harry Carr] gallops to a shock win over Irish champion Ballymoss [Tommy Burn] in the Ormonde Stakes at Chester, 8 May 1958.

a crucial amount. He was within three-quarters of a length at the furlong pole but Carr rode like a dervish to get the Queen's colt home by a length and a half.

Boyd-Rochfort, such a great trainer of stayers, made a rare mistake in plotting a campaign for Doutelle in the champion stayers' races including the Gold Cup at Ascot. It was misjudged because the colt plainly failed to stay a marathon trip. Agreement, who missed the Gold Cup, was the better stayer and would win two Doncaster Cups and a Chester Cup. Doutelle was returned to a more suitable trip for the 1958 King George VI and Queen Elizabeth Stakes where he would face Ballymoss once again and also his own talented stable companion, the four-year-old mare Almeria. She was by the champion stayer Alycidon out of the Queen's mare Avila who, when owned by her father, had won at Royal Ascot, prompting the dinner party at which Queen Elizabeth famously sat next to Lord Mildmay. Avila's sire was Hyperion and like others, notably Aureole, with plenty of that great sire's bloodline, Almeria was an agitated sort. She was also very talented. Where Doutelle was small, Almeria was a big, bold chestnut. Henry Cecil remembers her as a 'lovely big filly'. She was too backward to race more than once as a two-year-old and was beaten first time out the following year in the Lingfield Oaks Trial. Afterwards, Harry Carr told the Captain that he did not think she would be beaten again that season. Boyd-Rochfort told him, 'For goodness sake don't tell the Queen. Whenever one says that, something always goes wrong.'

This time Carr was right and Almeria breezed to four consecutive victories including the Ribblesdale Stakes at Royal Ascot, the Yorkshire Oaks at York and the 'fillies Leger' the Park Hill Stakes at Doncaster. She was by some margin the best middle-distance filly of the year and it was a pity that a slightly pulled muscle prevented her taking part in the Oaks. She was retired to stud but proved so intractable she was sent back into training for another year, with the King George her primary objective. Boyd-Rochfort was not that keen on having her back at Freemason Lodge, fearing that now she was such a 'madam' her form at four would not match her achievements of a year earlier. She was becoming more and more difficult to get on to the gallops but, somehow, he had her on peak form on the day of the King George. Events, however, conspired against her.

Harry Carr chose to ride Almeria with Doug Smith on Doutelle. The plan was hatched, with the Queen and the Captain's approval, that the royal runners would lie first and second, set a strong pace and force Ballymoss to challenge wide into the short Ascot straight, the tactic that had led to his downfall at Chester. Unfortunately Doug Smith had a fall the day before the big race and his place was taken by Joe Mercer who did not know Doutelle so well. The Queen was ill and unable to attend so Captain Charles Moore, then 77, stood in and, in the opinion of Bill Curling, gave the wrong orders to Mercer, telling him to ride a waiting race and challenge late. In effect he overruled Boyd-Rochfort and Carr.

The tactics were a disaster. Almeria had to make her own running but failed to burn off Ballymoss, who eased into the lead in the straight and won comfortably by three lengths from the filly with Doutelle a never-nearer third. Looking on the bright side, the Queen had the two placed horses in the best all-age middle-distance event in Britain. It was a disappointing result at the time but nothing like as unfortunate as Almeria's last race, the Doncaster Cup. Agreement was also in the field having a prep race for the Cesarewitch as Almeria's pacemaker. He started at 25/1 while the filly was joint favourite at 5/2, but in the race she refused to go past him in the straight even though she was going by far the best, in effect letting him win by a neck. Horses can make fools of you and it was definitely time for Almeria to retire to stud.

Doutelle was soon off to stud himself, standing at Sandringham while Aureole held court at the Queen's other Norfolk stud at Wolferton, three miles away. After just four years, at the age of eight, Doutelle was found dead in his box one morning. He had been playing with his 'rack chain', caught his teeth in the spring and while trying to free himself had torn his mouth and cheek so badly that he bled to death. It was particularly unfortunate because Bruce Hobbs clearly recalls that on the morning the stud groom arrived at Freemason Lodge to take the colt away he advised him of Doutelle's habit of playing with his rack chain and the fact that he was always put on a rope in his box: 'I told him, "Don't ever put the colt on a rack chain with a hook on it." He took no notice and, of course, a hook ended up in the side of Doutelle's mouth.'

It was a terrible end for a lovable and popular horse. He had already shown great promise as a sire and his death was a major blow to the Royal Studs and to the Queen, who probably gets more enjoyment from this side of the sport than from the racing itself. It would not be the last time she would lose a horse through an accident in his stable box.

❧ The Great Races
Carrozza: The Oaks, Epsom, 7 June 1957

Opposite: Noel Murless pictured in 1972.

For 10 supremely successful years the partnership of trainer Noel Murless and jockey Lester Piggott was the most feared classic combination in racing. Murless had chosen the impetuous Piggott as his stable jockey to succeed Sir Gordon Richards in 1955. It was a bold move to fill the great man's shoes with a 19-year-old, albeit one who had already won the Derby. Murless, a tall, slim Yorkshireman, had taken over Fred Darling's stable and with it responsibility for the royal horses leased from the National Stud. When he moved to the superb Warren Place stables in Newmarket in 1952 he continued to look after the horses for the new Queen. Although the Queen has always derived most pleasure from her homebred winners, it was more than useful having such a talented trainer as Noel Murless in her corner.

Murless and the Queen's principal trainer, Captain Cecil Boyd-Rochfort, were very different men. The Captain was robust and larger than life whereas Joe Mercer remembers Noel Murless as 'thin-framed and chesty'. Henry Cecil is in a unique position to judge the two men because, besides being Boyd-Rochfort's stepson, he also became Murless's son-in-law when he married the trainer's daughter Julie: 'Noel was a workaholic. They were both champion trainers and there was a touch of rivalry and jealousy between the two but Noel had a much bigger stable, far more horses. Uncle Cecil was from a different generation.' Whereas the Captain was a master of laying out a horse for a handicap and collecting from the bookmakers' satchels, Murless was only interested in winning big races and, in particular, the classics. He eschewed betting. They did, however, share two important qualities according to Bruce Hobbs, a friend to both men: 'They both paid 100 per cent attention to detail and knew the capabilities of each horse.'

The first couple of years at Warren Place were relatively quiet but, as at Freemason Lodge, 1957's crop of three-year-olds looked full of promise.

Expectation was not misplaced when Sir Victor Sassoon's Crepello took the 2000 Guineas and then the 'rough house' Derby. Two days after the Derby, Carrozza was on duty for the Queen in the Oaks but she was not carrying the first colours. That privilege was reserved for Mulberry Harbour, ridden by Harry Carr and representing the Captain. Both trainers were hopeful of providing the Queen with her first classic success. Carrozza was a small, brown, admirably tough filly who won her first race as a two-year-old in useful but unspectacular fashion at Hurst Park before rearing over backwards in her box, damaging her withers and being off the course for five months. She came back to be fourth in two late-season races at Newmarket, but was not particularly in the front line of the following season's classic contenders.

Lester Piggott had even chosen not to ride Carrozza in the 1000 Guineas in which Bill Rickaby brought her home in fourth behind the Aga Khan's brilliant filly Rose Royale II but was back for the Oaks, still basking in the glory of Crepello's Derby win. Harry Carr wore the black cap of the first colours while Piggott donned a distinguishing white cap. Carr, by now a veteran of the weighing room, had been a good friend to the young Piggott, particularly as they both survived on a diet of fresh air because of their weight problems. He was a great admirer of the young maestro and praised his riding: 'There are occasions when his riding has the sharp, cold sparkling brilliance of a diamond.' Piggott needed all that brilliance in the Oaks where Carrozza started relatively unfancied at 100/8. Mulberry Harbour was the more favoured, an 11/4 chance.

Rounding Tattenham Corner Carr had Mulberry Harbour perfectly poised in second behind Taittinger who was trying to give Sir Victor Sassoon a Derby-Oaks double. Piggott had Carrozza close behind in fifth and as they fanned out into the straight he showed all the bravado of youth by driving Carrozza up the inside of the leader. Mulberry Harbour collapsed like a paper bag full of water and Carrozza was in front with two furlongs to go. The Guineas winner, Rose Royale II, loomed up menacingly but was a nonstayer and faltered in the final furlong as Jimmy Eddery – father of Pat Eddery – brought the Irish filly Silken Gilder to challenge on the outside. Piggott was literally carrying Carrozza over the line in one of his famously determined Epsom finishes. Two strides past the post and Silken Gilder was clearly in front but they had passed the finishing line together in a blur of excitement.

Bill Curling called the race 'one of the most exciting I have ever seen'. In his report for the *Daily Telegraph* he wrote, 'In the last twenty yards with hopes of victory fading, Piggott rode like a man inspired, almost willing Carrozza to win. They flashed past the post together. There was a momentary hush. I thought from my position high up on the Press Stand that Carrozza had hung on by inches, a colleague on my right favoured Silken Gilder. The majority of people hoped for the best and feared the worst.' Needless to say, when the photo showed Carrozza had won by about 9 inches a tremendous roar went up. Generally speaking royal victories are so popular that you could almost feel sorry for the other owners.

The Queen leads in Carrozza [Lester Piggott], her first classic winner in the Oaks at Epsom, 7 June 1957.

The Queen, her face wreathed in smiles, rushed down to lead her heroine into the winners' enclosure. Carrozza, a little overwhelmed at the reception from the crowd and the clicking of the cameras, coquettishly refused to co-operate and started moving backwards. The Queen, fully practised in handling horses, simply wheeled the filly away from the battery of press cameras and firmly took her forward. It was the first time a monarch had led in a winner at Epsom since Edward VII brought Minoru through a celebrating crowd in 1909. It was the Queen's first classic victory. Spare a thought, though, for the unlucky Mulberry Harbour, who finished very distressed with her pupils dilated. Bruce Hobbs remains convinced that something 'happened' to her. Unfortunately no dope test was ordered – this was done only occasionally then – although the horse had clearly been 'got at'. If the Queen had not won the race anyway there might have been a greater inquest into what was in retrospect an enormous scandal, the suspected doping of a strongly fancied royal runner in a classic. It was especially galling for Freemason Lodge because Almeria, unable to take her place at Epsom, was a much better filly than Carrozza and was rated ahead of her at the end of the season. Carrozza, described a little unkindly by Lester Piggott as 'a fat little lady' only ran once more, finishing fourth and lame in the Nassau Stakes at Goodwood. But she had already secured her place in royal racing history. She was the major contributor to the Queen's second leading-owner title, although Boyd-Rochfort had to make do with runner-up spot to Noel Murless for the trainer's prize.

∾ Life at Freemason Lodge

The Queen never failed to impress everyone at Freemason Lodge with her equine expertise. She has always been a keen student of form but, more than that, has a genuine knowledge of breeding and an excellent memory for horses. Joe Mercer remembers his father-in-law Harry Carr telling the story of how the Queen rectified what might have been a serious mistake at the yard when she went to look at the two-year-old prospects for the coming season. Two of the colts were Doutelle and Agreement and they were led in that order from their boxes. At least that is what Captain Moore said. But the Queen instantly spotted a mistake and said, 'No, that is Agreement,' pointing to the one her racing manager had called Doutelle. She had known them as yearlings at Sandringham and had taken care to watch their progress, as she always liked to do.

A trip to watch the horses work on Newmarket Heath would invariably be followed by lunch prepared by Boyd-Rochfort's continental staff. Henry Cecil recalls, 'On one occasion when the Queen was visiting my mother had ordered a dessert she called a "Mars Bar Surprise". The idea was that the Mars Bars would be sliced and used as a topping to some ice cream. It was brought in but the staff hadn't quite got the point. The Mars Bars were piled up on the ice cream still in their wrappers.'

If the staff were a little bizarre at times, their employer was most eccentric. He could never remember anybody's name properly. Lady George Cholmondeley, a tall, striking woman who liked to gamble, owned several horses including the admirable Goodwood Cup winner Sagacity in the late Fifties and early Sixties. She was a regular guest at Freemason Lodge but the good Captain could never master her name and, recalls Henry Cecil, would introduce her vaguely as 'her'. One day Her Ladyship could bear it no longer and carefully put her gin and tonic down before boldly declaring, 'I am Diana, Lady George Cholmondeley, not 'er!'.

Boyd-Rochfort could never make the staff understand him. Henry Cecil remembers the daily exchange regarding his stepfather's hat when he was leaving in the morning, 'He would say to one "My hat" expecting them to fetch his hat from the stand. But the man would stare at him like Manuel from *Fawlty Towers* so he would bellow, "My hat!" He thought they would understand if he shouted.'

Growing up in the Boyd-Rochfort household was never dull. The Captain had taken on the Cecil brood when he was past 50 and subsequently had a son of his own, Arthur Boyd-Rochfort. His wife, Rohays, was not a great horse enthusiast and preferred to go shopping in London. But the twin boys, Henry and David, were always keen. Henry became assistant trainer before his stepfather retired and, during that time, was assigned to look after Queen Elizabeth who had joined her daughter to look at the horses one morning. Henry recalls, 'It was a very cold morning and I remember we grabbed one end each of a dining table and took it through so we could have lunch by the fire. I stuck her next to the fire and, after some time, with sweat pouring off her, she said to me, "Henry, do you mind if I move?".'

During the golden age of Freemason Lodge, 1953–1960, there was a triumvirate at the controls. Boyd-Rochfort was naturally captain, Harry Carr was a vastly experienced jockey in a wonderful age of horsemen and Bruce Hobbs, later to be a successful trainer in his own right, was a very talented stable lieutenant. Hobbs had won the Grand National on Battleship in 1938 at the age of 17, the youngest winning jockey. One Friday, just a week or so after he joined Freemason Lodge, the Captain called him into his office and announced, 'The Queen Mother is coming for a visit on Monday, Hobbs. I am off shooting so you'll look after, won't you?' Hobbs had already had a spell of training before he joined Freemason Lodge and his expertise and attention to detail were of enormous benefit with the more difficult horses like Aureole and Almeria. Unluckily for Hobbs, the Captain gave no hint of wishing to retire as he entered his seventies.

Despite a great period of success there was still no sign of a classic winner for the Queen from Freemason Lodge as the 1958 season took shape. The Captain was very confident he had the winner of the 2000 Guineas in the American-owned Bald Eagle, a big, commanding stamp of a horse. The Queen's representative, Pall Mall, a neat liver chestnut with three white socks and a long white blaze, was rated at least a stone behind his stable companion. Bruce Hobbs thought him no more than a 'goodish horse with bad conformation'.

Harry Carr had little choice other than to pick Bald Eagle for his ride, even though he would always choose to ride a royal runner if there was only a little between them in terms of ability. That was not the case here and Boyd-Rochfort told him that he would have made the same decision himself.

Doug Smith, the master of Newmarket's Rowley Mile, was engaged to ride the Queen's colt. The Queen was unwell at Windsor suffering from a heavy cold and could not travel to see her horse run. He was a 20/1 outsider while Bald Eagle was clear favourite at 7/4. Pall Mall also had the worst of the draw on the wide outside but Doug Smith bided his time and, although well back, the neat-actioned colt was always going easily. Afterwards Smith remembered catching one glimpse of Bald Eagle as that horse dropped back. As they met the rising ground coming out of the 'Dip', Pall Mall had caught Major Portion, ridden by Doug's brother Eph, and, resolutely galloping on, held that colt by half a length. Far behind, Harry Carr could not believe how the race unfolded. It may not have been an epic race but it was an epic result: the Queen's first homebred classic winner. Until now Pall Mall had appeared better named than bred. He was by the champion miler Palestine out of an undistinguished mare called Malapert, who Captain Moore thought so little of that she was sold after foaling Pall Mall for a paltry 910 guineas.

The Queen on Surprise gallops up the straight at Ascot before racing at the Royal meeting in June 1961.

No sooner had Carr recovered from his disappointment than his Derby mount, Alcide, owned by Sir Humphrey de Trafford, had to be withdrawn on the eve of the race. Boyd-Rochfort thought the horse had been got at in his box, receiving a blow which broke a rib. It is incredible how many top-class horses in the 'old days' were victims of suspected foul play. Alcide won the St Leger but another Derby had slipped by for Freemason Lodge. The Captain took the disappointment as well as ever. Henry Cecil recalls, 'He would be irritated when little things went wrong but he took the big things very well. One year we had a strong fancy for the Derby called Smooth Sailing who broke a leg. I remember he still stopped off to buy his kippers that day.'

Royal Racing

Changing of the Old Guard

From the lofty position of leading owner in 1957, runner-up in 1958 and third in 1959, the Queen's fortunes spiralled rapidly downwards. Freemason Lodge had its worst ever year in 1960. Plagued by a bout of coughing in the yard and a virus, the stable sent out just 13 winners all season, even though there were still 60 horses resident. The Queen's total number of winners trained by the Captain was a big fat zero. Noel Murless fared no better and it was left to the minor trainer Tom Masson, a superb horseman, to provide two winners. His stable at Lewes in Sussex had been sent three difficult three-year-olds in the hope that a change of scene might be beneficial. In this disappointing year he sent out the only winners from the Queen's total string in training of 22. Even more galling for the royal team, the champion sire was Aureole, whose son St Paddy captured the Derby for Sir Victor Sassoon, the owner's fourth success in the race in eight years.

No one factor caused the rapid decline in the Queen's fortunes, which did not recover until the mid-Sixties. It was the end of a very successful era for the two captains, Moore and Boyd-Rochfort, who had been at the helm of the royal racing empire for some 25 years. But perhaps the two old gentlemen hung on too long. Charles Moore was 80 in 1960 and showed no inclination to retire. He had always enjoyed a reputation as an excellent raconteur, particularly of anecdotes from his native Ireland. In later years he had appeared rather old-fashioned and set in the ways of the old school. But under his stewardship the Royal Studs had showed a marked revival. Looking back with 20/20 hindsight, he probably advocated too much stayers' blood and not enough speed. He had the perfect trainer for stayers in Boyd-Rochfort, who won three Gold Cups, six Goodwood Cups and seven Yorkshire Cups.

Changes, though, were inevitable during a great period of transition. Bruce Hobbs left Freemason Lodge at the end of 1960 to pursue his own training career. And who could blame him after such a wretched season? He recalls, 'I went to Freemason Lodge on the understanding that all being well I would take over when the Captain retired. But he never looked like retiring and I thought that time was marching on so decided to leave. He didn't like it at the time but we were perfectly all right again after a few months.' Moore was eventually persuaded to hand over the reins, reluctantly, in 1961 to his deputy, Brigadier Tony Wingfield, who looked after things for two years before Major Richard Shelley, who had achieved a good reputation managing Lady Zia

Below: The Queen with one of the foals at the Royal Stud, Sandringham.

Bottom: Master trainer Henry Cecil in pensive pose at Newmarket in October 1996.

Wernher's stud, took over. More and more at this time, the Queen turned to her great friend Lord Porchester for help and advice. 'Porchey', as she endearingly calls him, had been an officer in the Royal Horse Guards when he first started accompanying the then Princess Elizabeth to the races. He shared her great enthusiasm for racing homebred horses and his father, the Earl of Carnarvon, owned the Highclere Stud at Newbury which was to have a profound influence on royal racing fortunes in the 1970s. Lord Porchester was certainly instrumental in persuading the Queen to close the Hampton Court Stud and lease Polhampton Lodge Stud near Kingsclere. John Porter's famous stables in the village were then occupied by Captain Peter Hastings-Bass and it was decided to split the yearlings and send some to him and the rest to Freemason Lodge.

By 1963 Captain Moore's health was failing and the Queen and the Queen Mother went to see him at his Hampton Court apartment. He struggled out of bed to receive his visitors and was asked how he was feeling by the Queen. He replied, 'Well, Ma'am, I feel like a rabbit who has been bolted by a ferret.' The Queen laughed and said, 'I may have been called many things behind my back, but I have never been called a ferret to my face before.' Captain Moore died the following year when ill health also forced stable jockey Harry Carr to retire. He had been the royal jockey for 18 years. To mark the occasion he was invited to Buckingham Palace where he was given separate audiences by Queen Elizabeth, who presented him with a signed photograph, and the Queen who gave him an inscribed silver cigarette case.

Over the years he had enjoyed a very good relationship with Boyd-Rochfort, who always called him, 'Carr'. The Captain wrote an appreciative foreword to Harry Carr's autobiography *Queen's Jockey*, in which he praised the fact that the jockey had never been late on the gallops. After Carr had returned from the horrific fall from Hethersett in the 1962 Derby to win the St Leger on that same Dick Hern-trained horse, the Captain put his arm around the jockey and declared, 'Well done Carr. I am just as pleased as if I had trained the winner myself.'

The Captain's own team at Freemason Lodge began to wind down as he contemplated retirement. There was time for a final hurrah, however, when Canisbay, a big, chestnut son of the ill-fated Doutelle, provided an unlikely 20/1 triumph in the 1965 Eclipse Stakes: the new stable jockey Stan Clayton forced him home by a short head from the Roan Rocket ridden by Bill Williamson. Boyd-

Rochfort, as cantankerous as ever, decided to retire in 1968 and move back to Ireland to enjoy country pursuits, particularly fishing. By then he had trained 136 winners for the Queen, winning some £300,000 in 17 years. Although Henry Cecil took over the stables and would later move to Warren Place when his father-in-law, Noel Murless, retired, he did not receive any royal horses to train. And despite being the outstanding trainer of the last 30 years he still has not been sent a single one. Perhaps he has been too flamboyant or enjoyed too colourful a private life. It's the Queen's decision of course but, in a world of connections, you could not get a better-connected racing trainer than Henry Cecil. He still says, 'It would be a very great honour to train for the Queen but there are no hard feelings.'

The nearest he has been to training for the Queen was when he looked after two undistinguished horses called Zaloba and Castle Yard while he was learning his trade at Freemason Lodge. At least Zaloba had the distinction of becoming Michael Oswald's hack when he was running the Sandringham Stud in the 1970s. The retirement of the Captain closed the door on Newmarket as a training centre for the Queen for the next 20 years. Instead, she turned increasingly to the beautiful countryside of Hampshire and Berkshire, where Ian Balding and Dick Hern trained and where her mother would soon follow her example by sending her horses to Fulke Walwyn.

The Captain died in Ireland in 1983. At his funeral his nephew Angus McCall was told he had been left his boat. Henry Cecil recalls, 'We went to the boathouse to inspect the inheritance and it was nowhere to be seen. Then we looked down and there it was lying on the bottom, 30 feet down.' Boyd-Rochfort was not always universally liked, being a bit of an Edwardian relic, but his large frame bestrode racing for more than 60 years. Bruce Hobbs, who modestly attributes his own training success to his time with the Captain, observes, 'He had a sense of humour but it took a bit of finding'. Boyd-Rochfort could be militaristic and overbearing, not least in his refusal to queue for anything. Henry Cecil remembers being acutely embarrassed in supermarkets because his stepfather would always march straight to the front of the queue to pay for his tins of Irish stew. The Captain made a habit of embarrassing his family. Cecil also recalls how his stepfather would often go to South Africa in the winter and take with him many cases of luggage: 'He would always tip sixpence which wasn't a great deal of money even then. The porter would shout after him, "What are you saving up for?".'

Part Four

A Special Place

After Special Cargo's heroic Whitbread Gold Cup triumph, Colonel Bill Whitbread and his wife Betty held a dinner party for Queen Elizabeth. The other guests were Michael and Lady Angela Oswald, Fulke and Cath Walwyn, Bill Smith, Kevin Mooney, Princess Margaret and the Queen. After an enjoyable dinner they adjourned to another room to watch a film of the race one more time. They were a chair short so the Queen sat on the floor.

ᴄᴡ Changing Stables

When Peter Cazalet died the racing community, a very small world, was awash with rumours about who might take over from him as royal trainer. There were even fears that Queen Elizabeth, who was after all nearly 73, might sell her string of horses and retire from ownership. At the time the two most celebrated National Hunt trainers were Fulke Walwyn and Fred Winter. They trained next door to each other at Upper Lambourn, Berkshire, and enjoyed a keen rivalry as the winter game's top two trainers. Fulke and his wife Cath were at Epsom during Derby week when a distinguished-looking man came up to them and said that if they had room for a horse or two, then he would see them before the first race tomorrow. Neither Fulke nor Cath had a clue who he was but later, in the bar, Fulke was telling the story to Cath's brother-in-law Derek Parker-Bowles who asked him what the mystery man looked like. 'I bet it was Michael Oswald,' he said after hearing Fulke's description. Cath remembers, 'Fulke was astonished and said "It can't be!" but, of course, the next day it was.'

The Walwyns were sworn to secrecy, not even being allowed to tell their staff at Saxon House stables until they had met Queen Elizabeth at Ascot and finalized arrangements with her. Cath recalls, 'It was very funny because there was a lot of betting going on about who was going to get the Queen Mother's horses. Dave Dick, who was our jockey at the time, and who was a fun man, went to Fulke and said, "I bet you're going to get them" and Fulke replied, "No I shouldn't think so," which was all he could say really. So Dave said, "Well, it can't be you then because I've been told the person who's going to have them knows. I shall have a large bet on Fred Winter."'

Although Queen Elizabeth had decided to carry on racing she would never again have as many horses in training as she had at Fairlawne. At the beginning of 1973 she still had 16 horses at the Cazalet stables but only seven made their way from the Kent countryside to Saxon House. They included her favourite horse Game Spirit, proven winner Inch Arran, a couple of likely sorts in Isle of Man and Colonius and former flat racer Tammuz. The highly promising Black Magic was too unsound to be properly trained and was literally in one stable door and out the other for an early retirement.

Fulke Walwyn had been a champion amateur rider in the Thirties when he was with the 9th Lancers cavalry regiment. After turning professional in 1936 he suffered a number of nasty falls, including one at Ludlow in Shropshire

Opposite: Fulke Walwyn surveys the Lambourn gallops in 1982.

that ended his riding career in 1939. He took a crashing blow on the head and as a result he was never able to take his drink too well. But as Lord Oaksey remembers, 'However late and long he stayed up at night he was always there for work in the morning, sometimes in a pretty foul temper, it's true.'

Before he quit the saddle Fulke did, however, have one ride that was to change the course of his career. Golden Miller was the most famous steeplechaser before the Second World War and is still the only one mentioned in the same breath as Arkle. Until Queen Elizabeth's involvement promoted greater public interest in the sport, he was probably the only National Hunt horse the man in the street could have named. Golden Miller also had a well-documented dislike of the Grand National fences after winning the race in 1934. He had been strongly fancied for the 1936 National when Anthony Mildmay rode Davy Jones and Fulke was on the eventual winner, Reynoldstown. Golden Miller had fallen at the first fence, was remounted and then persistently refused at Valentine's. He clearly hated the whole business. That autumn, Fulke miraculously rode him round to complete the course and finish second in the Becher Chase. It was a remarkable piece of horsemanship and one that Golden Miller's eccentric owner, Miss Dorothy Paget, greatly appreciated.

Fulke Walwyn, the Lion of Lambourn, on his favourite chaser, Mandarin.

Dorothy Paget was the most important owner in National Hunt racing before Queen Elizabeth. She was very rich, very large and very distinctive. She always wore a blue felt hat and a long blue coat that reached almost to the floor. She was a legendary punter and an exacting owner and would hold interminable conferences with her trainers long after other racegoers had left for the comfort of their own firesides. After the Second World War she sent her horses to the young trainer Fulke Walwyn and helped make Lambourn the principal centre for training jumpers in Britain. It was an enormous boost for Fulke's career. He would train more than 350 winners for her before her death in 1960 including his first Gold Cup hero, Mont Tremblant, in 1952. By then all her horses were ridden by Dave Dick who was chosen after she fell out with Bryan Marshall in 1951. Dick was always able to charm Miss Paget where others failed and, when he was convalescing in hospital after a rail post splintered into his leg in a horrible accident at Cheltenham, she made sure that he was surrounded by every conceivable luxury refreshment throughout his stay.

Bill Smith, who rode 63 winners for Queen Elizabeth when he was Walwyn's stable jockey, was sitting in the great trainer's office soon after starting at

The eccentric Dorothy Paget (centre), wearing her famous coat 'The Speckled Hen', pats her chaser Golden Miller.

Saxon House in 1974 when he noticed a painting on the wall. He recalls, 'I looked up and there was a picture of five horses, all in their paddock clothing with their names underneath. It said they were "owned by Miss Dorothy Paget, trained by Fulke Walwyn, ridden by Bryan Marshall". They were five winners in one day and it was a month before I was born. And I thought maybe he does know what he's doing. He never really explained what he was doing. He would just sort of mumble to you. I don't think he was sure exactly what he was doing with a horse himself. He just did it by instinct. He really was a natural genius with horses.'

That genius had long been plain to the racing fraternity who had watched in awe as the maestro prepared such famous chasers as Mandarin, Mill House and Taxidermist for a string of big-race wins. Taxidermist, or 'Taxi' as he was affectionately known, was partly owned by Cath which led to a degree of marital strife within the Walwyn home. Taxi was the regular ride of Lord Oaksey, or John Lawrence as he was before he inherited his barony. The partnership had run in the Kim Muir Handicap Chase at Cheltenham in 1958 when they were beaten by Peter Cazalet's son Edward on Fairlawne's useful chaser Lochroe.

In those days Lawrence was able to juggle his riding with a blossoming career as a racing journalist. He had been taken on in the mid-Fifties by the *Daily Telegraph*, probably, he thinks, because the sports editor, Frank Coles, was impressed that he had his arm in a sling for the interview after breaking his collarbone in a race fall two days before. After a year Coles told Lawrence that he must have a pen name and from now on he would be known in the paper as 'Marlborough'. An astonished Lawrence asked, 'Why call me Marlborough? I wasn't at Marlborough College and I am nothing to do with the Duke.' Coles replied gruffly, 'Well, you keep reversing the charges from there.'

As a result it was 'Marlborough' who was on board Taxidermist when he took on the star chaser Mandarin, the apple of Fulke Walwyn's eye, in the 1958 Whitbread Gold Cup at Sandown. They jumped the last fence together before the large weight concession proved too much for Mandarin and Taxi easily drew clear, much to Walwyn's annoyance. 'It was no speaks for two days,' recalls Cath, who was, of course, delighted her horse had won.

Fulke Walwyn had an entirely different training strategy from that of Peter Cazalet. He was interested in big races and nurturing horses whereas Cazalet wanted to provide his owners, particularly his royal patron, with winners. The two men were good friends. Cath Walwyn observes, 'They were contrasting characters. Peter was very on the ball and ran things like a military operation. We would go and stay at Fairlawne which had lovely stables and a huge, beautiful house. It always annoyed me because he would never let me look at all his horses. He would always have some new buys which I would be dying to see. There were no other racing yards around Fairlawne but Lambourn is a racing community where we all used communal gallops.'

One marked difference between Fulke Walwyn and Peter Cazalet was in the former's attitude towards the jockeys. Amateur and professional were treated the same, and they would all be asked to join the trainer for breakfast after schooling on a Monday or Tuesday. They were not, however, allowed to sit in the chair to Walwyn's immediate left. That place was reserved for Rags, the trainer's much loved Cairn terrier. The jockeys did not share Fulke's affection for the pooch, who would regularly bite them on the calves. Bill Smith, always a target for Rags, recalls, 'The old man would usually have a boiled egg with soldiers. He would put little bits of leftover meat from the Sunday roast on to the soldiers and feed Rags off that. Rags was a pain in the neck.'

During schooling Rags would be there on a lead, barking at the horses. His master would conduct proceedings furiously chewing gum which he did every morning until breakfast. 'He would grind away all the time,' says Smith, 'and the more annoyed he got the more the gum would get some suffering. You were glad you weren't a piece of gum.' After breakfast the gum would be discarded and replaced by a cigarette holder and Fulke would sit in his favourite armchair for a leisurely smoke, something which he would do for most of the rest of the day.

ᴖ The Lion of Lambourn

Fulke Walwyn was a perfectionist, a worrier and the most patient man in racing. He was totally dedicated to his horses and, other than a two-week break in summer, could never bear to leave Saxon House. After the stable lads had left for the evening he would wander round the yard, checking to see if the horses had eaten up and inspecting every box. Most trainers become adept at examining horses' legs for the imperfections that can spell trouble but Fulke was particularly skilful. He had to be. It is one of the problem areas of training chasers, especially the three-mile specialists Fulke favoured. He liked to find inexpensive young horses and develop them over a number of years. His top chasers like The Dikler, Diamond Edge, Charlie Potheen and, of course, Queen Elizabeth's Game Spirit seemed to go on forever.

The secret is regular attention. The former head lad at Saxon House, Darkie Deacon, so called because of his jet-black hair, spent 30 years with Walwyn and explains, 'You have to catch a bad leg early and then you can do something for the horse. If you are feeling the same legs every day, you know if there's a difference.' It does not always work. In the case of Tammuz, his legs were so bumpy it was impossible to tell which of the lumps were new. If a 'leg' was discovered, a poultice would be put on it at once to try and take the soreness out. A horse would need to be left in his box to recover at leisure even if the injury was slight. Deacon remembers that Walwyn would only lose half a dozen horses a year to leg trouble because he would not put the rigorous demands on his stable's inmates that today's more competitive trainers are obliged to do to maintain a position in the commercial rat race that National Hunt racing has become.

Part Four ᴖ **A Special Place**

Walwyn could be very fierce around the yard. Deacon observes, 'He was a lion of a man and could swear with the best of them. But I found him a very fair man. He was very firm about everything. Everything had to be "just right" with the horses; martingales had to be the right length, the bridle had to be fitted properly, rugs had to be 4 inches above the hipbones. Even the tail string had to be a certain length. He missed nothing. His stable lads only looked after two horses. These days they might do six.' Walwyn was equally thorough on the gallops, varying work to keep the horses interested. He would never send them monotonously up the same gallop and was not interested in interval training. Each horse was treated differently with meticulous attention. 'He did what he was paid to do – train the horse,' says Deacon. When the doughty warrior Special Cargo had leg trouble, Walwyn would send him out in the dark to canter up and down a gallop of long shavings because he did not want him to use them after the other horses had churned them up. It was perfect ground for him.

Queen Elizabeth found the transition to Saxon House did not diminish her enjoyment of racing. There could never be another Fairlawne, a unique establishment. But Fulke Walwyn provided her with the biggest race winners of her owning career. Right from the start she made clear her intention to talk to him directly about the horses and plans for their racing careers. She would travel down to Lambourn on a Monday at least half a dozen times a year to look at her horses and chat to the stable lads. Deacon says, 'The yard was always tidy but we had a bit of a spring clean when she was coming.' Queen Elizabeth has a superb memory for the little details. If a lad told her he had just become a father, on her next visit she would ask him about the baby. It is quite a feat considering how many people she has to meet in an official capacity.

She also liked to watch the schooling sessions. On one occasion Bill Smith was on a horse called Winter Flag which he had just acquired and which he was hoping to persuade Queen Elizabeth to buy. Smith wanted the horse to look good so thought he would jump the three schooling fences, and then the rails of the paddock on the way back, to show off and make a big impression. At the first schooling fence Winter Flag tried to run out and all but wiped out the watching Queen Elizabeth, Fulke Walwyn and Rags. Bill had to put Plan B into operation. He pulled the horse up and trotted over to the apprehensive group. 'What a lovely horse,' he declared confidently. Queen Elizabeth was not fooled.

During the Seventies and Eighties Queen Elizabeth felt quite at home on the gallops of Lambourn. She appreciated Fulke's methods and his careful preparation. Cath recalls, 'She always said, "Don't run a horse just so I can see it if it's not the best race to run it in. If it can win somewhere I can't go, then run it anyway." She always felt that punters would think the horse was fancied if she was there.' That was certainly the case for one renewal of Queen Elizabeth's favourite race: the Horse and Hound Grand Military Gold Cup at Sandown. The race is a last hurrah of old racing traditions where regimental gentleman riders, stirrups scraping the ground, do battle around Sandown's exacting course. Queen Elizabeth has always had a cocktail party for the riders at Royal Lodge, Windsor the evening after the race. Some of them have to hobble in, bravely nursing their bandaged wounds. It is the one race above all others that she likes to win. Special Cargo triumphed on three consecutive occasions in the 1980s including one when his talented pilot Gerald Oxley's stirrup leather broke and he rode one of the great races to get the horse home.

On another occasion Oxley was on the warm favourite Sun Rising, a talented but injury-prone royal horse. The Walwyn yard had another

Special Cargo [Gerald Oxley] flies a fence at his favourite Sandown Park on his way to his third victory in the Horse and Hound Grand Military Gold Cup, 8 March 1986.

unconsidered runner in the race, a 50/1 shot called Columbus who had been recovering from a knock but on the morning of the race Cath Walwyn thought he was just well enough to take his chance. Michael Oswald was watching the race with Queen Elizabeth. 'We had a terrible run,' he recalls. 'Poor Gerald got bogged down in traffic and couldn't get Sun Rising out of a pocket. He worked like a demon and just failed to get up. An irate Fulke pointed to the winner, the unconsidered Columbus, and said, "Who trained that bugger?"– whereupon his wife told him, "You did!" He had forgotten the wretched thing existed even though it was technically trained by him.' Cath remembers that Queen Elizabeth did not find it at all funny. Mrs Walwyn told her sympathetically, 'It's very unlucky. We nearly didn't run the winner.' Queen Elizabeth replied, 'I wish you hadn't.'

The next time Queen Elizabeth visited the yard the conversation naturally returned to the race. She turned to Fulke and remarked with a twinkle in her eye, 'You think I didn't hear that naughty little word?' Poor Fulke was dumbfounded. He had forgotten all about it.

∾ Isle Of Man and the Hayling Island Slapper

On a bitterly cold November afternoon in 1973, two days after Princess Anne had married Mark Phillips in Westminster Abbey, Queen Elizabeth watched Isle of Man contest a novice hurdle at Ascot. Stable jockey Terry Biddlecombe, in his last season, was sidelined with injury and so the reliable stable number two, Aly Branford, took over with strict instructions from Fulke Walwyn not to hit the horse with a whip under any circumstances. It was to be a gentle introduction. But Isle of Man, a tall, handsome bay gelding, amazed everyone by jumping into the lead at the last flight and only just getting pipped on the run-in by the vigorously ridden Fervor, trained by arch rival Fred Winter. After the race Branford told the royal party that Isle of Man would definitely have won with one smack of the whip. It would be churlish to suggest the stewards should have inquired whether the royal runner was ridden to reach the best possible finishing position. No steward is that brave.

One thing, however, was plain for everyone to see. This was a decent prospect, just as Queen Elizabeth and Michael Oswald had hoped.

Sir Michael observes, 'He was a magnificent horse. He was big, long-legged and rangy and we were determined not to send him into training too early because that could ruin him.' Isle of Man spent his early life tucked away in Ireland before being wrapped in cotton wool at Hampton Court. His dam, Queen of the Isle, an undistinguished racehorse at Fairlawne, was the most important jumping brood mare in the royal story. She produced not just Isle of Man but also the powerful grey Inch Arran and Colonius, a flashy chestnut who won a series of races at the minor tracks when the going resembled a tarmac road. By a striking coincidence each of the three won 14 races for Queen Elizabeth.

Initial expectation that Isle of Man was a long-term Cheltenham Gold Cup prospect was a little dampened when he clearly failed to stay three miles in a long-distance hurdle at Cheltenham on his second outing. By this time Terry Biddlecombe was back in action. One of the most popular post-war jockeys and three times champion, Terry was at Saxon House for one year before hanging up his boots after the 1974 Cheltenham Festival. He discovered that the most important thing with the long-striding Isle of Man was to keep him balanced – under pressure he tended to run up and down on the spot. In March, after chalking up a hat trick of wins, Isle of Man was sent to Cheltenham for the Sun Alliance Novices' Hurdle. But even on his preferred soft ground he did not stay the two and a half miles. He was a horse for whom two miles would be the optimum trip.

Bill Smith took over from Biddlecombe as stable jockey at Saxon House. Like his boyhood idol David Mould, Bill was a Londoner but, unlike the former royal jockey, his was not a horsy background. His father had been a professional cyclist and owned a cycle shop. The family had moved to Hayling Island on the Hampshire coast near Portsmouth when Bill was a young boy and he started taking lessons at a local riding school with the ambition of becoming a show-jumper. But because he was a small lad it was suggested he try his luck as a jockey. After drifting in and out of racing as a teenager and working for Moss Bros as a gentleman's outfitter, he broke through riding winners for Bill Marshall who was then training at Marlborough. The young jockey was not the most stylish and had the habit of slapping a horse down the shoulder after the last fence, something the rules do not allow today. As a result Smith was christened the 'Hayling Island Slapper' by the press room.

By coincidence he had also followed Terry Biddlecombe into the job of first jockey to Fred Rimell, who sent out a host of big-race winners from his yard at Kinnersley near Worcester. Fred had been the trainer of E.S.B. who so fortuitously won Devon Loch's National. Bill Smith did not get on with Mercy, Fred's battle-axe of a wife, and his stay at Kinnersley was not a happy one. He recalls, 'Terry was a wonderful, flamboyant, outgoing sort of guy and had been there nine years. I was much quieter and didn't live there and it just didn't suit. Mercy Rimell didn't like me and I didn't like her much.'

By this time Smith had already had his first ride for Queen Elizabeth on a very moderate animal called Colonello who had been sent from Fairlawne to Jack O'Donoghue's bohemian stables. David Mould spotted the young jockey proudly putting on the royal silks and shouted across the changing room, 'Oh God they'll let anyone wear those now.' He did advise the young man how to behave towards the royal owner. He warned him not to wear gloves for the royal introduction. He should bow and call her 'Your Majesty' and subsequently 'Ma'am'. It was the same piece of advice that Smith was later able to pass on to his own successor, Kevin Mooney. Queen Elizabeth, as she always does with her jockeys, put Smith instantly at ease. She appeared more interested in the ride he had in the next race: the popular stayer Spanish Steps owned by her good friend Edward Courage. 'Be careful,' she advised, 'you've a very nice ride in the next race.' This did nothing to instil confidence in Smith, who decided self-preservation was clearly the best policy and pulled up Colonello at his earliest discretion.

Bill Smith's lobbying for the Saxon House job eventually paid off. In April 1974 he rode his first royal winner, Inch Arran, the horse that coincidentally had been David Mould's last winner in the blue and buff colours. It was one of very few wins for Queen Elizabeth at Cheltenham, albeit in an unimportant late-season race. Smith had a torrid introduction to the stable. He found it hard to establish a rapport with Walwyn, who could be very irascible but commanded the greatest respect in the yard. Teething problems in the relationship were compounded when Bill broke his shoulder and pelvis and bruised his kidneys in a fall and came back too soon after three weeks, anxious to please his new employer. He didn't click in an outing on the mighty Game Spirit. Fortunately David Mould, who knew the horse so well, was able to advise Bill not to bully him and they subsequently went from strength to strength together.

Opposite: Two fearless royal jumpers: *Above* Isle of Man [Bill Smith] in front-running form on his way to finishing fourth in the Old Year Handicap Chase at Newbury, 30 December 1978. *Below* The headstrong Colonius gives jockey Aly Branford a hair-raising ride to victory in the Bewdley Novices Chase at Worcester, 10 May 1975.

Part Four ✑ **A Special Place**

Bill missed Isle of Man's winning novice chase debut at Sandown in November. The horse jumped so brilliantly under Aly Branford that afterwards Fulke Walwyn declared him 'the best novice I have schooled since the Cheltenham Gold Cup winner Mill House'. Smith was back to ride him for the first time at Ascot two weeks later and again Isle of Man was not extended and led all the way. Things were also beginning to pick up for his jockey who completed a double on the very useful staying hurdle prospect Sunyboy. Isle of Man won again a week later at Newbury before Fulke decided to rest him for a couple of months with Cheltenham in March very much in mind.

Isle of Man was fast becoming a great favourite of Fulke Walwyn. Bill Smith observes, 'If you had a blank piece of paper and asked him to draw his ideal horse, he would have come up with Isle of Man.' Although he was magnificent to look at, Isle of Man was less than perfect in his box. He was what is known as a 'box-walker', a very restless type. Walwyn thought it would be a good idea to find a companion for the hyperactive chaser and asked Bill Smith if he had any ideas. Smith had a goat he had bought for a fiver and offered to sell it on to Walwyn. The goat was put in the box and Isle of Man promptly bit off one of its ears. 'There was no question of it being a companion,' declares Bill Smith drily. 'It was dinner.'

Isle of Man continued to be a handful. Whenever he raced the jockey literally had to be thrown on as the horse jigged by, unable to stand still for a moment. At the stables he would regularly take a bite out of his stable lad, 'Big Pete' Standon, who had looked after him at Fairlawne and come over with the horses from there. Darkie Deacon remembers, 'Big Pete used to think it was an honour to be bitten by one of the Queen Mum's. Thick sod.' Once, when Queen Elizabeth was visiting the yard, Deacon had to look after Isle of Man because Big Pete was away that day. She asked him, 'Does he bite you as well?' Deacon replied, 'No Ma'am, I don't give him the chance.' Queen Elizabeth laughed and said, 'Well, it's not an honour, is it?'

Isle of Man is keen and alert as he is led around the paddock before a race at Sandown.

❧ The Great Races

Tammuz: Schweppes Gold Trophy, Newbury, 8 February 1975

Tammuz winning the Schweppes was a coup, a masterful piece of training by Fulke Walwyn who carefully laid out a horse with dodgy legs to win the top handicap hurdle race of the year at the very acceptable price of 18/1. Tammuz had bad legs when he raced on the flat for the Queen. He was a big bay brute of a horse, who had matured slowly with Ian Balding at Kingsclere and, at three, had managed to win just a two-mile maiden at York in the autumn of 1971. He was certainly bred to be useful, being out of the mare – Highlight – who would a couple of years later produce the Queen's classic winner Highclere. It was decided to keep Tammuz in training as a four-year-old. He was gelded and prepared for a career as a staying handicapper, but it soon became clear that he was never going to be particularly sound. Having broken down yet again he was pin-fired and given, as a present, by the Queen to the Queen Mother.

The horse was sent to recuperate at the Hampton Court Stud before being sent to Saxon House the following year to see what Fulke Walwyn could make of him. Even Walwyn, a genius with bad-legged horses, would have his work cut out making something of Tammuz. Cath Walwyn observes, 'He really did have the most dreadful legs you've ever seen.' They were, as Darkie Deacon puts it, 'lumpy and bumpy'. After a couple of moderate-placed efforts in novice hurdles Tammuz was 10 lengths clear at Warwick with the inimitable Terry Biddlecombe riding when he ignored the last fence, stumbled, did the splits and dumped an embarrassed jockey on the grass. The partnership made amends just after New Year at Sandown when Tammuz jumped immaculately to win on the bridle in the manner of a very promising horse.

Afterwards his old leg trouble returned and this time all that could be tried was a 'split tendon' operation. It would mean another year off, and Tammuz would need a good measure of Walwyn's legendary patience to race again. The novice win at Sandown had shown him to be more than useful. Perhaps just as importantly, his fall at Warwick warned Bill Smith, who would be his regular pilot the following year, that he was apt to bulldoze a hurdle, especially if he was in front. Walwyn already had a tilt at the 1975 Schweppes in mind for the horse and he decided to bring him back for a six-week burst: two or three prep races and then Newbury. Tammuz was a heavy-topped, strong horse who took some getting fit so Walwyn had to tread a tightrope between getting enough work into him and nursing his fragile legs.

Bill Smith thought Tammuz had a 'good set of wheels'. He was not like some weedy sorts who graduate from the flat to jumps: 'He was a lovely big-shouldered horse with a touch of class. He was a lovely horse to sit on.' Tammuz came back from his lay-off in a Sandown hurdle race on unsuitably soft going and was looked after down the field. He then won on Boxing Day at Kempton, ears pricked and clouting the last hurdle when in front. In his last prep race at Wincanton in Somerset he was unimpressive or, as Bill Smith puts it, 'moderate'.

The Schweppes was always an ultra-competitive race and Tammuz, with a history of bad legs, breaking down and indifferent jumping over the last couple of flights, was not one of the more fancied runners in the eyes of the betting public. After all, the mighty champion hurdler Lanzarote and the talented Bird's Nest were running. But Lanzarote had to give Tammuz a whopping 20 lbs, an impossible task if Walwyn's charge was anywhere near his best. As Bill Smith attests, 'He was always ridiculously well handicapped.'

That was certainly the opinion at Saxon House where every stable lad raided the piggy bank to back their horse at such generous odds. By tradition the Schweppes is either a bog or falls victim to the weather, but this year the going was reasonably good. Bill Smith, who seldom walked the course, was taking no chances and trudged up the Newbury straight before racing: 'It was pretty rare for me so it must have been a major plan. I know the "old man" was pretty geed up. I felt it was better ground up the stand side so that was where we decided to go.'

Queen Elizabeth was in the paddock beforehand to talk to Bill Smith. She never gives instructions to a jockey. 'She never put any pressure on you for any race at all,' says Smith. 'She was much more likely to say "the favourite's a nice horse" as if trying to steer the conversation away from her own horse.' Sir Martin Gilliat was there, his normal enthusiastic self, keeping everyone cheerful.

As almost always happens in this race, the 28 runners set off at a furious gallop, charging from the gate like the cavalry at Balaclava. Bill Smith found himself sitting even further back than he planned, something which gave the watching Fulke Walwyn palpitations because he always hated horses being dropped out too far. Bill Smith recalls, 'I had a good feeling about the horse because I knew I had a very live one and he had a bit of class. I rode him like a good horse.' At Newbury there was then a cross flight which swept the field round to the left into the straight and there Smith made his move to the outside, which would bring him up near the stand rail over the last few flights. He moved Tammuz easily up to the heels of the leaders and was sixth turning in. By the second last he was practically disputing the lead with Tip the Wink and Roaring Wind and took it up between the last two flights, which was plenty soon enough for Tammuz: 'He never went clear if there were horses around him. We went to the last in front and he cocked his ears and had a good look at it. Then he flattened it but that didn't make

Tammuz [Bill Smith] demolishes a flight on his way to securing victory in the Schweppes Gold Trophy at Newbury, 8 February 1975.

any difference to him. He was challenged up the run-in by Legal Tender but always kept pulling out a bit more. He held what he'd got and kept moving up a gear. Although he only won by half a length, it was an easier half a length than you might think because he was always going to win.'

It was a perfect race, especially as the money was down. Sir Martin Gilliat had no doubt found a home in the ring for his fearless fiver but Queen Elizabeth never bets. Her racing manager, Sir Michael Oswald, is very firm on this point. If that is the case it's rather a shame that she does not follow the tradition of Edward VII and George V. For some reason there seems to be a stigma attached to having a little wager, but she could have won enough on Tammuz to pay her training bills for a decade or more. Judging by the three cheers for the Queen Mother that rang around Newbury as Tammuz was led back to the winners' enclosure, there were a large number of happy punters around that afternoon. And that evening there was a rollicking party at the Malt Shovel Inn, just a furlong from the gates of Saxon House.

Almost there, Tammuz [Bill Smith] leads Legal Tender [Robert Hughes] at the last flight on his way to his Schweppes triumph.

Fulke Walwyn said afterwards that he had never had a bigger thrill in his training life than winning the Schweppes for Queen Elizabeth. It was her biggest victory to that point and remains the most important hurdle race she has won. Poor old Tammuz broke down again in the Welsh Champion Hurdle at Chepstow. He came back three years later to try his luck at the larger obstacles. It was worth the try because he could have been Gold Cup standard if he had taken to them. Bill Smith pulled him up on his second try at the larger obstacles, much to Walwyn's annoyance, but the great trainer soon realized after further schooling at Saxon House that Tammuz was not a jumper of fences and he was immediately retired. 'He was frightened of them,' observes Smith. But this was a horse who literally didn't owe anybody a thing.

Royal Racing

❧ The Cheltenham Hoodoo

Queen Elizabeth had a strong hand for the 1975 Cheltenham Festival. Isle of Man, who had made an impressive start jumping fences, was going for the Arkle Challenge Trophy Chase, the championship race for novice chasers over two miles. Sunyboy, a tough and talented stayer, would contest the two-and-a-half-mile Sun Alliance Novices' Hurdle. Game Spirit would have another crack at the Cheltenham Piper Champagne Gold Cup, the blue riband event. At last Queen Elizabeth had every reason to be optimistic about the three days in March which represent the pinnacle of the jumping season.

Up to this point she had been a leading National Hunt owner for 25 years and was pushing towards 300 winners. Yet her record at Cheltenham was miserable. Only Antiar had triumphed, in the 1965 Spa Hurdle. He was a speedy hurdler who came into Queen Elizabeth's ownership when already a successful racehorse. She was left him in the will of the Contessa di Sant'Elia, another of Peter Cazalet's owners, and injuries to Bill Rees and David Mould gave the swashbuckling Dave Dick the opportunity to ride a royal winner at Cheltenham. Dick was at his most determined. At the last flight the new royal horse appeared to have the measure of his only challenger, Tobago, ridden by David Nicholson. But Antiar clouted it and Tobago headed him up the long run-in. Dave Dick, riding like a demon, forced Antiar back into the lead as the winning post loomed. It was the horse's very first run in the royal colours and it is a sobering thought that if the Contessa had hung on for another couple of months Queen Elizabeth's Cheltenham record would have been even more wretched.

All her best horses had tried their luck. Makaldar, Worcran and Escalus had been placed in the Champion Hurdle. Sunbridge might have won the four-mile National Hunt Chase but finished only third to his jockey John Lawrence's dismay. The Rip had been unplaced in the Gold Cup and Double Star likewise in the Two Mile Champion Chase. In truth, Queen Elizabeth never had that many runners as she never wanted to run her horses out of their depth. If Peter Cazalet had trained a horse specifically for Cheltenham the record might have been better. Fairlawne successes at the meeting were very sparse.

Fulke Walwyn, however, had a Cheltenham record to be envied. Mont Tremblant, Mandarin, Mill House and The Dikler had all been memorable winners of the Gold Cup and, although hurdling played second fiddle at Saxon House, he had still sent out Anzio and Kirriemuir to win the Champion Hurdle.

Surely he would be able to manage a hatful of Cheltenham winners for Queen Elizabeth? If only it were that simple.

The incomparable Game Spirit had been Walwyn's first royal winner, in November 1973. He was convinced the horse would stay the Gold Cup trip of three miles and two furlongs and, although a Cheltenham victory did not yet appear on his CV, it was decided Game Spirit would take his chance in the 1974 race when he would be Terry Biddlecombe's last big-race ride. He had been in top form, winning effortlessly around Windsor's figure-of-eight track in February, and took his chance alongside the other Saxon House stars, The Dikler and Charlie Potheen. Darkie Deacon remembers that Walwyn was 'tipping' Game Spirit of his three. The race was a dramatic one, best remembered for the fall of High Ken three fences from home. He brought down the favourite, Pendil, who had been cruising at the time. Pendil was destined to be one of the best horses never to win the chasing crown. At the time Game Spirit was going very well, even though slightly hampered by High Ken's fall. Biddlecombe reported that he suddenly weakened and 'died in my hands'. Game Spirit pottered up the hill in his own time to finish third behind Captain Christy and The Dikler. It was Queen Elizabeth's best result in the Gold Cup. Charlie Potheen struggled home a gallant fourth which meant that Walwyn had saddled all the placed horses, a statistic unlikely to have given him much pleasure because he always hated to lose.

The next season Game Spirit appeared to be as good as ever, striking up an understanding with Bill Smith. He warmed up for Cheltenham by taking the Geoffrey Gilbey Chase at Newbury in a canter. Smith was now following David Mould's advice about not bullying him. Instead of a lash with the whip, the horse would be rewarded with a pat and a kind word. Walwyn was still convinced Game Spirit would stay the trip at Cheltenham especially if the going was no worse than good.

The rains came to Cheltenham to dampen everyone's spirits – not just the odd shower, but torrential downpours that washed out the whole of the first day. There was little point in letting Game Spirit run on ground so heavy he could not possibly win and he was withdrawn. Isle of Man, on the other hand, was at his best on soft going and was in fine fettle after a 10-week rest. Bill Smith was confident: 'He loved the bottomless ground and was a fantastic jumper.' Isle of Man set off in front, long striding and confident, stretching

Antiar [Dave Dick] lands over the last flight just ahead of Tobago [David Nicholson] on his way to winning the Spa Hurdle, 11 March 1965 and giving Queen Elizabeth her only success at the Cheltenham Festival.

easily out and clearing his fences with panache. Two fences after the water jump, disaster came in a moment. His hind legs slipped from under him and he was down. Bill Smith is certain he would have won: 'I was having a great ride, just sitting on him, not doing a thing. I don't even know how he fell. He probably just stood off too far and maybe lost his footing on take-off.' The race cannot be rerun and Isle of Man's chance had gone forever.

Sunyboy, too, loved a bog. He also had unlimited stamina and when Smith had him disputing the lead at the top of the Cheltenham hill there was every reason to be hopeful he might stay there. In many ways Sunyboy was similar to Queen Elizabeth's fine hurdler Makaldar, off the bridle and being booted along practically the whole race. He had been a more than useful flat horse when trained by Dick Hern for Lady Beaverbrook and had finished second in the Irish St Leger. He was still an entire horse but, having developed an aversion to the starting stalls, he was given a shot at hurdling. Lady Beaverbrook was no great lover of the jumping game and was forever phoning Michael Oswald to make sure her former charge had returned safely home to the stables after a race. Sunyboy's jockey on the flat, Joe Mercer, told Bill Smith, 'It takes two men and a boy to push him along. He's so lazy.' Smith was pushing and shoving in the Cheltenham straight but Sunyboy just could not quicken and had dropped back to fifth place at the last flight. But he refused to give up and doggedly powered on up the hill to retake second place near the line. The winner, the Irish-trained Davy Lad, would win the Gold Cup two years later, putting Sunyboy's heroic effort into perspective as one of the best by any of Queen Elizabeth's horses.

Game Spirit and Isle of Man returned to Cheltenham in future years to do battle and both were placed in the Two Mile Champion Chase. Game Spirit was second to the Irish-trained Skymas in 1976 and Isle of Man third to the same horse in 1977. In all honesty Skymas was not the equal of the royal horses but they were never at their best at Cheltenham. Game Spirit was a world beater at Newbury and nothing could get past Isle of Man at Windsor. There in 1980 at the age of 13, his speed gone, he still gave a jumping lesson to his rivals to record his swansong victory for Queen Elizabeth. After registering a royal success in six different seasons Isle of Man owed nobody anything and was retired to end his days hunting with the Quorn in Leicestershire.

Sunyboy never tried his luck at Cheltenham again but he did have the honour of winning the 300th race for Queen Elizabeth when he took the Fernbank Hurdle at Ascot in February 1976. Game Spirit had been winner number 299 at Newbury and Isle of Man was expected to be the 300th the following day but could finish only second to the useful chaser Uncle Bing. Queen Elizabeth postponed some engagements in the hope that Sunyboy would be the landmark winner the following week. Although quite lightly raced, he was a good jumper and difficult to beat if the pace was a strong one because he would stay on so much better than most. The only niggling doubt was over the ground, which was a little firmer than the squelchy marsh he favoured. But Sunyboy travelled well throughout the race, kept close to the inside rail by Smith who gradually stoked him up to wear down the pacesetter, Prince Eleigh, and run out a decisive winner. Queen Elizabeth enthusiastically rose from her seat to applaud her runner home. Afterwards Fulke Walwyn and Bill Smith were invited to the Royal Box for a celebratory glass of champagne. Smith had barely been aware in advance that this might be the 300th winner: 'I appreciated it more for Fulke than for me. I wasn't the one who had to live with the horse and feel his legs every day and worry about him. I just had to turn up on the day and push him round.'

To mark the occasion there was a reception in London and Bill Smith was naturally invited. He remembers it well because he and his girlfriend Sue had to get engaged so that he could introduce her to Queen Elizabeth as his fiancée. They were married the following year. He was impressed by the way everyone had their three and a half minutes chat with Queen Elizabeth before she effortlessly glided on to speak to another guest: 'It was beautifully done. And she had a special way of speaking to you, her way. She would never say, for instance, "Have I got something nice for Cheltenham?" She would say, "Do you think we have something nice for Cheltenham?"'

She never really had something 'nice' for Cheltenham again, more's the pity. But Fulke Walwyn continued to try. That stout warrior Special Cargo managed third in the Sun Alliance Novices' Chase in 1981. Cath Walwyn confesses that her husband was frustrated at not being able to provide Queen Elizabeth with a Cheltenham winner: 'She always thought she was terribly unlucky at Cheltenham.' Nothing illustrates that misfortune more dramatically than the fate of Easter Ross in the 1999 Coral Cup. Strongly fancied by the Queen Mother's current trainer, Nicky Henderson, backed into second favourite by a public hungry for a royal victory, he promptly fell at the second hurdle.

Game Spirit [Terry Biddlecombe] has Pendil [Richard Pitman] on his outside for company during the dramatic Cheltenham Gold Cup, 14 March 1974. The Dikler [Ron Barry] is just behind.

Queen Elizabeth gives Sunyboy an appreciative pat after he had carried her colours to their 300th win in the Fernbank Hurdle at Ascot, 18 February 1976.

At the 2000 Festival, the Cheltenham Executive presented Queen Elizabeth with a picture to mark her support of the meeting and her nine winners at the course. It would have been impolite to draw attention to her meagre one festival winner. Far better to dwell on the fact that the Queen Mother Champion Chase is, for many, the highlight of the three days. The 2000 race in which Tony McCoy dynamically hauled Edredon Bleu over the line was one of the best ever. Afterwards there were no empty spaces as the crowd waited for Queen Elizabeth to arrive in her racing buggy decked out in her famous colours. The cheers and applause were as great as ever. You would have thought one of her own horses had won.

❧ Death of a Gentleman

Queen Elizabeth was at Newbury that dreadful afternoon and perhaps she had a shudder of impending doom when she said in the parade ring before the race, 'I do hope nothing happens to him in this race.' She was concerned because the horse in question was her favourite: Game Spirit, winner of a record 21 races for his royal owner and in the final weeks of his racing career. At the end of the 1976/7 season he was to retire from racing and enter the Queen's service as a charger to be ridden in her birthday parade. It would be an honour for the 11-year-old, renowned for his fine looks and lovely temperament.

Game Spirit had not been at his best since beating Bula in the Hermitage Chase at Newbury's October meeting. What a race that was! Two superb horses jumped the last fence as one and Game Spirit, relishing the fight, battled ahead up the run-in. No one knew it at the time but that epic victory had taken a crucial toll on the horse. He ran a lacklustre race in the Kenton Chase at Kempton over Christmas so Fulke Walwyn decided to give him some time off and in March take him back to Newbury where the horse had won seven times and invariably excelled. Game Spirit was lumbered with 12 stone 4 lbs in the Geoffrey Gilbey Chase and in the circumstances ran a fair race to finish fifth, although his regular pilot, Bill Smith, confessed to being disappointed, reasoning that the horse should have been at least third on the track he knew so well.

After the race Smith settled Game Spirit to a walk and guided him across the hurdles track, back through the gates of the main course area and on to the walkway where the stable lads met their returning charges. Fortunately they were just out of sight of Queen Elizabeth in the Royal Box. Smith recalls, 'Fred Rimell had told me years before that if a horse whinnies after a race, jump off it because it usually means it's going to drop dead. Game Spirit started to whinny. Andy Turnell and his mount were behind me and he could see quicker than I could that the horse was staggering behind. And he started shouting "Get off! Get off!" I instinctively half jumped and Game Spirit went down flat and flipped right over. He rolled over completely but somehow missed me. I jumped up and rushed to him but he was already dead.

'There was a vet near listening to a horse's breathing and he was with us within five seconds and just said, "He's dead". We got the saddle off and everybody just stood around looking. There's nothing worse than people standing around looking at a dead horse so we put a sheet on him and I took the saddle and went.'

Fulke Walwyn and Michael Oswald had come down the steps from the stand ahead of Queen Elizabeth when another trainer rushed over and told them, 'Quick, your horse is down!' They hurried to where Game Spirit, now lying on his side with the vet attending to him, had fallen. Sir Michael had the sad task of returning and stopping Queen Elizabeth before she reached the

Game Spirit [Bill Smith] going to post for his fateful last race, the Geoffrey Gilbey Chase at Newbury, 5 March 1977.

unsaddling enclosure and discovered Game Spirit was not there. She was coming down the stairs when he met her and told her they had lost Game Spirit. He recalls, 'Her first thoughts were to console Fulke, Bill and Peter, the lad who looked after the horse.'

Cath Walwyn remembers how terrible everyone felt talking about it to Queen Elizabeth, but adds wisely, 'She is trained not to show her emotions in public. She hides her disappointments.' Bill Smith remembers being invited up to the Royal Box later that afternoon with the lad, Peter Payne: 'She was marvellous. She felt so badly for Peter, quite openly. And we couldn't help feeling badly for her. I think she told us then that she was going to give him to her daughter as a hack. You hate any horse getting killed or dying but I was particularly cut up about him. The biggest shame of all was that he had other things in life to do. He could have had a marvellous life in retirement as a hunter or as a hack for the Queen. It was horrible for Fulke, who adored Game Spirit, and for Peter. He had to go back to the stables in an empty horsebox with a bridle and a rug and a head collar with "Game Spirit" written on it.' After racing Bill Smith had a spat with a moronic punter who told him that he was glad Game Spirit had died because he had lost money backing him. Bill was able to put him right.

An autopsy on Game Spirit was carried out by vets at Bristol University. They discovered he had died from a massive pulmonary haemorrhage. They also found he had suffered a previous haemorrhage, perhaps after the Hermitage Chase. Or perhaps when he had 'died' in the hands of Terry Biddlecombe in the Cheltenham Gold Cup. The vets had no idea how Game Spirit had even managed to finish the race. Never was a horse better named.

✎ The Great Races
Special Cargo: Whitbread Gold Cup Handicap Chase, Sandown, 28 April 1984

Not only did Special Cargo have the legs of a gnarled old sofa, he also had an allergy which resulted in great clumps of hair falling out. About two days before the Whitbread he looked particularly unsightly. Cath Walwyn recalls, 'He had dreadful patches all over him which made him look absolutely hideous. Fulke said, "We really can't have him walking round the paddock at Sandown looking like this. We must do something." I suggested we could try using boot polish. Fulke was a bit apprehensive and asked the vet if it could do any harm and if it would show and was told, "Of course not, you can put it on". So that's what we did.' On the day of the race an excited crowd gazed admiringly at Queen Elizabeth's black horse, a gleaming blend of highly toned muscle and Cherry Blossom.

Queen Elizabeth loves Whitbread Gold Cup day. Traditionally it has been the last big race of the National Hunt season, often run in spring sunshine around three miles five furlongs of the course, which probably offers the finest viewing facilities of any in the country. Colonel Bill Whitbread and his wife, Betty, were among her closest racing friends and Fulke Walwyn was aware that it would be particularly appreciated if she could have a runner. Special Cargo was a personal favourite of his, having been off the course with leg problems for two years before returning to win the Horse and Hound Grand Military Gold Cup the previous month. The going at Sandown would be firm which did not favour Special Cargo's brittle legs at all. He was a much better horse on soft going but, after dithering for a few days, Walwyn decided to let the horse take his chance.

Fulke had long been a master of producing a horse to win the Whitbread, having already won it six times including twice with stable star Diamond Edge

Queen Elizabeth toasts Bill Smith's 500th success as a jockey after he had ridden Special Cargo to win the Alanbrooke Memorial Handicap Chase at Sandown, 27 March 1984. Mrs Cath Walwyn (centre) enjoys the moment.

who had suffered almost as much as Special Cargo from bad legs. Although now 13, Diamond Edge was by far the more fancied at Saxon House because he could beat his stable companion 20 lengths on the gallops and could go on good or even fast ground. Bill Smith had already decided that this race was going to be his last ride. He could choose his mount and took the professional decision that Diamond Edge had the better chance in the conditions. A routine choice was made appreciably more difficult because Special Cargo was also a favourite of his, having carried him to his 500th success as a jockey at Sandown the previous month. Afterwards Queen Elizabeth and Fulke Walwyn had joined him to celebrate with a glass of champagne. Now, just a month later, he was deserting the royal runner. Kevin Mooney, stable number two, was handed the ride.

Kevin Mooney was a much underrated jockey and a very loyal stable stalwart. He was born and bred in Lambourn at a time when there were only two jobs to go to: Fulke Walwyn's yard or Fred Winter's next door. He took his chances when they were presented and Special Cargo was a great opportunity. Although he started at the ungenerous odds of 8/1, the racing pundits saw the race as a duel between Fred Winter's Plundering and Michael Dickinson's Ashley House.

Royal Racing

Dickinson also had a more than useful second string in Lettoch. In the paddock beforehand there was no pressure on Mooney from the connections. Fulke Walwyn told him to pull the horse up if he was 'feeling his legs'. Queen Elizabeth, not particularly hopeful, simply told him to 'do his best'.

The race unfolded with no more than an adequate pace on the first circuit. It was stepped up down the far side second time around when Smith let Diamond Edge stride on to the first of the fences down the back straight. Special Cargo dropped back as the leaders quickened and Kevin Mooney at that stage thought his race was over and considered pulling up. He recalls, 'They went 10 lengths clear and I was just pushing and kicking along. Fulke Walwyn had told me to go the shortest way round and, although I wasn't in contention, I pulled to the inside. He flew the "pond fence" and as we went round the corner into the straight, he's changed his legs and he's away, starting to go. He ran into the bottom of the second last but didn't lose any ground. I'm seventh but staying on and I thought, "I might be third here!" There was Diamond Edge, Plundering and Lettoch ahead but he flew the last. I gave him two cracks and he just took off. I knew I'd won.'

Special Cargo [Kevin Mooney] at halfway in the Whitbread Gold Cup, 28 April 1984. Stable companion Diamond Edge [Bill Smith] is in the lead.

Not everyone was so sure. Special Cargo, Lettoch and Diamond Edge had crossed the line in a blur with Mooney, whip in his left hand, doing a more than passable imitation of Lester Piggott riding a Derby finish. The roof of the stand almost came off with one almighty shout of excitement from the crowd urging the gladiators home. It was a triple photograph. Lettoch, badly hampered by a faller at the third fence, had performed wonders to finish so close. Bill Smith knew he had been beaten on Diamond Edge but had the consolation of believing he had done all he could and that the old horse, in front just 50 yards from the line, had run a terrific race. Mooney excitedly told him, 'I think I've won Bill.' The two jockeys shook hands.

Queen Elizabeth in the Royal Box would not move until the result was announced. Cath Walwyn, who was with her, recalls, 'She didn't want to come down until she knew. She could not have borne that. It was an agonizing two or three minutes.' The loudspeaker announced Special Cargo the winner from Lettoch with Diamond Edge third. The distances were a short head and the same. Lord Oaksey describes the race as 'the most exciting of all time'. Television commentator Graham Goode regards it as the best finish he has ever called. He told Channel 4 viewers, 'You would have to travel a million miles to see a better race.' Sir Michael Oswald simply says it is the greatest race Queen Elizabeth has won. Racegoers, sensing the sheer joy of the occasion, stampeded towards the winners' enclosure to applaud the contestants. Special Cargo's lad, Kevin Stone, was crying as he led his hero back. Kevin Mooney could not believe it: 'It was so emotional. They didn't want me to weigh in until I had spoken to the Queen Mother. She was speechless really because she couldn't believe her horse had done it. She was also concerned about Diamond Edge because both of the horses were very lame. They had given their all on the firm ground.'

Queen Elizabeth invited Kevin and Bill up to the Royal Box for a celebratory drink. Mooney recalls, 'She actually did say, "It's a pity there had to be a loser." Fulke was in tears. He couldn't believe it. He cried for days. Every time you saw him he would burst into tears. It was so great for him.' Smith remembers watching a rerun of the race and Queen Elizabeth pointing out where he was at various points and praising Diamond Edge's jumping: 'There was nothing like "I've just won a big steeplechase". She told me what a good ride I had given my horse and what a marvellous way to go out. It was such a lovely, unselfish attitude, making you feel you're the important one.'

Back at the Malt Shovel Inn that night there was a hooley for everyone at the stables. The celebrations might have gone on for weeks except that, four days after the race, the Jockey Club contacted Fulke Walwyn to say they were not satisfied with the results of Special Cargo's routine drug test. Cath Walwyn recalls, 'Fulke did his nut. He asked the vet if the boot polish could be responsible and was told it could have been. I thought Fulke was going to strangle the vet. He phoned up about 10 times a day to find out if everything was clear and eventually it came through all right. We never told a soul. Can you imagine if that horse had been disqualified?'

∾ Royal Champion

A few paces from Queen Elizabeth's side for most of her racing life stood the unmistakable figure of Sir Martin Gilliat, her private secretary. Well-dressed, slim and mostly bald, he was universally liked within racing and brought an air of enthusiasm into the game which lifted everyone who came into contact with him. The former army colonel could often be seen moving purposefully among the bookmakers' pitches searching for the best value before producing a £5 note and moving swiftly in to claim the price. When he suffered a loss he would return solemnly to the Royal Box and announce again that he would have to sell the car.

In his late 20s he had been captured by the Germans at Calais, a member of a battalion trying to slow up the enemy before Dunkirk. It was 1940 and he was to spend the rest of the war in captivity, much of it in Colditz, the famous prison, where he had been sent for causing his captors, as Sir Michael Oswald puts it, 'a lot of angst'. He received an MBE for keeping up morale. Sir Michael, who knew him for 23 years as part of Queen Elizabeth's 'team', observes, 'I can quite imagine him doing that. The sort of thing he would do would be to declare, "Oh my, what a smell!" and then turn round and say, "I'm so sorry Herr Major, I didn't hear you come in". It was lower-fourth-form humour. He was a very entertaining person who spread good will everywhere, which is why he did a brilliant job as private secretary.'

After he became Queen Elizabeth's private secretary in 1955, Sir Martin took on responsibility for organizing the social side of her racing, which has always been an important ingredient. He was a great extrovert and, says Sir Michael Oswald, 'could get away with saying very funny and outrageous things'.

Edward Cazalet remembers that he was a frequent guest at the Fairlawne house parties where he was always full of fun: 'He was such a character. He would address all the local women as "My good lady" and utterly charm them. He may have given the impression of being a bit buffoonish but he was very able and not to be underestimated.' One can imagine Sir Martin fitting snugly in as a house guest at Blandings Castle, the P.G. Wodehouse creation which Queen Elizabeth so much enjoys. Cath Walwyn fondly recollects, 'I think he was the funniest man I ever met.'

Sir Martin, who remained a bachelor, died in 1993, aged 80. The less well informed thought he was Queen Elizabeth's racing manager, an impression he was in no hurry to correct unless he was asked a question about the horses, in which case he would hastily ring Michael Oswald to find out the answer. He was, however, greatly instrumental in persuading her to allow Central Television to make the *Royal*

Queen Elizabeth accompanied by her popular private secretary Sir Martin Gilliat, walks into the winners' enclosure at Windsor after Game Spirit has won the Royal Windsor Handicap Chase, 20 January 1973.

Champion documentary. It took Gary Newbon, the producer, now Controller of Sport for Carlton Television which took over Central, five years to get the programme off the ground. A royalty to the Injured Jockeys Fund went a considerable way towards persuading Queen Elizabeth and her advisers to finally go ahead. Terry Biddlecombe also helped to move the project forward in the capacity of programme consultant.

One major stumbling block for Newbon was the question of an interview with Queen Elizabeth. She does not grant interviews but in this case he ingeniously persuaded Sir Martin that she might be filmed having a 'conversation' with an off-camera Terry Biddlecombe. Only one topic was

Royal Racing

banned: Devon Loch. When the film was eventually shown we did not hear any questions. The impression was that Queen Elizabeth was just chatting naturally and quite sweetly about the sport and some of the horses. Wearing her favourite blue, she was seen seated beneath an old oil painting, with flowers on the mantelpiece behind her, looking for all the world as if she was talking in the comfort of her own apartments at Clarence House. The programme showed soldiers marching by, a clever illusion. She was actually at Windsor racecourse where a room had been specially prepared.

Sir Michael Oswald remembers going to inspect the room in advance: 'It was decked out in rather ghastly prints and rugs. I asked "What's all this?" and was told, "It's Clarence House".' His doubts were firmly rising when a young woman approached him. 'Who are you?' he inquired. She replied, 'I'm the make-up girl' whereupon a now alarmed Sir Michael spluttered, 'Oh, no, no, no. The Queen Mother does not have a make-up girl.' As he was recovering his composure he was approached by a man who asked him, 'Would the Queen Mother like her microphone down her front or up her skirt?' The normally affable Oswald told him firmly that Queen Elizabeth did not have anything down or up. He added, 'I suggest you get your hands on a boom.'

Sir Michael need not have worried unduly. He remembers Queen Elizabeth sailing through her 'conversation': 'After a question or two poor Terry dried, but Queen Elizabeth, a consummate professional, serenely carried on a monologue for the camera. It was a triumph.' The programme proved very successful with an audience figure of nearly eight million. It introduced many of the characters who were so important to Queen Elizabeth's enjoyment of racing: Sir Martin and Sir Michael of course, Major Eldred Wilson, Fulke and Cath Walwyn, Rags, travelling head lad Tommy Turley, Kevin Mooney and Captain Charles Radclyffe who has been a very influential member of the team breaking in young horses. The captain was shown putting a young horse through its paces on a long loose rein. Unfortunately the one he had intended to use went lame so he drafted in an already broken horse for the cameras, much to the poor nag's bewilderment. Kevin Mooney, who by now was stable jockey at Saxon House, talked of the pride all jockeys feel putting on the royal colours. He also mentioned the old woman in Lambourn who was a portent of bad luck if seen on the way to the races. Kevin would drive miles in the wrong direction in a desperate attempt not to catch a glimpse of her.

Part Four ～ **A Special Place**

Insular [Eamon Murphy] is in front at the last flight on his way to a battling success in the William Hill Imperial Cup at Sandown, 8 March 1986.

Most of all, the film showed the horses of whom Queen Elizabeth confessed to sometimes getting too fond. The programme featured one of her best ever day's racing, Imperial Cup day at Sandown in March 1986 when Special Cargo, Insular and The Argonaut provided an unforgettable royal treble. Special Cargo was the first leg, once again finishing powerfully up the long Sandown run-in to take his third Horse and Hound Grand Military Gold Cup. By this time the old warhorse's skin complaint was being remedied by a pint of goat's milk every day, instead of the less medically sound boot polish. Insular, a useful flat horse for the Queen and still trained by Ian Balding, showed great guts to take the big race, the William Hill Imperial Cup. He looked like getting swamped when challenged by four horses on the run-in but stuck his neck out for an important win. The Argonaut, a promising New-Zealand-bred horse, won the Dick McCreery Handicap Chase named in honour of the excellent amateur rider, one of Queen Elizabeth's close racing friends. In the film she says that racing is 80 per cent disappointment but that it's well worth it when you get a winner. Here was the proof.

✎ Sunsets

Special Cargo's last stand would be the 1987 Horse and Hound Grand Military Gold Cup. He had won the race three times but no horse had ever managed a fourth victory. The 'old boy' as Queen Elizabeth affectionately called him had been enjoying a holiday at Raynham near Sandringham where Sylvia Palmer looks after a mixture of unbroken animals and invalids. Matilda the goat provided Special Cargo with his daily pinta to ease his skin allergy. Queen Elizabeth always goes to see the 'walking wounded' when she is in residence nearby, enjoying a stroll around the quiet paddocks.

It was decided that Special Cargo would go back to Saxon House to be prepared for the race, but that if he did not sparkle he would be retired. Fulke Walwyn was fairly confident that the old horse was still as good as he was when he had won the previous year, so it was decided to have another go with Gerald Oxley riding again. Old rival Burnt Oak set a good pace and the race went as per usual for Special Cargo around Sandown. He dropped back, not quite able to go the gallop, and ran on strongly from the Pond Fence.

Royal stalwart, The Argonaut [Gerald Oxley], jumping for fun in the Horse and Hound Grand Military Gold Cup Chase, 9 March 1990. It was to be his 12th triumph for Queen Elizabeth.

This time, however, he was never able to get close enough to Burnt Oak to challenge. Afterwards Sir Michael Oswald remarked, 'He jumped well and finished like a train, almost got third.' Gerald Oxley always thought Special Cargo was a bit of a prima donna who liked to show off up the Sandown finishing straight for the benefit of the crowd. It was a gallant effort. Queen Elizabeth presented the trophy to her friend Brigadier Roscoe Harvey. 'I'm so glad,' she said, perhaps with a tinge of disappointment. The valiant Special Cargo was retired having provided Queen Elizabeth with her most memorable racing triumphs. He went back to the leafy paddocks of Raynham where, according to Sir Michael, 'He could boss the younger horses'.

Special Cargo's retirement left a void in Queen Elizabeth's racing operation. Unable or unwilling to pay ridiculous prices for 'made' horses, she was concentrating more and more on homebreds. Nurturing them from foal to steeplechaser requires great patience and although she enjoyed the whole process of watching a horse develop it meant her colours were seen far less around the racecourses. She still had The Argonaut and a frustrating young chaser called Sun Rising to fly the royal flag. There had been hopes that Master Andrew, an 80th birthday present from the Jockey Club, would be a success. Sir Michael observes, 'He was actually quite a good horse but he had the extraordinary habit of getting stewed up in the paddock and then behaving very badly at the gate and consequently giving the others 200 yards start. He would then either win the race or just fail to get up. We always thought of what the wretched horse could do if he could get away on terms.' Clutching at straws, a plan was hatched to seek help from an outside agency so a lock from Master Andrew's mane was sent to a spiritual lady who put a spell on it, like a talisman. Sir Michael recalls, 'The effect was miraculous. Master Andrew behaved like an old sheep in the paddock, like an old sheep at the start. Unfortunately he ran like an old sheep.'

Queen Elizabeth had sold her useful hurdler Sunyboy for a career at stud but had often said she would have liked one of his offspring to race. Cath Walwyn was staying in Yorkshire when she heard that there was a Sunyboy colt nearby. He was a three-year-old, just broken: 'He was a huge great horse, about 17 hands as a three-year-old, and I just loved him. I phoned Michael Oswald who said he would come with me to look at him and we bought him quite cheaply on the spot.' Queen Elizabeth adored her new giant whom she called Sun Rising but, although clearly talented, his massive frame put great strain on his legs throughout his career. Kevin Mooney suggested early on that the horse would do better in blinkers because he was such a tough ride. He finished third on him in a chase at Newbury but felt Sun Rising could have done better: 'I said either put blinkers on him or he'll be such a hard ride that you'll have to keep beating him up to win races. I was having a struggle to keep this horse concentrating. Blinkers were the making of him.'

Mooney was in the saddle for the Bagshot Handicap Chase at Ascot in October 1988, a race which still rankles with everyone involved. In a pulsating finish Sun Rising and Bajan Sunshine, ridden by Peter Scudamore, battled neck and neck for the line. It seemed impossible to split the two horses after three gruelling miles. Kevin Mooney confesses, 'I thought they would give a

Grim faces all round: Queen Elizabeth and Fulke Walwyn are far from amused after the photo finish goes against Sun Rising in the Bagshot Handicap Chase at Ascot, 29 October 1988.

Kevin Mooney galvanizes Sun Rising en route to success in The Rip Handicap Chase at Ascot, 21 November 1987.

dead heat.' Everyone thought the same as the minutes passed. A couple of races were run while the judge agonized about what must surely have been no more than the width of a cigarette paper. Eventually Bajan Sunshine, trained by Charlie Brooks at Fred Winter's old yard, was called the winner, much to everyone's astonishment. On inspecting the photo the Walwyn camp were in no doubt that Sun Rising's white nose had gone against him. Cath Walwyn is still furious about it: 'When they showed the photograph it was the most absurd thing you've ever seen. I think it was because he had a white bit on his nose that you couldn't quite see. If ever there was a dead heat this was it. Who would have objected if they had called a dead heat? I've always said that after three miles there ought to be two white finishing lines and that, if they're both between them, it ought to be a dead heat. It was just so stupid to deliberate for an hour and a half. He was such a sweet horse and Queen Elizabeth was very disappointed about it.'

Darkie Deacon, who used to ride out Sun Rising most mornings, believes the horse had actually won the race if you looked closely at his white nose. He remembers, 'The Queen Mum came round a few days afterwards and she said it was very close. That's all she would say. If she'd have thought the judge was bloody blind, she wouldn't say so.'

At least Sun Rising had given Queen Elizabeth reason to cheer when he won The Rip Handicap Chase at Ascot, named in honour of her popular chaser of the Sixties. Eventually Sun Rising's bad legs won the argument and he was retired. He was due to go to Raynham but Cath Walwyn asked Queen Elizabeth if she

Royal Racing

might have him because the stable lass who looked after him, Lin Eliot, loved the horse. The Queen Mother agreed and Sun Rising has spent a long and happy retirement in a paddock behind Cath's house. He is 23 now. 'No horse in training could be better looked after,' says Cath. 'Lin buys all the sheets and warm rugs. She built a stable for him in the paddock and there's carrots put out for him, and the best straw and hay. The Queen Mother thinks it's absolutely wonderful. He's too old to be ridden now but he's as happy as Larry. The moment it rains Lin's out there with a sheet to make sure he's all right'.

The Argonaut, a nearly black, powerful horse very much in the Special Cargo mould, is also in robust health as a 23-year-old. He still manages the occasional half-day hunting, ridden as he has been for many years by Lambourn vet Bobby McEwan. He also paraded at the 2000 Cheltenham Festival, looking magnificent and sprightly, before the Queen Mother Champion Chase. Gerald Oxley rode him when he gave Queen Elizabeth a fourth victory in the Horse and Hound Grand Military Gold Cup in 1990, the last year Fulke Walwyn held the training licence at Saxon House. When Fulke's health faded Cath took over the licence.

She had never intended to train but did not want the stable to close while her husband was still alive. He died in February 1991, on a morning when Queen Elizabeth came to the stable to look at the horses. His wonderful record of training long-distance chasers to big-race successes stands unequalled even by the phenomenal standards set today by Martin Pipe and company. Lord Oaksey simply says, 'He was the best there's ever been.'

Smiles all round when the Queen presents her mother with the trophy after The Argonaut's win in the Horse and Hound Grand Military Gold Cup at Sandown, 9 March 1990.

Celebrations and Controversy

A few days after winning the 1000 Guineas on Highclere Joe
Mercer received a handwritten letter from the Queen: 'I was sad
that I had to dash back to London at once and so I did not have
the opportunity to thank you personally on the success of that
short head. For once I don't remember much about the race
owing to the excitement but I do know that a homebred Guineas
winner has given me more pleasure than anything for a long time.'

New Ventures

Noel Murless was memorably described by the late racing author Roger Mortimer as a 'lean, lined, worried looking man who walks as if his feet were giving him hell. It is difficult to visualise any sort of party of which he could possibly be the life and soul.' His son-in-law Henry Cecil simply says that he was a workaholic, while former champion jockey Joe Mercer always thought he was an 'ill man'. It did not stop him being champion trainer nine times and training 19 classic winners, one memorably for the Queen. Although Carrozza won the Oaks, it was the very last horse Murless trained for the Queen, Hopeful Venture, who turned out to be the best. A change of policy had resulted in the National Stud giving up homebreeding and its mares and foals were sold at auction in 1964. It was appropriate that the final colt the Queen leased under the old arrangement with the stud should be by her old favourite, Aureole.

Hopeful Venture was Noel Murless's daughter Julie Cecil recalls, 'very ugly as a yearling'. He was a big, backward youngster but grew into a well-proportioned bay colt, 16.1 hands with black pointing, and was brought along in typically patient fashion by Murless who chose not to race him as a two-year-old. Instead he started him off in the Wood Ditton Stakes at Newmarket, the race at the Craven meeting in April where leading trainers have often produced one or two 'dark' three-year-olds which have been kept under wraps until they had matured a little. Hopeful Venture next showed his adaptability by whizzing round the tight turns of Chester in the Grosvenor Stakes over one mile and two furlongs. Here was a horse who was steadily improving. He was not entered in the 1967 Derby, which was just as well as Murless had the favourite, Royal Palace, one of the outstanding colts of the Sixties, who won comfortably at Epsom and would probably have taken the Triple Crown if injury had not intervened.

The accomplished Australian jockey George Moore rode Hopeful Venture in all his races as a three-year-old. Moore, regrettably, spent only one season at Warren Place before returning home but he rode three classic winners, had a strike rate of more than 30 per cent and was regarded as one of the best judges of pace since the Second World War. Hopeful Venture should have retained his unbeaten record in Royal Ascot's 'Derby', the King Edward VII Stakes. Going nicely entering the straight, the colt stumbled and lost a few vital lengths which certainly meant the difference between victory and defeat.

Opposite: Noel Murless taking breakfast at Warren Place, March 1972. Clockwise around the table are seated Julian Wilson, Julie Cecil and William Hastings-Bass, who would later train for the Queen.

Part Five ∾ Celebrations and Controversy

He went down by a fighting short head to Mariner ridden by Greville Starkey. Victories in the Princess of Wales Stakes at Newmarket and the Oxfordshire Stakes at Newbury showed Hopeful Venture to be in the top flight of the year's crop of three-year-old colts. With Royal Palace injured, Hopeful Venture represented Murless in the St Leger at Doncaster. He was joint favourite at 7/2 with the Lester-Piggott-ridden Ribocco, second in the Derby and winner of the Irish equivalent. On a good day Ribocco had a more than useful burst of speed and, nursed by Piggott in a strongly run race, he came with a well-timed run to beat the Queen's horse by one and a half lengths.

During 1967 the Queen enjoyed a three-day private visit in May to some of the best-known studs in Normandy. It was hardly a surprise that she then decided to have her first ever runner across the Channel. Hopeful Venture, still in good form, was dispatched to contest the Prix Henry Delamarre at Longchamp in October. He won nicely, quickening in the straight to win by three-quarters of a length from In Command ridden by Brian Taylor. Unfortunately, Moore had not prevented his mount crossing over in front of In Command. The manoeuvre had made no difference to the result and today Hopeful Venture would have stood a good chance of keeping the race. But back in 1967 there was no chance, especially in front of the harsh French stewards who always stuck rigidly to the rules governing interference. The dreaded klaxon sounded doom and Hopeful Venture was unceremoniously disqualified, a rare royal occurrence. 'It was dreadful,' says Julie Cecil. Another excursion to Longchamp was equally fruitless when the colt ran poorly in the Prix du Conseil Municipal but, mindful of the improvement his sire Aureole had shown at four, the Queen decided to keep Hopeful Venture in training for another season.

When George Moore returned to Australia, Murless appointed the Scottish-born lightweight Sandy Barclay as stable jockey. It was a bold move. Barclay, just 19, had been champion apprentice but was hardly of the stature of Piggott and Moore. But then Lester Piggott had been relatively unproven when he joined Murless. Barclay struck up very good relationships with both Royal Palace and Hopeful Venture, who between them mopped up the premier all-age races.

The Queen's colt began his campaign back at Chester in the Ormonde Stakes where he slammed the great mare Park Top by five lengths. He went back to Royal Ascot for the Hardwicke Stakes and made up for his previous defeat

there by coasting in as an odds-on favourite should. The decision to keep the horse in training was looking like a good one when it was decided to try again in France, with the Grand Prix de Saint-Cloud, worth £54,000 to the winner, as the target. The opposition included the brilliant Vaguely Noble who would end the year as Europe's champion colt. Sandy Barclay was able to kick Hopeful Venture on rounding the final bend and

Hopeful Venture [Sandy Barclay] cruises to victory in the Hardwicke Stakes at Royal Ascot, 21 June 1968.

he held Minamoto by a neck with Vaguely Noble a disappointing two lengths behind in third. It was the only defeat Vaguely Noble suffered in a year that climaxed with a runaway win in the Prix de l'Arc de Triomphe.

This was Hopeful Venture's finest hour. He came back for the traditional Arc trial, the Prix Henri Foy at Longchamp in September, but was disappointing, returning with a badly swollen hock. He never raced again. Comparing horses in different races is always subjective. Sandy Barclay did not think there was much between him and Royal Palace as four-year-olds. And the latter won the Eclipse and the King George VI and Queen Elizabeth Stakes. If Almeria is the forgotten filly of royal racing, then Hopeful Venture is the forgotten colt. Take Royal Palace out of the mix and he is champion of his generation. Bearing in mind the colt's aptitude for Chester, always a good guide to horses that will act around the undulating Epsom track, there is a very good argument indeed for believing that Hopeful Venture could have squeezed home first in the 1967 Derby if Royal Palace had not been selected for the race by the stable. Perhaps that is wishful thinking. Julie Cecil, while admitting that Hopeful Venture was one of the Queen's very best horses, believes he was still too backward to have raced in that particular Derby.

By a quirk of fate both Noel Murless and Captain Cecil Boyd-Rochfort trained their last winners for the Queen in 1968. The Captain's final victory was with Castle Yard in the Zetland Gold Cup at Redcar. The horse had the distinction of being looked after individually by Henry Cecil. At the beginning of his final year the Captain was knighted in the New Year's Honours. Noel Murless was knighted after his retirement at the end of 1976, in the Jubilee Honours of 1977, at the time a suitable addendum to one of the Queen's greatest ever racing years. He retired to look after his stud interests, although not in the best of health. He died 10 years later in 1987. Unusually, he himself had bred most of the good horses he trained at Warren Place. They included the Derby winners Crepello and St Paddy. Julie Cecil remembers affectionately, 'He was very shy and had more interest in animals than people. He had limitless patience as a trainer. I used to think he was very good.'

The Queen and her trainer Ian Balding watch the horses at morning exercise at Kingsclere.

During the two great trainers' final royal season, the emphasis of the Queen's racing interests had switched to the Newbury area – to the stables of Dick Hern at West Ilsley and of Ian Balding at Kingsclere, racing villages a few miles either side of the Berkshire town. They were near enough to Windsor for the Queen to have more chance of monitoring the 20 or so horses she split between the two stables. They were also close to Lord Porchester's family home at Highclere where the Queen was a regular guest. Balding had in fact trained his first royal winner, a two-year-old filly called Menai, in 1964. Royal patronage of Kingsclere had resumed in late 1963, for the first time since the days of John Porter, when Captain Peter Hastings-Bass was sent half the Sandringham yearlings as part of a new broom aimed at lifting the Queen's racing fortunes out of a slump. Sadly, he died from cancer in June 1964 at the age of 43 and Balding, then his assistant, took over at Kingsclere and began a royal association that would last 35 years.

❧ Examples of Disaster

A popular perception that Ian Balding has always been the Queen's second-string trainer is not strictly true. For more than 10 years there seemed no discernible bias towards Major Dick Hern until, in the late 1970s, the Kingsclere stables spent two years heavily affected by a virus. The Queen wrote to Balding explaining that he could no longer expect to be sent the yearlings bred from the good fillies he had trained for her in the past. It was a bitter blow for the trainer, who then had to endure years of mainly second-rate stock. It had not always been the case. With a couple of notable exceptions, Balding matched Hern's early successes as a royal trainer. But from the outset her horses at Kingsclere were plagued by misfortune. Balding recalls that his first good horse for her, Magna Carta, was also 'my first disaster'.

Magna Carta was a handsome bay colt with two white feet who Balding quickly realized was a slow-maturing type, the sort of stayer with which his predecessor Captain Boyd-Rochfort would have excelled. He was by the French Derby winner Charlottesville but, more pleasingly, out of the Queen's admirable filly of the Fifties, Almeria. He was bone idle at home and only made progress in the middle of his three-year-old campaign when he won a two-mile plod around Nottingham. The Queen, on Balding's advice, decided to keep him in training as a four-year-old with the objective of winning a race at Royal Ascot, her favourite meeting, in 1970. He warmed up for the Ascot Stakes with a luckless fourth around the tight turns of Chester before enjoying a confidence-booster at Wolverhampton. The popular and shrewd Welsh jockey Geoff Lewis, then retained by Kingsclere, took the ride in the Ascot Stakes, a marathon slog of two miles and four furlongs. Lewis had the secret of Magna Carta, just as David Mould knew how to handle Queen Elizabeth's hurdler Makaldar. The horse was as game as you could wish but lazy. It appeared from the stands that with at least a mile to go Lewis was pushing and shoving the lumbering Magna Carta along more in desperation than hope. In the straight it looked certain that Sir Humphrey de Trafford's colt Pride of Alcide, trained by Henry Cecil, would last home but Lewis, still stoking up Magna Carta, came down the wide outside in relentless fashion to claim the spoils in the last hundred yards. It was an inspired piece of riding.

The Ascot race was the making of Magna Carta. He won two competitive handicaps, the Greenall Whitley Gold Challenge Trophy at Chester and the W.D. and H.O. Wills Trophy at Newcastle, after just missing out to Parthenon, another Henry Cecil colt, in a fierce battle for the Goodwood Cup. Late in the season he took the Doncaster Cup, reversing the form with Parthenon, thanks to an astute ride from Lewis who was able to pounce late in rain-softened ground, proving again that Magna Carta had some priceless finishing speed at the end of a staying race. Henry Cecil, who has won five Gold Cups at Ascot, believes speed to be the most important ingredient for a stayer. He explains, 'A horse will either stay or it won't. You can't make it. I believe that

**Ian Balding on the
Kingsclere gallops at dawn.**

you should run them over a mile and a half to build up their speed.' Magna
Carta had that precious acceleration, which augured well for the following season
in which as a mature five-year-old he would be aimed at the Gold Cup, a race
the Queen had not won.

Training is not a job for those of a nervous disposition. You would never
get to sleep wondering what unexpected fate might befall a horse during the
night. No one could have foreseen the sight that greeted Kingsclere's head
lad, Bill Palmer, when he opened up the stables one morning early in 1971.
Magna Carta was on the floor of his box with one foot trapped in his hay
net. Palmer cut the net and was relieved when Magna Carta got to his feet.
But the horse did not touch his feed that morning. The vet was called and
told Balding that the colt had a broken jaw and would need an immediate
operation, because a horse cannot survive if unable to chew. Magna Carta

Royal Racing

was dispatched to the Equine Research Centre at Newmarket where he was found to have broken his jaw in two places trying to free himself from his hay net. Balding remembers that they were bad fractures. The Queen was kept informed of Magna Carta's progress. He was operated on by Professor James Roberts, later to save the life of the great Mill Reef, who thought the procedure went well. Magna Carta, however, had been under anaesthetic for some seven hours and was unable to recover. He died two days later. Balding recalls, 'It was very upsetting for the Queen. Magna Carta could have won the Ascot Gold Cup. None of my horses ever have hay nets now.'

Ian Balding had bought a handsome yearling called Musical Drive for the Queen in 1968: 'He was a hell of a nice horse.' On the gallops one morning some of the string got loose and Musical Drive, then a two-year-old, was fourth or fifth of those that were charging about. He had given a buck and a kick and fired his lad off his back. He galloped fully one mile and at the end smashed into some white, metal gates. It is still a vivid picture in Ian Balding's memory: 'This poor horse literally dragged itself back to me and died at my feet.' Balding then had the distressing task of ringing the Queen and telling her what had happened.

Smart stayer Magna Carta [Geoff Lewis] powers past Pride of Alcide [Frankie Durr] to take the Ascot Stakes at Royal Ascot, 16 June 1970.

He remembers how sympathetic she was and that she asked particularly about the unfortunate stable lad, Peter Williams.

The flat-racing season of 1971 was the highlight of Ian Balding's career as a trainer. He was champion trainer and Mill Reef, running in the famous black and gold colours of American millionaire Paul Mellon, was one of the best and most popular of Derby winners. The Queen could be seen in the Royal Box cheering the colt home,

much to Balding's appreciation: 'She'd seen him here as a two-year-old. He'd won at Royal Ascot the same day as Magna Carta and I think she got more than normal pleasure out of seeing him win the Derby.' After Mill Reef's career was cut short by a broken foreleg he stood as a stallion at the National Stud and Paul Mellon gave the Queen a free nomination to the great horse. Two of her best colts, Milford and Special Leave, were by Mill Reef who would prove to be an excellent sire.

It was not all doom and gloom for the Queen at Kingsclere in 1971. A late-maturing filly called Example gave her good reason to cheer in the second half of the season. The horse was a big flashy chestnut with a white blaze and, says Balding, 'easy to train'. By this time Richard Shelley, who was not in good health, had retired. For the first time his job was shared: Lord Porchester became racing manager while Michael Oswald assumed responsibilty for managing the Royal Studs. It was Porchester, a great admirer of Lester Piggott, who engaged the maestro to ride Example in the Park Hill Stakes at Doncaster in September. The race is traditionally regarded as the fillies' St Leger. Piggott had not sat on the horse before the race but immediately found the key to the filly. He dropped her out a remote last of the eight runners and, riding her for a burst of speed, brought her past the entire field in the last two furlongs. Piggott rode the filly again in her next race, the Prix de Royallieu at Longchamp, when she again came from last to first laughing at some high-class French fillies on the way.

The decision to keep Example in training as a four-year-old was only a partial success. She had a blow-out in the John Porter Stakes at Newbury, finishing third to the good stayer Rock Roi, before Piggott produced her with a now customary final flourish to claim the Prix Jean de Chaudenay at Saint-Cloud in May, another masterly performance by the jockey that secured the spoils by a neck. Soon afterwards Kingsclere was hit by a mid-season virus and Example never won another race. But the highest hopes were held for this strapping filly as a brood mare and the Queen decided to start her off at the very top by sending her across the Atlantic to the great Nijinsky standing at stud in Kentucky. She returned in foal to the Royal Stud at Wolferton near Sandringham. Tragically, Example was injured while giving birth when the foal put a foot through her uterus and she died from a ruptured colon a few hours later, a terrible loss to the stud. The foal, neatly called Pas de Deux, was saved when Michael Oswald found a foster mother.

Pas de Deux bore little resemblance to her mother. Ian Balding remembers she was 'very small' where Example was a lovely, big sort. She did manage to win but was a disappointing racecourse legacy for a brood mare of such potential.

Example had died at five, when she might reasonably have expected to produce foals for another 10 or 15 years. For the Queen, who so enjoys the strategy of breeding, it was a particularly sad loss. Looking back over the racing careers of both the Queen and the Queen Mother, Ian Balding sadly reflects, 'Between them they have had as many disasters as it is possible to have.'

Ian Balding holds the bridle of his great racehorse Mill Reef.

◌ The Mayor of West Ilsley

During the Second World War Dick Hern and Michael Pope were stationed in Africa and North Italy with their regiment, the North Irish Horse. They became firm friends after discovering they shared a great enthusiasm for horses. At the end of hostilities the two majors were billeted with their regiment in and around the Grand Hotel, Rimini, waiting to be recalled to England. They wasted no time in organizing race meetings for the troops at the nearby bomb-ravaged Ravenna track which, with the help of assorted German prisoners of war, they restored to a raceworthy condition. The horses were also the spoils of war and went into training on the local beaches. Hern, a very accomplished rider, was the star jockey at the track where the majors even introduced a tote for betting purposes, donating all proceeds, of course, to the regimental benevolent fund. It was an agreeable way to start the peace.

On his return to England Major Hern was determined to make his living working with horses. He joined the Porlock Riding School in north Somerset as an instructor. An acknowledged expert, he was drafted in to help coach the three-day-event team for the 1952 Olympics. He would undoubtedly have ridden in the team himself if he had not been deemed a professional and thus disqualified from competing in those days of true amateur spirit. He did, however, ride in point-to-points and a growing association with racing was cemented when, in the autumn of 1952, his old comrade Pope asked him to join his fledgling stable at Blewbury in Berkshire as assistant. Hern jumped at the chance. Pope had an endearingly cavalier attitude to the game, and together the two majors had some hilarious adventures which were later described with great relish when Pope wrote a light-hearted column for *The Sporting Life*.

On one memorable occasion Hern was dispatched to Warwick to orchestrate a coup on an old selling chaser called Teddy Tail. It was vital not to alert the professionals and bookmakers at the track that there was anything afoot. Accordingly, Pope himself kept well out of the way to avoid any embarrassing questions from punting friends while Hern was told to put the tack on the horse as early as possible and then make himself scarce. He was not to speak to anyone or even be seen until the announcement was made for the jockeys to mount up. The future royal trainer hid himself in the gent's toilet close to the weighing room and locked the door. It was not a savoury waiting area and the only reading matter available was a railway timetable. Hern stuck it out until the loudspeaker called the jockeys. Then he shot out, hurled jockey Derek Weeden into the plate and gave him the instruction to 'jump off, make all and don't win too far'. Weeden carried out the instructions to the letter and won by three-quarters of a length, hard held. For many years Dick Hern insisted he could recite the entire train timetable from Warwick to Birmingham.

Less felicitous for the two majors was the time when Pope was hauled before the Jockey Club and fined a maximum of £100 for misleading the stewards at Wolverhampton over the declaration of a jockey. Pope told them the jockey in question had been held up in traffic but they sneakily rang the stables only to be told by Hern, not fully aware of the significance of what he was saying, that the jockey was in the yard 'doing' his horses. Coincidentally, a far more important case came before the Jockey Club that same day. It involved the formidable presence of the Queen's trainer, Captain Cecil Boyd-Rochfort, and concerned a race which Pope called 'the most hilarious I've ever witnessed'.

The race in question, the Winston Churchill Stakes at Hurst Park, featured the Captain's St Leger winner Premonition, who had defeated the Queen's Aureole in the classic, and a pacemaker called Osborne. Harry Carr rode Premonition who started at the rich man's price of 1/8 on. Osborne, an unconsidered 25/1 shot, was ridden by a Freemason Lodge work rider called Roy Burrows.

The daily routine at West Ilsley Stables where Dick Hern trained the Queen's horses.

According to the Captain's biographer, Bill Curling, Burrows was given the instruction to finish second if he possibly could. The rider, anxious to please, did exactly that although he could probably have won by five lengths! Fully four furlongs out Carr was pushing and shoving along on Premonition as Osborne sailed serenely on. A furlong out and Burrows was straining to anchor his mount. Pope observed, 'Burrows was now standing up in his irons like a cowboy, trying to pull Osborne back, but the more he tugged the better the horse went.' Carr, riding like a man possessed, brought Premonition up level on the line. The photo finish went in favour of the odds-on shot. Pope thought, 'the judge sportingly declared Premonition as the winner by a short head'.

After the race, Winston Churchill himself was heard discussing the Captain with Christopher Soames. 'I would not want to be in his shoes,' declared Churchill, impishly. Boyd-Rochfort was fined £100 by the Jockey Club for not giving concise orders under Rule 39. It was deeply embarrassing for the royal trainer although, it has to be said, he was somewhat fortunate not to be suspended for a lengthy period. Osborne later showed himself to be a very smart stayer but that is hardly the point. The implication of skulduggery was plain for all to see although the history books conveniently blame it on the stupidity of the jockey carrying out his instructions too much to the letter. Pope could consider himself unlucky that his case was heard the same day, because in no way was it comparable, but his misdemeanour diverted a little attention from the shenanigans involving the royal trainer.

After five years with Pope, in which he rode several winners himself, Hern was offered the chance to become the private trainer in Newmarket to one of the leading owner-breeders of the postwar period, Major Lionel Holliday, and showed himself to be to the manor born where training was concerned. Holliday was a notoriously crotchety and cantankerous Yorkshireman but Hern struck up an immediately successful partnership with his new 77-year-old employer. He showed himself to be an extremely talented trainer who, as future stable jockey Willie Carson explains, 'was a man who knew about horses'.

The Major, as his stable staff would always call Hern, never looked back after winning the Brocklesby with Plaudit, then traditionally the first two-year-old test at the season's opening meeting at Lincoln, and won 40 races for his patron in his first season. After just four years he was champion trainer for the first of four times, winning 39 races worth more than £70,000. The most important winner was Hethersett who landed Hern's first classic success in the 1962 St Leger after unluckily falling in the Derby – which subsequent form showed he probably would have won. At the end of the season Hern accepted an offer from the Astor family to return to Berkshire to succeed Jack Colling at West Ilsley stables near Newbury.

From this base he would send out three Derby winners. He recalls, 'The place was pretty run-down. Jakie Astor did a lot of work on it. He rebuilt the place putting in cottages for the stable staff. You always need to fill a stable with married men. I remember Lord Wigg coming to the stable when he was chairman of the Tote. "Dick," he said, "you're not a trainer, you're a mayor."' West Ilsley was soon one of the best training centres in the country and the Astor/Hern partnership dispatched Provoke to win the 1965 St Leger by 10 lengths in a Doncaster bog. The mud-splattered jockey was Joe Mercer, whom Hern had inherited at West Ilsley. The pair already knew each other well. Mercer had ridden for both Michael Pope and Major Holliday, and his father-in-law, Harry Carr, had ridden Hethersett. Racing is really just a family business.

Although Hern ran the West Ilsley stables in a very no-nonsense militaristic fashion that might be considered old-fashioned today, Joe Mercer observes,

'He was very methodical. He'd stand no nonsense at all. But if you wanted to say something he would call all the troops together, stand on the top step himself and you would have your audience. Everybody who worked for him was very loyal. Dick was very charming with the most terrific sense of humour.' That sense of humour was severely tested in 1966 when the stable was struck down for the first time with a dreaded virus, the first of several years when it would be laid low. The only sunshine in a wretched season was provided when Hern was asked by the Queen's racing manager, Major Shelley, to take some yearlings for the following season. He recalls with typical pragmatism, 'The first ones were useless which was a pity, just a bad patch I suppose.'

Hern's appointment seemed a very sensible one. His stables were convenient for travelling from Windsor. He had already been champion trainer, won two classics and was a military man in the tradition of both Boyd-Rochfort and Peter Cazalet. He was at the time on good terms with Lord Porchester for whom he also trained. The only horse of any note from the first batch of yearlings was St Patrick's Blue, who won a race at Ascot a month after Boyd-Rochfort had saddled his last royal winner. The first to catch the eye was a dour stayer called Charlton, a soft-ground horse with dodgy joints. Like the ill-fated Magna Carta he was by Charlottesville and he took that unfortunate colt's place in the 1971 Ascot Gold Cup but was comprehensively outstayed by Rock Roi and Random Shot. He did, however, win the Henry II Stakes at Sandown and the William Hill Gold Trophy at Doncaster. He finished fourth in the Ebor at York, a race he almost certainly would have won but for breaking down near the finish. Dick Hern, never one to overpraise a horse, assesses Charlton as 'dead honest but short of speed. He did his best and stayed well. But he stayed in the same place a little too long.'

ᘒ Bring on the Girls

After the lull in royal fortunes in the Sixties, during the changing of the old guard, the Seventies was a period of considerable success, brought about by a parade of exceptional homebred fillies. After Example, Ian Balding trained Escorial

St Patrick's Blue [Joe Mercer] was Dick Hern's first winner of note for the Queen when he won the Cranbourn Chase Stakes at Ascot from Archook [Eric Eldin], 26 July 1968.

and Joking Apart. Dick Hern, meanwhile, had care of Albany followed by the classic-winning fillies Highclere and Dunfermline. Albany, recalls the Major, was 'quite a nice filly but not top class'. She was a contemporary of Example and, sentimentally, had the perfect royal pedigree being by the Queen's 2000 Guineas winner Pall Mall out of her talented filly of the Fifties, Almeria.

For some reason Almeria never seemed to pass on her own excellent, strapping physique to her offspring. Albany was a neat chestnut, but on the small side. She also, thought Hern, would be very difficult to train as a three-year-old because she was coming into season every couple of weeks. Lord Porchester came up with the idea of sending the filly over to his stud at Highclere to be covered by Queen's Hussar and then, hopefully in foal, sent back into training. It worked like a treat for Albany. She was a changed filly almost at once, less fractious and showing far more zest in her work. The Queen came to West Ilsley to see her horses work, have lunch with the Major and Sheilah Hern and then adjourn to the local Newbury races to watch the expectant Albany battle home by a length in the Sandleford Priory Stakes.

Joe Mercer remembers the Queen's visits well, not least because the yard would always be swept before she arrived: 'She would come down once or twice a year for a proper look at her horses, but might pop in if she was going to Newbury races. She was always very relaxed and very much at home. She would bring the corgis with her. Prince Philip was with her once and walked with her round the boxes while she discussed the horses with us. He turned to us and said, "It's a completely different jargon. I'm not with this at all." But the Queen was very knowledgeable about horses.'

Although on breeding it looked unlikely that Albany would stay a mile and a half, she took her chance in the Oaks and finished a creditable fifth – on ground too firm for her – to the Noel-Murless-trained filly Altesse Royale. She finished her career with two races in France, winning the Prix de Psyche over 10 furlongs at Deauville in August when four months into her pregnancy. There is no doubt that being in foal greatly improved Albany's form. The foal in question, Allegiance, was a small, undistinguished filly – hardly surprising considering Albany's tender age. Allegiance never won a race, although it could be argued that she actually won two if you count those she won with her mother.

Highclere, by contrast, was a most elegant filly. Dick Hern approvingly observes that she 'stood over plenty of ground – a long-striding filly with bags of scope'. She too was by the Highclere stallion Queen's Hussar, the sire of Brigadier Gerard, one of the greatest horses of the century. Her dam was Highlight, a Royal Stud favourite and a daughter of Hypericum, thus maintaining the strong Hyperion bloodlines in royal racing. Highclere might have been called more appropriately 'Highly Strung' because she was a terrible handful when she arrived at West Ilsley. Joe Mercer recalls, 'She could be an absolute madam one minute and a perfect doll the next. You always had to go to her head when you went to get on her because she would lash out like a right cow.'

The first problem for the Major was finding someone willing to look after the big, bay filly. Fortunately a stable lass called Betty Brister, the only girl in the yard, volunteered and struck up a great rapport with Highclere. Hern recalls, 'If it hadn't been for Betty, Highclere would not have been half the filly. She was very tricky, especially in her box, kicking and biting, but Betty never lost patience with her.' Patience was clearly what was required for Highclere who, Hern realized, would need plenty of time to grow up. He started her off in a race for maidens at the Newmarket July meeting of 1973 when she finished second to future rival Polygamy. Highclere was already demonstrating a lovely high galloping

The Queen's brilliant filly Highclere [Joe Mercer] canters to the start before the 1000 Guineas at Newmarket, 2 May 1974.

action. Another second, this time at Ascot, followed before she won her division of the Donnington Maiden Stakes at Newbury. Although she appeared to labour a little, Joe Mercer was impressed, and the time was more than a second quicker than Ian Balding's royal filly Escorial took to win the other division.

Dick Hern's astuteness was in waiting patiently for a horse to find some form. He explains, 'When you are with the animals every day they tell you when they are improving.' That was the case as the 1000 Guineas of 1974 approached. Highclere was beginning to show some form on the gallops and it was decided to go straight for the classic without a prior run. Hern had pulled it off with Brigadier Gerard when he took the 2000 Guineas three years before. The problem with Highclere was that her high leg-action combined with a high head-carriage was tending to unbalance her and there were fears she might not realize her full potential. Hern decided to try galloping her in a set of black blinkers and they instantly did the trick. He saw immediately that she concentrated better and galloped a lot straighter with them on, while Mercer thought they brought her high action down a little.

She wore the blinkers in the Guineas. Polygamy ridden by Pat Eddery was favourite, with Highclere an insulting 12/1. Joe Mercer had his filly near the pace throughout and sent her into the lead with two furlongs to run. He observes, 'You couldn't do anything quick on her. You just had to let her use her long stride.' Highclere set off for home, running straight as an arrow tight to the rails. As the line approached Eddery had Polygamy flying up the hill and the two brave fillies crossed the line together. The Queen's first classic-winning filly, Carrozza, had prevailed in the closest of finishes in 1957 and here was another nail-biter. Dick Hern watched the race with the Queen in the stewards' box. Slightly pessimistically, he turned to his royal patron and said, 'Well Ma'am, she has run a very good race.' The Queen, Lord Porchester and Michael Oswald all felt Highclere had just been beaten. Hern rushed off to greet his game filly: 'I saw Bob McCreery on my way to the unsaddling enclosure and he had watched the race by the winning post. He said, "I think you've won." He was very knowledgeable and if he said that, he was probably right. It was quite a long time before they announced it but she had won by a short head.'

Highclere's victory was the Queen's third English classic success. Hopes were raised a few weeks later that Escorial might make it four in the Oaks. She had been one of the winter favourites for the classic and had her warm-up race in the Musidora Stakes at York's spring meeting. Unusually, the Queen travelled to York to watch her prospect run. Ian Balding remembers being a little apprehensive because Escorial was quite a flighty filly, so he took the precaution of having three staff with her to make sure she remained calm: 'We were in the royal box and we could see the runners being led across the course from the stables. I said to the Queen that we should be seeing Escorial any

moment. We had taken every precaution. Halfway across she rears up, falls over and gets loose. I was horrified.' From their position high in the stand, Balding and the Queen watched a riderless Escorial cantering back towards the stables. Balding rushed off to help but, fortunately, by the time he reached the stables Escorial had been caught by northern trainer Joe Mulhall. It did not put her off and, dropped out by Lester Piggott as he had done with Example, she came with a storming run up the middle of the straight to win easily.

Escorial started second favourite in the Oaks but did not act round the Epsom bend and finished disappointingly in the ruck behind Polygamy. She failed to win again. Ironically, after the Musidora the Queen was in the unsaddling enclosure to welcome back the filly. Lester Piggott jumped off the horse next to her and a voice from the crowd shouted, 'Arise Sir Lester!' Sadly, that will never be the case.

Despite running loose before the start, Escorial [Lester Piggott] coasts to victory in the Musidora Stakes at York, 15 May 1974.

❧ The Great Races

Highclere: Prix de Diane, Chantilly, 16 June 1974

Highclere's long, raking stride did not look tailor-made for Epsom. The French racetrack Chantilly, with its much flatter aspect and a finishing straight of nearly half a mile, would suit the Queen's classic winner much better. Crucially, the Prix de Diane, the French Oaks, was run over one mile and two and a half furlongs, a distance more appropriate to Highclere's breeding than the one mile four furlongs of the Oaks at Epsom. The Queen herself had told the racing press the plan when she led Highclere back into the unsaddling enclosure at Newmarket. Forewarned of the Queen's presence, her French hosts turned the day into the most memorable of all royal racing occasions.

Dick Hern, his wife Sheilah, Joe Mercer and his wife Anne flew over to France in a light aircraft, taking off from Newbury racecourse and clearing customs at Shoreham in Kent. Sheilah was a very popular figure at West Ilsley. Joe Mercer observes, 'She was an absolutely adorable lady. If she had a house party for 10 people, you could guarantee that she would have everyone working within a matter of half an hour. "Joe darling, just pop down to the village and do that." She'd give the orders out and we would all do it.' The plane landed at Orly airport and the Herns and Mercers took a taxi to the course. Dick Hern recalls, 'The traffic was very heavy and time was getting on so we asked the French cabby why it was so bad. "Pour la Reine," he said. When he realized that we were the trainer and jockey of la Reine's horse he shouted, "À l'extérieur!" and went past all the traffic on the outside. He overtook everything.'

Meanwhile the Queen, more sedately, was the lunch guest of Marcel Boussac, then 85, one of the leading European owners of the century. The President of France, Valéry Giscard d'Estaing, sent a bowl of red roses as a mark of esteem. It was the Queen's first ever visit to Chantilly, which could legitimately hold claims to be the most beautiful of all courses. For French Derby and Oaks days there is an easy charm and sophistication in the crowd. It may be the chance for French racegoers to dress up but perhaps they do not try quite so hard as those attending Royal Ascot. On a sunny June day there is no finer sight than a group of classic horses galloping down the back straight with the Prince of Condé's magnificent chateau forming a natural backdrop.

The Queen was driven down the course in an open car before the second race. She went to see Highclere being saddled and was told by Betty Brister that the filly was in a fiery mood, a sign that she was on very good terms with herself. It was a big field of 22 runners so Joe Mercer had to be aware of possible traffic

problems during the race. Fortune smiled that day because he had a dream run. It was a strong pace and he settled Highclere in the leading group, turning third into the straight behind Hippodamia, owned by Nelson Bunker Hunt and one of the Queen's filly's main rivals. Highclere was trapped on the rails behind Hippodamia and it looked as though Mercer would have to wait for his chance to pull her to the outside. Unexpectedly, Hippodamia drifted away from the rails and Highclere was through like a ferret down a rabbit hole. 'She took off, and just shot through the narrow gap on the inside, and that was it,' says Joe. The leading French hope, Comtesse de Loir, came out of the pack to mount some sort of challenge but, in truth, Highclere won comfortably by two lengths.

In the stands the Queen watched, her hands clasped together as if in prayer. On either side of her Lord Porchester and Michael Oswald were on their feet, binoculars waving, arms aloft in an uninhibited declaration of excitement. 'An example of how not to behave at the racecourse,' observes Sir Michael, still revelling in the victory 25 years later. The photograph that captures the joyous moment hangs on the wall of his Norfolk home. Scenes of near pandemonium ensued around the unsaddling enclosure with Porchester and Oswald forming a human

Highclere [Joe Mercer] pulls clear of Comtesse de Loir [Jean-Claude Desaint] for an unforgettable win in the Prix de Diane at Chantilly, 16 June 1974.

Part Five ❧ Celebrations and Controversy

shield to protect the Queen from any French backslapping. Oswald remembers, 'It was a complete riot. The Queen was wearing a pillbox hat and all you could see of her was the hat. I was embraced by all manner of large French matrons who I had never met before in my life.' Highclere was the first filly to win both the English 1000 Guineas and the French Oaks.

On the flight home the Herns and the Mercers settled down to toast their victory with a couple of bottles of champagne they had bought on their way back to the airport. Hern recalls, 'We finished the champagne and were feeling rather sweaty and tired when the pilot received a message that we were to go to Heathrow, where a limousine would be waiting to whisk us off to Windsor for dinner. We were badly in need of a wash and brush-up.' Mercer adds that the instructions were to come dressed exactly as they were. At Heathrow they were met as arranged and driven to the Queen's private quarters at Windsor. There, in the pouring rain, she came out to greet them. 'Come in my warriors,' she declared. The Duke of Edinburgh, Princess Margaret and Lord Mountbatten were there to join in the welcome. Joe Mercer recalls, 'The Major and I were both in jeans. The Queen wasn't in jeans!' They all went into the dining room and there on the table stood the gold cup for winning the race. 'The perfect end to the perfect day' says Hern.

Joe Mercer, who has enjoyed many great racing triumphs, simply reflects, 'It was the finest day in my memory.' The occasion provided a real insight into the great joy the Queen derives from racing. This was no half-hearted celebration. The excitement her mother gets from racing has always been self-evident, but here was a peep into the Queen's private world of simple, relaxing family enjoyment. It is a world the representatives of the press never get the chance to witness.

The heroine herself, Highclere, went on to run possibly her finest ever race when runner-up to the great filly Dahlia in the King George VI and Queen Elizabeth Stakes at Ascot. She finished strongly, beating the Derby winner Snow Knight in the process, but she was never the same filly again. She had done her best over a trip of one mile and four furlongs, which sorely tested her stamina. Perhaps, in retrospect, she should have been kept to a mile and a quarter, but the rewards over that distance are far greater now than they were 25 years ago. As Dick Hern wisely comments, 'She ran really well in the King George but she didn't really get the trip. If you run fillies over a trip too far, it can dishearten them.'

❧ Ten Feet Tall

Even though Lester Piggott has ridden plenty of good winners in the royal colours he has never been described as a 'royal' jockey in the same way as Harry Carr, who practically had the silks glued on for 20 years. In reality there is no such thing as a royal jockey. Carr was retained to ride all the horses at Freemason Lodge and the Queen was just one of the owners who paid a proportion of his retainer. Of course, a jockey always feels a bit special wearing the scarlet and purple. Willie Carson explains, 'When you put those colours on you feel 10 feet tall. More jockeys get the chance today to wear them but when I was a boy it only ever seemed to be Harry Carr.'

If Carr was the first jockey indelibly associated with riding for the Queen, then Joe Mercer was the second and Willie Carson the third. As Carson confirms, the honour has been shared among many more jockeys since he stopped riding in the colours at the end of the 1980s. When the Queen chose to send horses to West Ilsley she was effectively keeping the royal colours in the family. Joe Mercer, the stable jockey, was Harry Carr's son-in-law. His hero and mentor in racing, however, was his elder brother Manny, a supremely gifted young jockey in the 1950s. They grew up in the Yorkshire wool city of Bradford, two of eight children whose father, Emmanuel, was a coach painter. By 1947, when Joe was 12, brother Manny had won the Lincolnshire Handicap and become attached to George Colling's Newmarket stable, one of the biggest in the country. Encouraged, Joe joined the Dickensian establishment of Major Fred Sneyd near Wantage in Berkshire where the brilliant Eph and Doug Smith had been apprenticed. Life had not become easier since they were there. The young Joe had to put on a little white coat and serve the old tyrant his dinner. However, Major Sneyd may have mellowed a little over the years because the apprentices were allowed one trip to the cinema per week. They were also permitted two afternoons off a week which gave them the chance to cycle into Wantage and, like all good jockeys-to-be, find someone to take a bet.

Although Joe received a good grounding as a jockey from Major Sneyd he developed his smooth style from watching his brother ride. While Manny was riding successfully for George Colling, Joe joined Jack Colling, George's brother, at West Ilsley as a 19-year-old apprentice. In his very first season he took the Oaks for the yard with Ambiguity. It was the start of a 23-year association with

The superb jockey Manny Mercer, elder brother of Joe Mercer. He was killed on 26 September 1959, when his horse threw him on his way to the start at Ascot.

the stables that continued when Dick Hern took over in 1963. Joe was by then the only Mercer riding. His brother Manny had been killed instantly when he was thrown by a filly called Priddy Fair on his way to the start of a race at Ascot in September 1959. The jockey smashed into the rails and was kicked by his unnerved mount. Concrete posts have no place on a racecourse.

Dick Hern and Joe enjoyed classic success with Provoke in the St Leger before their association with one of the outstanding horses of all time: Brigadier Gerard owned by Mr and Mrs John Hislop. They were also associated with Remand, considered by Hern to be the unluckiest horse of his whole career. He was fourth in Sir Ivor's Derby in 1968 even though it was subsequently revealed that he was carrying a virus. Highclere's victories in the royal colours in 1974 cemented Hern and Mercer's stature as one of the great trainer-jockey combinations in racing. Yet within two years Joe was packing his suitcase, having been replaced by the Scottish dynamo Willie Carson.

The announcement came during the Epsom Derby meeting in June 1976 and was greeted with general incredulity. Mercer and Hern were hardly going through a slump. The villain of the piece, as far as Joe was concerned, was Sir Arnold Weinstock, later Lord Weinstock, who had bought the West Ilsley stables from Jakie Astor. He was not a fan of Mercer although the official line was that they were going for a younger man. Joe was at the time an 'old man' of 41. When Weinstock, with his father-in-law Sir Michael Sobell, bought West Ilsley the stables effectively became a private establishment. Their horses had been trained by Sir Gordon Richards until his retirement and he still had a say in their management and in those owned by Lady Beaverbrook, who also transferred her horses to Hern. Although the Queen's horses were still with Hern, the choice of stable jockey was not hers. Joe explains, 'When I left West Ilsley it was nothing to do with Dick and nothing to do with the Queen.'

Mercer was part of the furniture at West Ilsley and could be forthright in his views on the horses, opinions that did not always sit easily with Sir Arnold or his son, Simon. Joe explains, 'In those days young Simon thought he knew everything and even questioned my riding one day at Newbury when I was beaten on a horse of theirs called Cupid.' Simon Weinstock thought

Royal Racing

Joe should have made his challenge on the outside instead of going for a gap on the rails. The jockey told him in no uncertain terms that there was 'enough room to drive a double-decker bus through and the horse simply wasn't good enough'.

The most unsavoury thing about Joe Mercer's sacking was that, because it was kept so secret, it acquired the whiff of skulduggery. Willie Carson had been approached at the end of 1975 and told not to breathe a word. Racing prides itself on being a sport where loyalty counts, something the Queen herself was to discover when her association with Dick Hern ended some years later. The cold facts are that Sir Arnold, the chairman of GEC, was the owner of a multi-million-pound racing stable and had an absolute right to have whom he pleased as jockey. Carson, already twice champion jockey, was only 33 and there was the prospect of a long employment at West Ilsley.

Although his departure from the stables still rankles with Joe Mercer today, it did give him the chance to enter the most successful stage of his career. He might have drifted towards retirement in pipe-smoking contentment at West Ilsley but for the ruthless decision-making of Sir Arnold. Instead he found himself on his way to Warren Place in Newmarket as first jockey to the champion trainer Henry Cecil. He rode over 100 winners in four consecutive seasons and was champion jockey in 1979 with 164 winners. Carson, meanwhile, was the unwelcome guest as far as the staff at West Ilsley were concerned.

Carson was used to fighting a battle. His cackling, chirpy persona has often belied an exemplary dedication to reach the pinnacle of his profession and stay there. He has always been popular with the general public, revelling in the increased awareness television has brought to his sport. His never-say-die, punchy style found favour with betting-shop habitués who always felt he was giving value for their wager. He was born in Stirling, Scotland, and saddled with the famous name of William Hunter Fisher Carson. The unexpected middle names were in honour of an uncle who had been a missionary in America. His father, Tommy, was a warehouseman and his mother, May, a waitress and there were no family connections with racing. But, like many young lads of small stature, he was always being told he was the right size to make a jockey.

The young Carson, who was always called Billy – the more familiar Willie was a courtesy of the press – was inspired by a 1950s film called *The Rainbow*

The elegant style of Joe Mercer is seen to good effect aboard Milford, winning the Lingfield Derby Trial, 12 May 1979.

Jacket, the story of a young jockey's involvement in a blackmail plot to lose a big race. It starred Bill Owen, later to become a national treasure in the television series *Last of the Summer Wine*, and featured a cameo role by then champion Gordon Richards, who had won the Coronation Derby on Pinza in 1953. Carson was hooked and would cycle nine miles to Dunblane once a week for a riding lesson paid for by his paper round. At 15 he was sufficiently accomplished to travel to the Yorkshire training centre of Middleham and join the stables of Captain Gerald Armstrong as apprentice.

When Captain Armstrong retired, Carson transferred to brother Sam Armstrong's yard in Newmarket. Sam, the father-in-law of Lester Piggott, was a renowned improver of young jockeys and advised Carson to model himself on Doug Smith, then still first jockey to Lord Derby. When that great erstwhile royal jockey retired at the end of 1967 it was Carson who stepped into his shoes at the Stanley House stables of Bernard van Cutsem. The dream move for Carson was nearly finished before it started when he was involved in a horrific car accident on the A1. His Jaguar ran into a lorry attempting a U-turn in fog and he suffered a broken leg, jaw and wrist and needed 27 stitches to facial wounds. He later remembered the words of an ambulanceman, 'Look at the driver, he's a goner.' Carson's legendary determination had him back riding five months later.

Lester Piggott was 18 when he won his first classic as was Joe Mercer, but Willie Carson was 29 years old when he captured the 2000 Guineas in 1972 on the van-Cutsem-trained High Top. He was never a boy wonder or a young pretender. He first caught the eye of Sir Arnold Weinstock in the 1974 Gordon Stakes at Goodwood when he gave a typical Carson bravura ride to a 25/1 outsider called Grey Thunder, who came to pip the West Ilsley hope Straight Flight, ridden by Joe Mercer, on the line. It was a style and attitude that Hern, too, admired. Without the Major's support, Carson's move to West Ilsley would almost certainly have been a disaster. He recalls, 'Dick was great. It was a bit acrimonious to begin with at West Ilsley. A lot of people thought Joe shouldn't have been going.'

The horse that bridged the gap between Mercer and Carson was the Queen's promising filly Dunfermline.

❧ The Great Races
Dunfermline: The Oaks, Epsom, 4 June 1977

Willie Carson's pride and joy was a gleaming black Ferrari which would be carrying him in some style to Epsom. After riding early work for Ian Balding he was back at his home at Eastbury, near Lambourn, in plenty of time to prepare for what everyone hoped would be a royal celebration. This was Silver Jubilee Year and even the effervescent Scot admitted to feeling 'a bit of pressure'. He left home at midday in plenty of time to cruise up the motorway to Epsom. Unfortunately, taking a short cut through the village, the Ferrari cruised head-on into an old banger of an Austin driven by a local man out with his wife and kids. Willie, a little shaken, was considerably stirred at the prospect of being late for his first big royal ride since taking over as the stable

Three of the greatest jockeys who all achieved classic success in the Queen's colours. Willie Carson *below*; Lester Piggott with his hand on the shoulder of Joe Mercer *bottom*.

jockey at West Ilsley. The stricken Ferrari was nursed back home where, by a stroke of good fortune, a brand-new VW Golf convertible was waiting in the garage. It had only been delivered the day before and Willie had yet to take it for a spin. He charged off while his girlfriend at the time called to reassure an anxious Dick Hern that his jockey was on his way.

Major Hern, as trainers invariably do on these occasions, went into a panic and put Joe Mercer on stand-by. Joe had already ridden the royal filly in her two-year-old days so knew her well. Watched by the Queen, the combination had managed a second in the May Hill Stakes on St Leger day when Dunfermline was still inexperienced and had not really gone through with her effort. The Queen had also watched the filly first time out as a three-year-old when Carson had made full use of her stamina to win the Pretty Polly Stakes at Newmarket during the Guineas meeting. The filly herself was not particularly pretty, carrying a rather plain head, and had not impressed Carson when he arrived at West Ilsley. He freely admits he barely noticed her.

As the runners charged out of the stalls for the first race Carson sped into Epsom. It had been a bad start to the day's proceedings. Disappointingly, the Queen was not at the course that afternoon, busy with Jubilee business and waiting to welcome the young Prince Andrew home from Canada. She was having to make do with watching the race on television at Windsor. Instead, Carson presented himself to the Queen Mother, Lord Porchester and a relieved Dick Hern. The mood was a hopeful rather than a confident one. Dunfermline was, however, well backed on the day and the odds came in to 6/1, fourth favourite to Durtal ridden by Lester Piggott.

Fate intervened dramatically to play a potentially catastrophic hand for Piggott, who was going for a Derby/Oaks double after a breathtaking triumph on The Minstrel in the colts' classic three days earlier. Durtal's saddle slipped on the way to the start and the filly panicked and careered into some rails, breaking Piggott's left stirrup leather. Unbalanced, he was thrown off but not before he had been dragged some yards with his foot still in the right leather. It is not an exaggeration to say that the great jockey could easily have been killed, especially as there were some very solid rails in the vicinity. Durtal was caught and withdrawn.

Meanwhile Carson was doing his best to keep the royal filly calm during the 10-minute delay. She had sweated up during the parade but appeared reasonably relaxed. Carson intended to play to her strength which was stamina. He remains adamant that Dunfermline would have beaten Durtal anyway

Royal Racing

because that filly would not have properly stayed the mile and a half. The race proved once again that even the best-laid plans can go astray. Carson jumped the filly off close to the pace on the inside as he intended, but was shuffled back nearer to last as they passed the mile marker and the horses drawn on the outside started to drift across for the first left-hand bend. Dunfermline was trapped on the inside, took a bad bump as she tried to overtake Geoff Lewis on Brightly and then was chopped off trying to pass Philippe Paquet on Anya Ylina. Halfway and Dunfermline had only two runners behind her. The race was not going well.

'I began to panic just a little,' Carson admitted later. He had to take action quickly or the chance would be gone. He recalls, 'I pulled her out, gave her two backhanders and to my amazement she took off like a rocket. I went round half a dozen horses and running downhill into Tattenham Corner we were flying.' Once in the straight Dunfermline's reserves of stamina came into play. She had the other horses beaten a furlong out but started to hang into the left. Thankfully, Carson held her together to pass the post three-quarters of a length in front of Freeze The Secret, ridden by his great friend Gianfranco Dettori, father of Frankie.

Queen Elizabeth and Dick Hern greet Dunfermline in the winners' enclosure at Epsom after the filly's success in the Oaks.

Carson returned to the unsaddling enclosure, his face creased in that familiar Cheshire cat grin. Dunfermline probably would have won comfortably given a trouble-free race but she had proved herself tough and honest. She had an even better payday to come in the St Leger, but the enduring image for Willie Carson on Oaks day remains the look of girlish excitement on the face of Queen Elizabeth the Queen Mother celebrating a Jubilee classic winner. Subsequently Willie called it his greatest ever race although future triumphs may have tempered that view a little.

Royal Racing

❧ Queen of Fillies

In terms of sheer, undiluted racing joy nothing could top the thrilling classic victories of Highclere for the Queen. She was there, able to revel in the pre-race excitement, rejoice at the moment of triumph and lead in her brave heroine with the cheers of the crowd ringing in her ears. Dunfermline, however, is generally acknowledged to be the better filly. Sir Michael Oswald, who witnessed the exploits of both superb horses, is in no doubt: 'Dunfermline would be the best horse the Queen has owned. Then Highclere with Aureole third.' The disappointing element in Dunfermline's success was that the Queen missed her two greatest races: the 1977 Oaks and St Leger, the race that sealed the filly's position as the number one royal horse of the past 50 years.

After her hard-earned Oaks triumph Dunfermline was rested until the York Ebor meeting in August, where she warmed up for a tilt at the Leger in the Yorkshire Oaks. A slow gallop did not allow Carson to bring her stamina into play and she was caught flat-footed in the straight, trailing in third. It was hardly an inspiring warm-up but did have the merit of blowing away the cobwebs. The extra two furlongs of the St Leger and a better pace would surely suit the royal filly better. Her form on the gallops started to improve and Carson's own confidence in her had grown. The major stumbling block to an unprecedented second English classic for the Queen in one season was the formidable partnership of Vincent O'Brien and Lester Piggott with the powerful galloper Alleged, unbeaten in five races and, according to the betting market, a near certainty at 4/7 to remain so.

The Queen had hoped to fly down to Doncaster for the race but the prime minister, James Callaghan, and his wife were arriving at Balmoral and she stayed at the castle to welcome them formally. In the end, like millions of others, she watched the drama unfold on television. On the day, Dick Hern produced Dunfermline at the very peak of her ability. Even so, Willie Carson believes he was a little bit lucky to beat Alleged: 'I think Lester was too confident on his horse. He went to the front too soon and I just followed him through.' In Lester Piggott's defence he was merely reproducing the tactics that had already worked so spectacularly at York when he won the Great Voltigeur Stakes by seven lengths. Dunfermline's stamina won the day and she wore the colt down inside the final furlong, both of them well clear of the rest of the field.

Just after the start, Dunfermline [Willie Carson] and Alleged [Lester Piggott] are side by side in the St Leger at Doncaster, 10 September 1977.

Willie Carson, however, was far from being all smiles at the result. He knew that Dunfermline had given Alleged a clear bump as she went past him and a steward's inquiry was announced. Carson recalls, 'I did give him a little nudge as I went by. It was terrible waiting for the inquiry. Lester didn't object – I think he was very kind to me.' Even so, 20 agonizing minutes ticked by before the stewards decided to let the result stand, much to the relief of the royal jockey who admits he was 'trembling' outside the weighing room.

Nothing can beat the topsy-turvy world of racing for knocking you off a pedestal just as soon as you have climbed on. The Prix de l'Arc de Triomphe over one mile and four furlongs at Longchamp at the beginning of October had grown in stature to become the climax of the European flat-racing season, with justifiable claims of being the premier race in the calendar. The Queen would never have a better chance of winning it, although the suspicion that Dunfermline was better over the Leger distance – two furlongs longer – slightly dampened enthusiasm.

Lester Piggott rode one of his greatest races on Alleged while Willie Carson, with customary candour, confesses he was outridden and rates it one of his worst efforts in the saddle. Piggott dictated a slow pace from the front and when he quickened the gallop on the run to the final bend Dunfermline was trapped on the rails with Carson sitting and suffering. Carson observes, 'If I'd ridden her 10 years later I would have thrown the orders out the window, gone through and made the running. But Piggott got in front of me and I just accepted the pace, even though it was too slow for me. I wasn't riding with the same confidence then as I was later. And as it turned out, the filly

Royal Racing

did not get the best ride on the big occasion. She was a staying filly and galloped. Piggott stuck his horse in front and slowed the pace. In the end she finished a close fourth, but deep down I knew she hadn't been ridden to the best of her ability. I'm not saying I would have won, but it's a bit grating.' Dick Hern is philosophical about the result: 'All jockeys ride moderate races sometimes. We had a pacemaker in the Leger and Piggott went a bit soon. In the Arc we didn't have one. Dunfermline was an animal who wanted a bit of pace because she could produce a bit off a fast gallop.'

Alleged was a great Arc winner and emphasized the point by winning the race more easily the following year. Piggott rated the horse among the top five he had ever ridden. Although Alleged was probably at his best over one mile and four furlongs, the performance of Dunfermline on Leger day should not be underestimated. The royal filly had just one more race, a tired third in the Prix Royal-Oak, the French St Leger, one trip too many to the well. By the time she came to herself the following season the decision to retire her had already been made. It was a pity because, as Hern remembers, she had 'really bloomed' and the prospect of a third encounter with Alleged would have been a mouthwatering one.

The finish of the St Leger and Dunfermline has won the battle.

❧ Derby Days

Lester Piggott was wearing the royal colours for the 200th Derby at Epsom in 1979. The colt he was riding was Milford, an exceptionally good-looking chestnut, bred to be a champion: his sire was the inspiring racehorse Mill Reef, who won the Derby in 1971 for Ian Balding. His dam was Highclere, the royal classic winner. It would be the racing story of the decade if, in this of all years, the Queen could cheer home her first Derby winner. The crowds that flocked to the Epsom Downs on a sweltering summer afternoon were willing it to happen. The stage was set for the perfect result.

At West Ilsley it was a slightly different story because stable jockey Willie Carson had chosen to ride Troy, a muscular colt owned by Sir Michael Sobell. Carson never really had any doubts as to which horse was destined to be a true champion. He recalls, 'Milford was a playboy. He was the sort of character who went out and would have his head stuck in the air like a peacock. He'd see a filly and think "Phwoar, let's get hold of her!" He thought he was a good-looking character. But when it came down to the hard work, the nitty-gritty, his little eyes would roll back and his ears would go back and he didn't like it. He had a little bit of white at the bottom of his eye when things were getting tough for him and you could feel him tense.'

Troy, Milford's stable rival, could not have been more different. Where Milford pranced and preened, Troy behaved in a laid-back fashion. 'He was the sort of guy who would go down the road kicking a can with his head down. He wasn't worried about anything,' observes Carson. On form, as the Derby approached, there looked to be little between the two colts. Milford, after showing some promise as a two-year-old, began the following season by scorching home in the White Rose Stakes at Ascot. Carson had a nasty fall at the Chester May meeting which left him with a broken collarbone and torn knee ligaments, so Joe Mercer donned the royal silks in the Lingfield Derby Trial. Milford started at the prohibitive odds of 4/11 and romped in by seven lengths. Carson was back in time to ride Troy in his Derby warm-up, the Predominate Stakes at Goodwood, and, looking absolutely magnificent, the colt stormed home – by seven lengths. As with all the classic trials, you are never sure of the calibre of the opposition until the cards are played in the big race itself.

At home Milford appeared the better worker. But Carson, always a very astute judge of a horse, was in no doubt that Troy would do for him. Brian Proctor, chief work rider at West Ilsley, remembers a gallop in which he rode Milford while Carson was on board Troy. As they pulled up, Carson shouted over to him, 'This is the one, Brian. This is the one.' The Major was of the same mind, confessing that he too 'would rather have had Troy in the Derby'. The professionals knew the score even if Lester Piggott was engaged to ride the Queen's colt. Troy was 6/1 second favourite while Milford was 15/2. Lester Piggott had ridden eight Derby winners while Willie Carson had yet to break his duck. Joe Mercer on Lyphard's Wish led the way round Tattenham Corner and into the straight with Milford, surprisingly close to the pace, in second.

Opposite: Milford [Lester Piggott] circles before the start of the 1979 Derby at Epsom.

The Royal Box at Epsom is always a crowded place on Derby day. The 1996 event was no exception.

Suddenly, two furlongs from home, the watching crowd became aware of a horse challenging on the wide outside, powering down the course like a jet-propelled bulldozer. It was Troy, who passed six horses in a furlong and strode away to win by seven lengths from Irish challenger Dickens Hill. Milford came home in the middle of the pack. Like all playboys, he had flattered to deceive although the riding tactics were surprising. Perhaps Piggott wanted to make sure the royal colours were noticed from the stands.

Another Derby had passed in disappointment. To be fair to Milford, he came back to win the Prince of Wales Stakes at the Newmarket July meeting in a record time. He was not, however, a Group One colt, let alone a champion like Troy. In truth, since Aureole in the Coronation Derby, the Queen has had very few horses who have gone to Epsom with a real chance. Doutelle had a most unlucky run but a place was all he could realistically have hoped for. Hopeful Venture never went to Epsom. The best placed horse from West Ilsley was Church Parade, who was fifth in the 1981 Derby and who Dick Hern describes as 'nearly a good horse'. Willie Carson remembers him well, for embarrassing reasons. He once told the Queen that he thought Church Parade would win the Derby for her. In the end he was left praying for a bit of Dick Hern magic to improve him but the colt was in truth just a stayer. That really is the story of too many royal homebred horses throughout the years. They just did not have enough speed in their pedigree.

The one horse that 'got away' as far as the Derby is concerned was Special Leave, another Mill Reef colt, this time trained at Kingsclere by Ian Balding who still describes him as 'an outstandingly good horse'. He was a lovely, big bay who had been lucky to be born at all. His dam, Light Duty, had to undergo major surgery for an ulcer while she was carrying her foal. As a two-year-old in 1982 Special Leave won the Hyperion Stakes at Ascot with such authority that Balding was convinced he was a serious classic prospect. Although he ran poorly in the Guardian Classic Trial at Sandown the next spring that defeat was put down to the heavy going, and there was every reason to be optimistic that the colt would show his true colours on better ground at Epsom. A training setback meant he missed the race and then one morning on Balding's gallops there was a crack like a gunshot wound and Special Leave had broken a leg. So sudden, so unexpected and so many hopes dashed.

Church Parade [Willie Carson] *top* winning the Lanson Champagne Stakes at Goodwood, 31 July 1980 and *above* Special Leave [Joe Mercer] on his way to post at Sandown for the Guardian Classic Trial on 20 April 1983, were two Derby hopefuls who would prove disappointments for the Queen.

❧ Height of Fashion

Bustino, even though he never raced in the Queen's silks, was one of the most popular of royal horses. Queen Elizabeth the Queen Mother was a particular admirer of the muscular, golden bay horse when he was resident stallion at the Wolferton Stud near Sandringham. She would always take the time to visit him as well as going to see her own young horses at nearby Raynham. He had been a superb racehorse for Lady Beaverbrook. His trainer Dick Hern still considers him very unlucky not to have won the 1974 Derby when he was fourth behind Snow Knight on ground a shade too quick for him. Joe Mercer had been unable to position Bustino, a confirmed stayer, as near to the pace as he wanted and was finishing best of all. The horse did manage classic success in the St Leger and in the following season took part in what many regard as the 'race of the century' with Grundy, that season's Derby winner, in the King George VI and Queen Elizabeth Stakes at Ascot. In a pulsating duel Bustino was beaten by half a length, although Mercer maintains his brave colt broke down half a furlong before the finish. Even the great filly Dahlia, back in third, smashed the course record. Bustino never raced again.

In the autumn of 1974 the great horse Aureole, who had stood at Wolferton for so many years, was finally retired at the age of 24 and there was a vacancy for a new stallion at the stud. Bustino fitted the bill. He was particularly attractive to the Queen because his dam, Ship Yard, was by one of her favourite colts, Doutelle. She bought 10 shares in the syndicate formed to buy the colt for stud duties and, although Lady Beaverbrook retained the majority interest, he arrived at Wolferton at the end of 1975. The filly Highclere had already produced the useful colt Milford and there was considerable optimism that a match with Bustino could produce something special. The result was Height of Fashion, a tall, leggy filly who went into training at West Ilsley. Willie Carson recalls, 'She was very lean and not pretty. She had a great big head and was tall but she had a lovely stride on her. She had to have blinkers on her to get the best out of her.'

She proved herself an outstanding two-year-old, remaining unbeaten in the 1981 season. She won the May Hill Stakes at Doncaster over a mile on St Leger day and then captured the Hoover Fillies' Mile at Ascot. Carson had been badly injured in a fall at York that season and she was ridden in both races by Joe Mercer, who had steered the filly's parents to classic success. At two she was already taller than her sire, Bustino, who was by no means a small horse. Hern and Lord Porchester decided not to go for the Oaks with Height of Fashion, reasoning that she was too big to act around the Epsom turns. Instead she achieved her finest hour in the Princess of Wales' Stakes at the Newmarket July meeting when she trounced the admirable stayer Ardross, twice winner of the Gold Cup. In so doing she broke the course record for a mile and a half held by the Queen's colt Milford.

Soon after a chain of events was set in motion that would have a profound effect on the history of royal racing. Sheikh Hamdan al Maktoum of the Dubai ruling family, which was then becoming increasingly influential in British racing, offered the breathtaking sum of £1.2 million for Height of Fashion. This was a considerable sum of money for a homebred filly and the Queen, advised by Lord Porchester, who inherited the title Earl of Carnarvon in 1987, decided to take the money and use it to purchase the yard at West Ilsley as her private stables. The question remains 20 years later: Was it good business or the biggest mistake of the Queen's racing life?

Willie Carson observes simply, 'It was very good business because it was a lot of money.' That opinion looked unquestionably the right one when Height of Fashion ran two poor races following the sale and was packed off to stud. It did not look quite so bombproof when her first three foals at stud were all group winners of outstanding quality and one in particular won the Derby. Nashwan was that colt. In the same season he won the 2000 Guineas, the Eclipse and the King George VI and Queen Elizabeth Stakes. He was undoubtedly one of the very best post-war Derby winners.

The leggy Height of Fashion [Joe Mercer] on her way to post for the Hoover Fillies' Mile at Ascot, 24 September 1981.

It is too simple to say that the Queen missed her best chance of a Derby winner in the pursuit of prudent business. As Willie Carson explains, 'What stallions would the Queen have been sending this mare to? There is no way she would have been sending Height of Fashion to the top sire Northern Dancer or to other great stallions in America. The mare might have bred good horses but she would not have had the added advantage of going to the best stallions in the world.'

The acknowledged expert on breeding, Tony Morris, wrote at the time of Nashwan's success, 'The chance of Height of Fashion actually proving to be worth the amount offered must have seemed remote, the chances of a similar or higher offer ever arriving from another party remoter still. Bear in mind too that Height of Fashion's parents were still in residence at Sandringham and the material was there to produce others as good, if not better.'

The Queen's former trainer, Ian Balding, is very critical of the whole business: 'The argument that the Queen could not have afforded to use Northern Dancer is absolute rubbish. It was appallingly organized. She should have used Northern Dancer, Nureyev, The Minstrel, Blushing Groom, all the top stallions, which she could have done. She or Lord Carnarvon would say they couldn't afford to but they would have given her nominations. They sold Height of Fashion to buy West Ilsley. It was crazy – selling your best mare when you breed your own stock and when you don't need to buy a racing stable anyway.'

Part Five ⸰⸱ Celebrations and Controversy

The purchase of West Ilsley appears to be the imponderable in the whole saga. Owning the stables did not improve the Queen's racing fortunes or those of her studs at all. In fact, the 1980s were for the most part disappointing. Why were some of the profits from the sale of Height of Fashion not put aside to send some of the mares she still owned – Highclere among them – to the very top stallions? Only Lord Carnarvon could answer that and he has always kept his cards very close to his chest on the sale of Height of Fashion.

Happier times for the West Ilsley team. *From left to right:* Lord Porchester, Princess Margaret, Willie Carson, the Queen, Queen Elizabeth and Dick Hern crowd into the winners' enclosure after Expansive has won the Ribblesdale Stakes at Royal Ascot, 19 June 1979.

◌ The Sacking of Dick Hern

When the Queen purchased the stables at West Ilsley her relationship with Dick Hern inevitably changed. From being just one of the many owners in the yard she became the boss. And in practical terms that meant the stables were under the more direct scrutiny of her racing manager, Lord Carnarvon. Major Hern, on whom the Queen had conferred the honour of Commander of the Victorian Order (CVO) in 1977, remained there, of course, and was given a new seven-year lease in 1982. These were not happy years and they ended in a manner which still leaves a bitter taste in the mouths of the racing community. The sacking of Dick Hern – for there is no other way to describe the extraordinary train of events – when he was paralysed from a hunting accident and hospitalized because of a serious heart complaint – has cast a long shadow over the Queen's entire career as an owner.

Lord Oaksey is just one of a number of distinguished figures in racing who are forthright and outspoken in their views: 'The Queen blotted her copybook comprehensively by effectively sacking Dick Hern. I think it's common knowledge that the Queen Mother was absolutely furious. I had always heard that the Queen Mother was absolutely disgusted and so was I disgusted. It was an extraordinary thing for her to do. I very much admire the Major. He's a splendid and very skilful trainer and was, in his prime, a marvellous horseman.

Royal Racing

He's a wonderful man and he genuinely was very badly treated. It was a diabolical, extraordinary departure from normal employer relationships within the Royal Family. The one thing they don't do is sack people, probably excessively they don't sack them.'

In the Queen's defence it was not easy for her to ignore the counsel of Lord Carnarvon, her best friend and advisor for well over 40 years. She was in a difficult position and it does seem out of character. The chain of events began on 7 December 1984: the community of West Ilsley stables was thrown into turmoil when Major Hern took a horrible fall from his horse Badger while out hunting with the Quorn in Leicestershire. They had been unable to see a stone water-trough lurking on the other side of a fence and, in an effort to avoid it, horse and rider parted company in mid-air. Hern was taken to Stoke Mandeville Hospital suffering from a broken neck and unable to move. He remained in traction for six weeks and had surgery in February before finally discharging himself in March, partially paralysed and confined to a wheelchair. The Major, stoutly supported by his wife Sheilah, had made impressive progress spurred on by an indomitable spirit and a desire to resume day-to-day charge of West Ilsley.

Fortune, however, did not favour the brave on this occasion. By the end of April there were signs that the horses were going down with a mystery virus, memorably described by Hern as a 'thief in the night. You don't see it come and you don't see it go.' A completely miserable season for the stable was avoided by the exploits of Petoski, a three-year-old colt owned by loyal patron Lady Beaverbrook, who surprised everyone by winning the King George VI and Queen Elizabeth Stakes at 12/1. It was a triumph for the never-say-die style of Willie Carson, who powered the colt past the brilliant filly Oh So Sharp in the final strides. The victory gave Hern a record fourth win in the race and allowed him to continue in the very top flight of trainers despite a virus-ravaged season.

The 1980s were a wretched period for the Queen's bloodstock. Neither Hern nor Ian Balding had much ammunition as the Royal Studs were, like many others, left trailing behind the blossoming empire of the Maktoums, not to mention Prince Khalid Abdullah and Robert Sangster. Sheikh Hamdan al Maktoum was becoming more influential in Hern's yard and would eventually provide the Major with some of the greatest triumphs of his career through Nashwan and Dayjur. Balding had a useful filly called Soprano who was

Nashwan's win in the 2000 Guineas at Newmarket, 6 May 1989, was an emotional triumph for jockey Willie Carson.

placed in the 1985 Coronation Stakes at Royal Ascot, but she was nothing to get wildly excited about and pickings were generally very lean.

The tide began to turn for West Ilsley – if not for the Queen – in 1988 when an excellent bunch of three-year-olds, including Unfuwain and Minster Son as well as a nice two-year-old Nashwan, caught the eye. In Unfuwain and Nashwan the influence of Height of Fashion was becoming increasingly apparent. At a time of considerable optimism disaster struck when Hern had a heart attack during Royal Ascot and had to undergo major surgery. The signs were not good. He was in a hospital bed and Lord Carnarvon took a more active part in the yard. Carson recalls, 'He was coming over playing trainers every night. He was going round every horse looking at their legs. And the lads were not leaving until seven o'clock at night and everyone was getting upset. After a couple of weeks of this, everyone started getting itchy. He was there as unofficial trainer, and making decisions. And everyone had to take notice of what he said. And, of course, somebody had to go and tell Dick. He had to get Carnarvon over and tell him, "Don't go to the stables". And that was the crunch. That was it. Carnarvon told him, "Out!" That's obviously what happened.'

At this point the roof fell in. Carson, who won many friends within racing by his unswerving loyalty to his trainer and his courage in speaking out at his treatment, reveals that Hern was still in hospital when he was told he had just two weeks to vacate the West Ilsley stables. Carson still recalls the tears as a bewildered Sheilah Hern tried to come to terms with the ultimatum that she had a fortnight to quit her house. She also had to cope with the very genuine fears regarding her husband's life. Carson acknowledges, 'Carnarvon wanted to get out of the situation quickly. They obviously took the view that Dick Hern's life was in danger – or, at least, his training life was in danger. It was the wrong view to take and it certainly wasn't done in the right manner.'

Ian Balding, who arguably had most to gain if Hern was packed off, went in to bat for his friend and professional colleague. He sought out the Queen's second private secretary, Sir Robert Fellowes, while on holiday in Barbados and warned him of the consequences of sacking the royal trainer while he was in intensive care: 'I went to see him and said, "If you don't make some sort of arrangement for Dick Hern it will be the most unpopular thing the Queen has ever done and she risks having her horses being booed in the winners' enclosure. That's just how strongly people in racing feel and I think she should know that." I also went and saw Carnarvon after I had been to see Dick in hospital. I told him this was unbelievable and he couldn't do it. I think that helped to get Dick Hern another year at Ilsley.'

An official announcement was made at the beginning of September that Neil Graham would be the caretaker trainer at West Ilsley until the end of the season and Minster Son's victory in the St Leger later that month is ostensibly credited as a training success for him. In reality Hern, from his hospital bed, and his wife Sheilah continued to run the show and could be forgiven for being upset that the Major was not credited with a seventh Leger success. The author Michael Seely observed that Sheilah Hern hung back from the celebrations at Doncaster. When Hern eventually returned home the following month the stable had its best crop of horses for 10 years.

The Queen and Dick Hern admire the trophy after Nashwan has won the King George VI and Queen Elizabeth Diamond Stakes at Ascot, June 1989.

The 1988 season emerged with the dark clouds of rumour and speculation still hanging over Hern's head. William Hastings-Bass, brother-in-law of Ian Balding, was tipped to take over at West Ilsley. Just when everyone's attention was focused on the Cheltenham National Hunt Festival in March an official announcement was made: the Queen had appointed Hastings-Bass to take over when Major Hern's lease expired at the end of that season. Both press and public perceived this to be the most cruel treatment of a disabled employee and the announcement was greeted with a mixture of incredulity and furore. Willie Carson threatened retirement if the Major could not find a yard. The 'royal' jockey was effectively casting off the scarlet and purple colours for ever.

And then came Nashwan. It seemed like a divine judgement when the colt by Blushing Groom out of Height of Fashion scorched down the Rowley Mile to win the 2000 Guineas. The *Daily Mail* journalist Colin Mackenzie observes, 'I have never seen Newmarket like it. There was an almost anti-royal feeling.' To further underline royal discomfort Nashwan won the Derby easily, adding the Eclipse and the King George VI and Queen Elizabeth Stakes for good measure in a glorious summer for Hern, Sheikh Hamdan and Willie Carson. Behind the scenes a compromise had been reached by the York May meeting and it was announced that Hern would share the yard for another season with Hastings-Bass. Later, Sheikh Hamdan again came to the rescue when he agreed to build a new training complex for the Major and offered Carson the job of jockey.

Carson himself, who has had nothing to do with Lord Carnarvon since the controversy, highlights how the Major's great popularity in racing was

Royal Racing

sorely underestimated by the Queen and her advisers: 'Dick Hern was one of racing's favourite people. He was a Jekyll and Hyde character as far as the press was concerned. He would talk to nobody on a racecourse because his mind was on his horses. He didn't want any distractions and if a press man asked him a question, he might well get a rebuff. Yet, when he got home and closed the front door at night, he'd get a glass of whisky in his hand and have a singsong. He's one of the boys and the nicest, kindest person you would ever come across.'

Ian Balding's robust support for Hern also sounded the death knell for his own long-term future as a royal trainer. He observes, 'Ever since then I've been on my way out. I was told in no uncertain terms that my loyalty should have been to him [Carnarvon] and the Queen and not to Dick Hern.' Even Willie Carson admits, 'If I had been in Ian Balding's shoes, I would not have said what he did. He is one of the bravest people of all for what he said. I told him not to do it. I told him to shut up but he didn't.'

When Hern left West Ilsley he took over at the new Kingwood stables until his retirement in 1997 after 40 years as a trainer. Now sadly a widower, he still lives in the village and is always happy to offer advice if asked by his successor Marcus Tregoning. In the *Racing Post*'s list of the 50 greatest British and Irish trainers of the twentieth century Tony Morris and John Randall placed Hern at eighth, just ahead of Sir Michael Stoute and Captain Sir Cecil Boyd-Rochfort. He was champion trainer four times and won 16 classics, but will be best remembered for training Brigadier Gerard, Nashwan and the Queen's filly Dunfermline. In 1998 he received a CBE in the Queen's Birthday Honours List which partly put the record straight, although few would have begrudged him the knighthood Boyd-Rochfort and Noel Murless received. He comments, 'There were so many highlights in my career that it is difficult to differentiate but I suppose winning the Oaks and St Leger in Jubilee year for Her Majesty were probably the best.'

Meanwhile the old hunter Badger, who accidentally started the unfortunate chain of events, has enjoyed a long and happy retirement being pampered in a field behind Lord Oaksey's Cotswold farmhouse. Sometimes in racing, horses are treated with more compassion than people.

Part Six

A Thousand Winners

On a cold, damp early spring morning Queen Elizabeth accompanied Ian Balding to watch her horses work on the downland gallops near Kingsclere. Noticing that the Queen Mother was wearing unsuitable high-heeled shoes, Balding politely suggested that the ground was very wet and she might prefer to put on some Wellington boots he had in the car. 'Oh no dear,' she said. 'These are my walking shoes.'

❧ Four Hundred Up

For a horse with a decent reputation in New Zealand, Nearco Bay was a big disappointment to Nicky Henderson when he arrived at Lambourn. Henderson had taken over as Queen Elizabeth's senior trainer after the death of Fulke Walwyn. Fulke's widow, Cath, soldiered on with a loyal staff for a year after her husband's death but she had never really intended to be a trainer. In any case, the yard was cruelly affected by a virus during her time in charge and good cheer was thin on the ground. It was up to Henderson, one of the most popular men in the sport, to put a smile back on the face of royal racing. The plodding Nearco Bay looked a most unlikely harbinger of better tidings. 'He was horribly slow,' recalls Henderson.

The team at Seven Barrows settled down to do their best with the bay gelding. The first thing they did was give him a year off to acclimatize and recover from a number of niggling ailments he had brought with him from the other side of the world. Under Jockey Club rules for foreign imports, he was required to race three times off automatic top weight in order to be assessed for a realistic handicap mark for future races. Henderson remembers, 'I was struggling with him in a big way but, although I didn't think he was very good, two things happened which improved things. Firstly the ground dried up which suited him and secondly he became very well handicapped by not performing terribly well. That certainly wasn't intentional, he had just been extremely disappointing.'

By this time Nearco Bay, a strapping 17-hand bay gelding, had reached the veteran age of 12 so, at the tail end of the 1993/4, season it was now or never for him. Henderson found a little race for him at Hereford at the beginning of April and the horse struggled home in front, having struck up a useful partnership with the stable's second jockey, Johnny Kavanagh. Henderson decided to strike while everything was in Nearco Bay's favour and so brought him back to Hereford to win twice more in five weeks. The secret was to let him bowl along at his own pace and get him jumping. Kavanagh recalls, 'His jumping would keep him in things. He had a good enough cruising speed if he had a nice lead.' At this point it dawned on everyone that Queen Elizabeth needed just one more winner to reach the quite astonishing landmark of 400 winners.

A week or so later Henderson bumped into the executive producer of Channel 4 Racing, Andrew Franklin, who asked him if there was anything

Opposite: Nicky Henderson and his wife, Diana, watch the horses work as dawn rises over the Lambourn downs.

Nearco Bay [John Kavanagh] jumps exuberantly ahead of Buddy Holly [Tom Grantham] on his way to recording Queen Elizabeth's 400th win in the Neville Lumb Silver Jubilee Handicap Chase at Uttoxeter, 30 May 1994.

interesting happening before the end of the season. The trainer told him that the big thing at the moment was trying to secure Queen Elizabeth's 400th winner. The target for the event was not a glamorous race at one of her more favoured tracks like Sandown or Ascot. Instead the unlikely sounding Neville Lumb Silver Jubilee Handicap Chase at rural Uttoxeter in Staffordshire on the Whitsun Bank Holiday Monday was selected for the potential landmark victory. Franklin, wisely realizing that this could be big news, decided that Channel 4 should cover the race because it dovetailed perfectly with their main coverage from Sandown. Sir Michael Oswald observes, 'It was a very bold decision. They thought the horse might win but, even so, they stuck their necks out and took pictures from rural Uttoxeter, which, at the time, was not normally a course they covered. It took a lot of initiative.' Franklin admits, more disarmingly, 'We took a flyer.'

It was lucky for Queen Elizabeth that the cameras were there that day because she had decided not to travel to the Midlands course. Instead Captain

Charles Radclyffe and his wife Duse had invited her to lunch, with Sir Michael and Lady Angela Oswald, at Raymond Blanc's acclaimed restaurant Le Manoir aux Quat' Saisons near Oxford. Queen Elizabeth particularly wanted to visit the restaurant because Monsieur Blanc travelled each year to Captain Radclyffe's home – they are old friends – to prepare a special lunch for her when she went to inspect her horses, which were being broken in there. Captain Radclyffe explains, 'There is no fuss or glory-seeking. Queen Elizabeth always makes a point of going through to our kitchen and shaking everyone's hand. She never loses sight of the fact that others are making a tremendous effort on her behalf. It is never too much trouble to put a smile on someone's face or a spring in their step. It is also rather splendid to sit down to a small lunch prepared by Raymond Blanc.'

Monsieur Blanc recalls that the day of the race was a glorious English spring day: 'Queen Elizabeth had an aperitif under the cedar trees in the garden and then took a short walk around the grounds. She particularly wanted to have lunch in the Conservatory

Le Manoir aux Quat' Saisons, the Oxfordshire restaurant where Queen Elizabeth celebrated her 400th winner. Master chef Raymond Blanc *top* prepares lunch in his kitchen.

with our other diners. Afterwards I provided a small room with a television for them to watch the race.' Meanwhile Nicky Henderson, somewhat nervous, was at Uttoxeter, aware that the sole reason the cameras were there was to film Nearco Bay. He recalls, 'They had come just in case he won – as if we needed any more pressure!' The race itself was an uneventful handicap chase, a five-runner plod over an extended three miles. Kavanagh jumped Nearco Bay, the 13/8 favourite, off in second, moved him into the lead two out and pushed him out strongly to the line. Back at Le Manoir, Monsieur Blanc was uncorking the champagne as the horse jumped the last fence. Sir Michael declares, 'It was a magical moment.'

Afterwards Queen Elizabeth was in an exuberant mood. Monsieur Blanc observes, 'She was so happy.' His royal visitor asked him what he considered his proudest achievement. Tongue in cheek, Monsieur Blanc replied the occasion on 14 July, Bastille Day, when he had persuaded 200 people at Le Manoir to sing the 'Marseillaise', the French national anthem. Queen Elizabeth was delighted and told him, 'If I had been there I would certainly have sung.' With that, she suddenly burst into song there and then: 'Allons enfants de la Patrie, Le jour de gloire est arrivé…'

Before she left, she insisted that she would like to speak to everyone at Le Manoir who had made her day so special. 'I would like to see them all,' she said, even though Monsieur Blanc warned her that there were close to 70 people involved.

In accordance with her wishes they were all presented in a very long line at the front of Le Manoir. Queen Elizabeth spoke to every single one.

❧ Top Hats and Turquoise

The Queen loves Royal Ascot. She owns the racecourse and, in a way, she is host to all the thousands who attend the meeting or watch the action unfold on television. It is her favourite racing week of the year and the four days in June are always the first to be blocked off in her annual diary. Although foreign tours did intrude a little in the early part of her reign, something akin to a nuclear war would now be required to force the Queen to miss Royal Ascot, although the great British weather did accomplish that feat in 1964 when both Gold Cup Thursday and the following Friday were washed out. She solved the problem of a large house party kicking their heels at Windsor by taking them to the course in a parade of eight Rolls-Royces and Daimlers. They lunched in the Royal Box and subsequently roamed around the empty stands and the weighing room. The Duke of Edinburgh was even reputed to have answered a call in the press room.

The BBC employs a fashion commentator for Royal Ascot week. It is her task to make suitably witty, sarcastic or enthusiastic comments as the camera darts around amid the pinks, the turquoises and the ill-judged feathers that parade around in the Royal Enclosure. Most important, however, are the

The Queen studying the action from the Royal Box at Ascot in 1991.

invariably gushing remarks about what the Queen, the Queen Mother and assorted members of the Royal Family are wearing for the traditional carriage-ride down the course before racing. It is a unique combination of social event and sport which the strawberries and cream of Wimbledon or the straw boaters and champagne of Henley come nowhere near to matching. It is so very British, and would be completely inconsequential if the racing itself were not of the highest quality.

The Queen's trainers, mindful of her enjoyment, have always tried particularly hard to provide winners in the scarlet and purple colours at the Berkshire track. Invariably, a horse is saved for the Royal meeting rather than wasting a speculative entry in the Derby or Oaks a few weeks earlier. Queen Elizabeth shares her daughter's enthusiasm for the week and always accompanies her for each of the four days. She even celebrated a rare race victory on the flat in her colours when Bali Ha'i III won the Queen Alexandra Stakes in 1959. Even the normally sensible racing journalist Ivor Herbert was moved to write,

Part Six ∾ A Thousand Winners

'Ascot that year was warm and sunny and Queen Elizabeth walked down the paddock in a pale blue floral silk coat and matching hat to look at Bali Ha'i.' The Duke of Edinburgh joins his wife and mother-in-law for the carriage procession down the course and always raises an elegant topper to an appreciative crowd. He then retires to the Royal Box where, according to numerous chroniclers, he settles down to enjoy coverage of the test match on television. While he enjoys his wife's successes, Prince Philip has never been a racing man.

As Duchess of York in the 1930s, Queen Elizabeth and the future George VI would always have a house party for Ascot at Royal Lodge, Windsor. During Coronation year in 1937 the new King and Queen travelled down the course each day. The present Queen has enthusiastically embraced her parents' traditions and, right from the start of her career as an owner, has enjoyed success at the Royal meeting – although she has yet to win the premier race, the Gold Cup. On the first day of Royal Ascot in the Coronation year of 1953 she invested her trainer, Captain Boyd-Rochfort, as a Commander of the Royal Victorian Order in a special ceremony in the Royal Box. The following day the Captain saddled Choir Boy in the Royal Hunt Cup, the traditional cavalry charge down the straight mile. Choir Boy, a small, honest, brown colt, had already had the distinction of being the Queen's first ever winner as monarch when he won the Wilburton Handicap at Newmarket the previous year. He had not raced in her colours, however, because it was not considered appropriate while the court was in mourning for her father. Instead he had raced in the colours of the Duke of Norfolk.

He had the chance to break new ground again by providing the Queen with her first Royal Ascot winner in the Royal Hunt Cup. The Wednesday handicap is usually the biggest betting race of the meeting. Harry Carr once again missed out, unable to do the weight, and was replaced by Doug Smith. It proved to be one of those races in which the horses drawn on the stands' side might as well have stayed at home in their boxes. The first six home were all drawn on the far side and Choir Boy, drawn two off the far rail, won comfortably. At one stage he had looked likely to be a good deal better than a handicapper but had split a pastern the previous season. Like Aureole he was by Hyperion and bred to be distinctly useful. His overall form, however, was nothing like as good as that colt's and so, while Aureole enjoyed a long career as a stallion in the paddocks at the Royal Stud, Choir Boy was sold and shipped off to Uruguay.

Opposite: Colour Sergeant [David Harrison] ends a 13-year drought for the Queen at Royal Ascot when he storms to victory in the Royal Hunt Cup, 17 June 1992. Afterwards, the jockey is greeted by a jubilant Lord Carnarvon, The Queen, Lord Huntingdon and Michael Oswald.

Royal Racing

The Hunt Cup proved a lucky race for the Queen again in 1956 when her colt Alexander won one of the most thrilling and nail-biting of all Ascot races. For once Harry Carr was wearing the royal colours for a big-race win. A compact, well-made colt, Alexander had been thought good enough to run in the previous season's 2000 Guineas but was a shade below classic standard. He just lacked a little size. Bruce Hobbs remembers that he had rather a 'plain head'. He was by the brilliant stayer Alycidon and inherited some of that colt's waywardness, although Carr always maintained he did not deserve the label of unwillingness. This particular day the draw made no difference with the two main protagonists, Alexander and Jaspe – who was ridden by the master tactician Rae Johnstone – drawn on opposite sides of the course. Carr held Alexander up behind the leaders hoping to conserve his finishing speed until the last moment. Two furlongs out the leading horses weakened quickly, leaving the royal colt in front far too soon. His ears went back and his head carriage became higher and higher. On the far side Johnstone was driving Jaspe up to challenge. Poor Carr could not go for his whip because he knew his mount would duck away from it and give up. The two horses passed the post with no one sure who had won. When Carr came into a deathly quiet unsaddling enclosure he shrugged at the Queen. Unusually for a jockey in these circumstances, he had no idea which horse had taken the spoils. Amazingly, when the result was announced, Alexander had prevailed by half a length.

The Queen enjoyed some very successful Royal Ascots in the Fifties and Sixties when a whole selection of her best horses won, including Aureole, Landau, Almeria and Hopeful Venture. She may not have won the Derby at Epsom but she took the King Edward VII Stakes, often referred to as the 'Ascot Derby', with Pindari in 1959. Ironically, the colt was a son of the mighty Pinza who had thwarted her Epsom ambitions for Aureole. The Seventies were not quite so memorable and the Eighties were a disaster. Not one winner at the Royal meeting. When Colour Sergeant stormed home in the 1992 Royal Hunt Cup he was not only her first winner in that particular race for 36 years, he was her first winner of any kind at Royal Ascot since 1979. Colour Sergeant's victory was a triumph for the Earl of Huntingdon, the former William Hastings-Bass, who had succeeded Dick Hern at West Ilsley.

Unknown Quantity [Bruce Raymond] gamely keeps Gulf Palace [Tyrone Williams] at bay to win the Royal Hong Kong Jockey Club Stakes at Sandown, 7 July 1989.

Hastings-Bass was in an unenviable position, taking over from the popular Major Hern under controversial circumstances. He had a very strong royal racing background. His father, Peter Hastings-Bass, had trained for the Queen before his untimely death and his brother-in-law was Ian Balding. Despite these impeccable credentials Hastings-Bass has always seemed to be a bit of a maverick. He was born plain William Hastings and acquired the beer handle when his father, complying with the will of his brewing-magnate uncle, changed the family name by deed poll. William also rejoiced in the middle names of Robin Hood, a proud acknowledgement of the popular legend that the famous custodian of Sherwood Forest was in fact the outlawed Earl of Huntingdon.

Hastings-Bass must have felt like an outlaw when it was announced in March 1989 that he would succeed Dick Hern. Ian Balding recalls how embarrassing it was when his brother-in-law took over. Fortunately the new royal trainer pulled off a spectacular success in the same season when, in August, he provided the Queen with her first ever winner in the United States. It took everyone by surprise, not least American racegoers who allowed the royal runner, Unknown Quantity, to start a 10/1 outsider in a field of five for the Arlington Handicap at Arlington Park near Chicago. Unknown Quantity, another product of the mare Pas de Deux, was lucky to be racing at all. He had been hit by a car as a two-year-old and patiently nursed back to health. The popular Panamanian jockey Jorge Valesquez took the mount and never looked in trouble, cruising into the lead at the two-furlong pole and pulling away for a three-length win. Unknown Quantity collected $120,000, which at the time converted to some £67,000, for his efforts.

Hastings-Bass, who had become Lord Huntingdon in 1990 when he inherited the title from a second cousin, produced an even better training performance with Colour Sergeant. The four-year-old bay colt had not raced since the previous November and had only ever won one race, a nondescript affair on the Midlands all-weather track at Southwell. The stable apprentice, 19-year-old David Harrison, claiming an allowance of 5 lbs, had the ride in the Royal Hunt Cup and, not surprisingly, the colt was a 20/1 outsider in a massive field of 31 runners. Huntingdon told Harrison to stay handy and go on two furlongs out. The jockey carried out the instructions to the letter and Colour Sergeant ran on to hold Gymcrak Premiere by a neck. It was a training feat of which the old handicap maestro, Boyd-Rochfort himself, would have been proud.

∾ A Sense of Relief

Ian Balding's 35-year stint as one of the Queen's trainers finished at the end of the 1999 season when it was announced he would not be receiving any royal horses for the start of the next millennium. Far from being upset or angry, he admits to a sense of relief: 'I no longer have to ring her up and say, "Sorry, we've got three useless animals". It's no pleasure if you're just training the cast-off yearlings. We were struggling to win a race. The moment the classic entries used to come up, we would have a long conversation about what we were going to put in the classics. One's never had anything that's well enough bred to consider putting in a classic. We've had rubbish and all the best ones have gone to Ilsley.'

Although his departure as one of the Queen's trainers was not accompanied by the acrimony and rancour associated with the sacking of Major Dick Hern, the longest serving royal trainer of the twentieth century makes little effort to

The Glums: Ian Balding, The Queen and Lord Carnarvon have had little to celebrate in recent years.

conceal his opinion of the Queen's racing manager, the Earl of Carnarvon. And it is not just the circumstances of Hern's dismissal which have nurtured ill feeling, although Balding's support for the Major was almost certainly a decisive factor. The animal that crystallized his feelings was Insular, a grand servant in both the Queen's colours and in those of Queen Elizabeth the Queen Mother for whom he was a brave and battling winner of the William Hill Imperial Cup at Sandown in 1986. He was a son of Pas de Deux, the only foal of Balding's high-class filly Example, and, as such, a tangible reminder of more successful times for the royal owner at Kingsclere. The bay gelding, who had won eight races for the Queen, had returned to the flat but had put in a couple of bad performances when Lord Carnarvon contacted Balding in May 1988. The trainer recalls, 'It was extraordinary and embarrassing. He rings me up and says, "That horse must either be put down or he can be given to you as an apprentice horse." I couldn't believe it. I said, "Well he owes nobody anything. You can't put him down just because he's run two bad races. I'd love to have him as an apprentice horse, obviously."'

Shortly after Insular was transferred into his ownership Balding was rung by Reg Griffin, the chairman of Timeform, who asked him if he would consider entering the horse in the Queen Mother Cup on Timeform Charity Day at York in June. Griffin had the excellent thought that Insular could run in the Queen's colours and be ridden by Princess Anne. It would generate great interest and be good publicity for the event. Balding had to tell him that, sadly, Insular would have to run in his own turquoise-blue and brown colours but he would certainly ask Princess Anne to ride. He recalls, 'She came down, rode him at home and was absolutely thrilled to ride him in the race. I remember ringing Lord Carnarvon up before the race and saying, "Would you like him to run in the

Princess Anne, wearing Ian Balding's colours, after the Queen's former gelding Insular's win in the Queen Mother Cup at York, 11 June 1988.

Queen's colours for this race because I can fix it?" He said, "Certainly not. In your colours and he's your responsibility." Those were the very words.'

In the race itself Princess Anne held the horse up, four or five lengths behind a fast pace, came through one-and-a-half furlongs out and strode clear to win very easily by 12 lengths. Afterwards the Princess modestly said, 'Insular knows more about racing than I do. I just sat and let him get on with it.' A delighted, if slightly embarrassed, Balding picked up £8000 in prize money and a similar amount the next time Insular ran at Sandown, when he won a handicap. During a lunch at Windsor soon afterwards, Balding was placed next to the Queen and the subject of Insular came up. The Queen told him how pleased she had been when he had won for Princess Anne, although she had been less delighted when he won his next race, again not wearing the royal colours. Balding admits, 'I wasn't brave enough to say, "It's all your stupid manager's fault".' Insular, at 21, is still a much loved resident at Kingsclere where he enjoys an honourable retirement as a companion to the younger horses.

Balding, unusually for a royal trainer, did not have a military background. He was, however, an accomplished athlete rather in the manner of Peter Cazalet. He played rugby union for Cambridge and Bath and also boxed for his university. As an amateur rider he won the National Hunt Chase at Cheltenham in 1962 on a horse called Time. He enjoyed a mercurial rise to the top of the tree thanks to Mill Reef and the patronage of his owner, the American millionaire Paul

Mellon, whose horses were far more successful than the Queen's at Kingsclere. Silly Season, Glint of Gold and Diamond Shoal were just three of Mellon's superb colts. Balding also trained Lochsong, one of the most popular sprinters of recent times.

Not everything was doom and gloom for the royal residents of Kingsclere over the years. Soprano was just beaten by Al Bahathri and Top Socialite in a desperately close finish to the Coronation Stakes at Ascot in 1985 and was, reflects Balding, just about the best filly he has trained. Spring to Action was another who was just short of top class. He ran in a graduation race at Beverley in Yorkshire early in the 1993 season and was narrowly beaten by a colt called White Muzzle, trained by Peter Chapple-Hyam. On dismounting, jockey Gary Carter told Balding that the winner would never beat them again. White Muzzle went on to win the Italian Derby and was one of the outstanding colts of the year. Spring to Action did manage a victory in a listed race at Newmarket, but at the end of the year was not even given a rating in the international classification for three-year-olds which placed White Muzzle joint-first in the 11 furlongs + category. Timeform rated Spring to Action fully 22 lbs below White Muzzle. Sometimes jockeys can get it laughably wrong.

Balding remains a great admirer of the Queen's affinity with horses. She once gave him a Shetland pony which both Prince Charles and Princess Anne used to ride and whenever she visited Kingsclere would always make a point of going to see the pony. She would also look at the horses belonging to her mother. Balding observes, 'They both enjoy each other's successes. And they talk about it a lot together. The Queen is an expert and a brilliant horsewoman. She could have trained.'

He still trains three horses for Queen Elizabeth so the royal connection at Kingsclere is not totally severed. Two of them – Double Brandy and Cherry Brandy – were bred at Sandringham from a former mare of the Queen's called Brand. Balding is particularly hopeful that Double Brandy, an athletic chestnut gelding, can pick up a nice handicap or two over a mile. Even though she is a jumping owner Queen Elizabeth is also a great fan of flat racing. Hopefully, therefore, royal winners will continue to be sent out from the historic stables of Kingsclere.

The last in the famous scarlet and purple colours of the Queen was Dancing Image, who bolted up in the Trundle Limited Stakes on the last day of Glorious Goodwood in 1997. Balding recalls, 'I rang the Queen and she was thrilled

Opposite: The unmistakable flying dismount of Frankie Dettori after Dancing Image has provided Ian Balding with his last winner as a royal trainer in the Trundle Condition Stakes at Goodwood, 2 August 1997.

to bits. And we discussed his previous races and his possible next race and so on. And then I get a phone call saying they've sold the horse.'

❧The Purple Patch

The Queen moved quickly to replace Lord Huntingdon when he decided to retire towards the end of the 1998 season. It had been a question of economics. The royal trainer was losing money at West Ilsley and the honour of training for the Queen does not pay the bills. He left to live in Australia where in late 1999 he needed a life-saving operation for heart and lung problems. Fifteen clots were removed from his lungs but thankfully he made a remarkable recovery. His departure led to an important change in royal racing. Within a week of the announcement that Huntingdon was going, Lord Carnarvon contacted Sir Michael Stoute and Richard Hannon, who trains at East Everleigh Stables near Marlborough, and invited them to train for the Queen. Clearly Huntingdon was not going to be replaced at West Ilsley and the yard was sold to Mick Channon for a reported £2 million. Colin Mackenzie, writing in the *Daily Mail*, described the sale as a startling parable of our times: 'A man born in a two-up, two-down council house in a tiny hamlet has just bought the Queen's magnificent stables at West Ilsley in the Royal County of Berkshire.'

The change of stables for the Queen was inspired. Of Sir Michael Stoute's first eight royal runners, six won, including a Royal Ascot victory for the regally bred colt Blueprint that was one of the most popular royal victories for many years. At least, by appointing Stoute as her principal trainer, the Queen will not have the problem of whether to recommend him for a knighthood. The present master of Freemason Lodge already has one. There is a satisfying symmetry about the Queen returning to Freemason Lodge, and the burst of success seems to hark all the way back to the golden age of Aureole and the other fine horses of the Fifties.

Although he is a pillar of the British racing establishment Sir Michael, like Boyd-Rochfort before him, does not hail from the United Kingdom. He was born in Barbados where his father was commissioner of police. (His knighthood in 1998 was in fact for 'services to sport tourism in Barbados'.) His love of racing grew because the island's renowned Garrison Savannah racetrack was conveniently near the family home. He came to this country aged 20 to work at Pat Rohan's stable at Malton in Yorkshire, although at the time he would probably have swapped

Richard Hannon has made a smart start to his career as a royal trainer.

a career in racing for playing test cricket alongside Gary Sobers and Clive Lloyd. He nearly failed to start a training career at all when he was short-listed for the position of BBC racing correspondent. Julian Wilson got the job and Michael Stoute embarked on a path to five training championships and care of one of the most famous horses of all time, the Aga Khan's Shergar.

He began training at Newmarket in 1972 and captured his first classic when Fair Salinia won the Oaks in 1978. Three years later came Shergar's unforgettable Derby triumph when he cantered away from the opposition. Michael Stoute was on his way to the very top. Excluding the unique Godolphin operation of Sheikh Mohammed and the Maktoum family of Dubai, only Henry Cecil can match his phenomenal level of success in the past 20 years, although Richard Hannon and John Dunlop would not be too far behind. Sir Michael particularly excels in gradually improving a horse each year.

Sir Michael Stoute (right) shares a joke with Henry Cecil.

He did it with Pilsudski and Singspiel, first and second in the 1996 Breeders Cup Turf as four-year-olds. While Blueprint could not match those heights, the colt had no pretensions to being a group winner when he was a modest inmate of Lord Huntingdon's West Ilsley stable. He took his chance in the Duke of Edinburgh Handicap on a bright sunny Wednesday at Royal Ascot in 1999, ridden by Gary Stevens, the renowned American jockey who spent an all-too-brief summer riding for Stoute. Stevens's stay in Britain was reminiscent of that of the Australian jockey George Moore in 1967. He impressed everyone with his masterful judgement of pace and his ride on Blueprint was no exception. Close up behind the pace early on, he moved the colt, a 4/1 favourite, into the lead soon after turning into the straight and swept majestically clear. Ten days later, guided by Frankie Dettori this

Richard Hannon watches his string on the gallops at East Everleigh.

time, Blueprint moved up a grade to listed company to win the Fred Archer Stakes at Newmarket.

Blueprint's June victories were part of a wonderful purple patch for the Queen which yielded seven winners in just 17 days. Besides Blueprint, both Holly Blue and Fairy Godmother were sent out by Roger Charlton to win listed races, which gives them what is known as 'black type', essential for the market value of a potential brood mare or stallion. Stoute also managed a listed win for the filly Fictitious in the same month, although she left Freemason Lodge in September to join the American stables of Christophe Clement. It was a daring departure for a royal runner but proved a sensational one when she won a race at Calder in Florida on Christmas Eve.

The 2000 season saw the Queen with a superb string of horses in training. Although none, as yet, compared with Highclere or Dunfermline Sir Michael Oswald says, 'I am very proud of them because I was stud manager when they started'. They represent a happy legacy for Sir Michael, who retired at the end of the 1998 season to be succeeded by Joe Grimwade. The intriguing aspect of the horses in training is that the sires read like a *Who's Who* of the current crop of stallions – Sadler's Wells, Rainbow Quest and Fairy King

Royal Racing

among them. Sir Michael Oswald explains, 'There has been a shift in the balance of power over the past seven or eight years from America back over to Europe. The Coolmore Stud in Ireland and the various Arab studs around Newmarket are now the best in the world.' The Queen's leading brood mare of today, Highbrow, would rank highly alongside her best of all time. In three successive years the horse has produced Blueprint, Fairy Godmother and Request.

Blueprint himself went from strength to strength, and improved yet another grade when he won the Group Two Sagitta Jockey Club Stakes on his first outing of the 2000 season. He was then unsentimentally sold to the USA.

❧ Unsung Heroes

When Queen Elizabeth's promising young horse Sorrento saw a racecourse for the first time on a chilly May afternoon last year at picturesque Worcester, he embodied all the ingredients that make up a royal winner. First and foremost he had been given time. Even in her 100th year Queen Elizabeth is in no hurry to rush her horses on to the racetrack because, as all lovers of horse-racing know, there is so much more to the sport than the thrill of victory and the well-planned raid on the bookmakers' satchels.

The magnificent stallion Bustino in his paddock at the Royal Stud, Wolferton.

Sorrento is following a trend of homebred horses for Queen Elizabeth. Unlike her daughter, she has relied on astutely bought animals for most of her career but now enjoys following a horse's career from the moment it is foaled at Sandringham. As Sir Michael Oswald observes, 'To buy a horse in cold blood at the sales costs a fortune these days.'

Sorrento is by Neltino out of Lunabelle, who had won one hurdle race and one chase when trained for Queen Elizabeth by Ian Balding. Neltino was a son of Queen Elizabeth's great favourite, Bustino,

and looked likely to prove a successful jumping sire, but unfortunately became prematurely infertile. Queen Elizabeth first saw Sorrento on her July visit to Sandringham in 1996. After being weaned, he was taken the few miles along the road to the Raynham estate of Lord Townshend to be looked after by the inimitable Mrs Sylvia Palmer, described by an appreciative Sir Michael as 'the original horse nanny'.

Sir Michael, who was knighted in 1998, lives close by and is able to keep a watchful eye on the progress of Queen Elizabeth's horses. Now retired as director of the Royal Stud, he is ever present when one of her horses runs and he and his wife, Lady Angela, lady-in-waiting to the Queen Mother, are very influential in maintaining her enthusiasm for the sport. Sorrento stayed in the care of Mrs Palmer until the late summer of his second year. Sir Michael enthuses, 'She is a very hard-working lady and Queen Elizabeth is very fond of her. They share an enthusiasm for homeopathic remedies and Mrs Palmer has often proved the vets wrong. She has her own remedy for heel bug, a sort of fungal infection in very wet weather, which has the vets baffled. But it works.'

By this time Sorrento was ready for his stay at the 700-acre farm of Captain Charles Radclyffe at Lew near Oxford. Now in his 80s, Captain Radclyffe is one of the unsung heroes of racing who has broken in some of the most popular horses of recent years: Corbiere, Morley Street and Mole Board are just three of the household names who learnt their jumping trade charging around his loose school. Such is Radclyffe's reputation within racing that the inestimable Martin Pipe has sent many horses to him, including the game grey, Baron Blakeney, who first brought Pipe to everyone's notice when he won the 1981 Daily Express Triumph Hurdle at Cheltenham. Pipe was so impressed by Radclyffe's schooling ring that he vowed he was going to go away and build one for himself. The captain also has the unenviable record of being the man who just missed out on buying both Arkle and Mill House in the same season.

Radclyffe had assumed the mantle of Major Eldred Wilson in Queen Elizabeth's racing operation in the mid 1980s. He explains, 'The horses come here as two-year-olds. They are so well handled up at Raynham that they are

Top: Jockey David Harrison is determined to claim a royal victory aboard the grey Arabian Story in the Steventon Stakes at Newbury, 19 July 1997.

Above: Captain Charles Radclyffe, one of the unsung heroes of royal racing.

Royal Racing

really half-broken by the time they get here. We get them broken in thoroughly here. They start off being driven around a paddock with no saddle. Then they try some road work to get them used to light traffic and noise before we teach them to jump.' The 'classroom', or loose school as it is called, is a surprisingly small, circular, covered building with two fences at three and nine o'clock. A pulley system adjusts the height of the fences which are covered in layers of foam rubber, the sort of material that used to cushion the fall in a pole-vault pit. 'You don't want a horse doing a knee the first time he jumps,' declares the no-nonsense captain, who likes to run his establishment like a military operation, just as the majority of those involved in royal racing have preferred to do.

Sorrento, a very well-made brown horse, was quickly established as the apple of Captain Radclyffe's eye and the one everyone wanted to see put through his paces when Queen Elizabeth made her annual trip to Lew in April. This is the occasion when Raymond Blanc travels the 20 miles from Le Manoir to prepare lunch. To whet their appetites, guests watch the horses in the loose school. Sir Michael Oswald observes, 'It is a hair-raising performance.

Sorrento [Mick Fitzgerald] runs out a game winner of his first national hunt flat race at Worcester, 24 May 2000.

Part Six ✸ A Thousand Winners

Easter Ross [Mick Fitzgerald] makes his way out onto the course for the Coral Cup at Cheltenham, 17 March 1999.

First of all we see them ridden, usually bare-backed in a covered yard. Then they go riderless round this loose school. We all stand in the middle and there is a fearful clatteration as they whirl round. It certainly makes them pretty quick on their feet.'

Afterwards Queen Elizabeth, Sir Michael and Captain Radclyffe discuss the options for each horse. If the animal is still backward it might return to Raynham for another year, or go to Mary Crouch who has a stable on the

Royal Racing

north side of the Ridgeway in Wiltshire where the horses can do plenty of work up hills and down dales. Sorrento stayed with Charles Radclyffe for the summer to avoid getting too fat before being sent to Nicky Henderson for serious training. Every autumn Queen Elizabeth visits the trainer's yard to watch the horses on the Lambourn gallops. Henderson explains, 'She loves to come and see them, especially at the beginning of the season because it gives her the chance to look at the horses before it all begins.'

Sorrento impressed Henderson as a decent prospect from the start and the most forward of that year's crop of royal runners. He was, however, very young and needed time to prepare for his first run. He had two jaunts to the racecourse in April 2000 without racing. On the first occasion he behaved very badly and was reluctant to go into his horsebox. By the time he was ready to actually race at Worcester the following month he was behaving like an old sheep. He started second favourite at 11/4 in a field of 15 for a bumper, a National Hunt flat race for horses who have never run on the flat. They are designed to give inexperienced animals an education.

Henderson's stable jockey, the brilliant horseman Mick Fitzgerald, held Sorrento up on the heels of the leaders, reluctant to give away too much ground on going that, while described as good, was quite tiring. The royal colours could be seen moving up five furlongs out and quickening smoothly into the lead in the straight. The Sue-Smith-trained After the Boys challenged strongly but Sorrento, showing a good attitude, held on by a head, the pair clear in a good time. It was an ideal introduction and Sir Michael was delighted: 'He travelled well but was very green and pricked his ears in front. Even though he only won by a head, he held off the second quite comfortably.' All the painstaking and patient preparation over four years had reached a perfect conclusion in just three minutes and 47 seconds.

To round off what he hoped would be a highly satisfactory day Sir Michael sped off to watch Easter Ross take part in a hurdle race at Uttoxeter. Like Sorrento, the gelding was homebred and, just a few months earlier, had looked up to Cheltenham standard when, jumping superbly, he bolted up in his first chase at Kempton Park. He was beaten but ran very creditably at Sandown next time out although, for some unknown reason, he gave each fence a good three feet of air when he cleared them. At Taunton in Somerset he was never travelling well and connections were concerned that he might have a bug. Schooling at home over fences, however, he appeared to have lost his nerve for some reason so was running back over hurdles to regain some confidence. He jumped the first four flights at Uttoxeter well, but never showed any enthusiasm and dropped progressively further behind horses he might well have expected to beat a season before. John Kavanagh wisely pulled him up. A disappointed Sir Michael declares, 'He is one hell of a problem.'

ᘐ Reflections

A former Bradford drain-digger called Stewart Andrew went to Newbury for the 1999 Hennessy Cognac Gold Cup hopeful of a good showing from his strapping and hugely talented chaser Ever Blessed. The seven-year-old was backed down to 9/2 and stayed on from the last fence for a three-and-a-half-length triumph. Stewart Andrew, still sporting the imposing stature of a rugby league wing forward, was jubilant. These days he has swapped his council overalls for business suits and runs his own plastics-recycling company, employing 12 men.

'I'm doing all right now,' he told the assembled press. 'I've done all sorts and was on the dole for a while. But I'm just an ordinary bloke and who would have thought I'd be standing here next to the Queen Mum.'

Queen Elizabeth the Queen Mother, in her 100th year, had made his day. She attended the race, one of her favourites, to present the trophy and make the day not just for the owner but also for many thousands of racegoers. It is too easy to knock the affection the racing world has for her as oversentimental and toadying to the aristocracy. Although the sport has an enormous legacy of class structure, the regard for Queen Elizabeth is very real. There is a special cheer when one of her horses wins. Everyone wants to catch a glimpse of her and, because of her great age, they are mindful of the efforts she makes to attend. As Jack Logan wrote in *The Sporting Life* after the death of Game Spirit, 'If there is a shorter cut to a bloody nose in Tattersalls than to criticise the Queen Mother in any way, I do not know it.'

Queen Elizabeth's enthusiasm for the sport is not just evident in public or in front of photographers. A few years ago she was unable to present the trophy for the Queen Mother Champion Chase at Cheltenham to the owner of

Remittance Man, Tim Collins. Instead, Mr Collins was invited to the home of Charles Radclyffe where she was having lunch. He joined the party for drinks in the garden and was presented with his trophy there. Captain Radclyffe observes, 'That is so typical of Queen Elizabeth. She recognizes the enormous pleasure the owners would get from that gesture.'

Queen Elizabeth has absorbed herself totally in racing. She has become part of it. Cath Walwyn explains: 'Racing offers so much. It's a world of its own. There's all the horses to think of, the breeding and watching them even when you don't have a runner. Every day she used to read the *The Sporting Life* – now, it's the *Racing Post* – and read it from top to bottom. She loves her day's racing. She loves talking to the jockeys and finding out their versions of what happens.'

Nicky Henderson recalls an example of her enthusiasm when he and his wife, Diana, joined her and Sir Michael Oswald for lunch at the Berkeley Hotel in London. Realizing that they would miss watching a race in which they had a runner, and with no racing channel on hand, the party decided to rush back to Clarence House: 'Michael and Queen Elizabeth sped off in her official limo. Diana and I had to get into a taxi. I had the great pleasure of saying, "Follow that car!"'

The Queen holds her great mare Dunfermline outside the gates of the Royal Stud at Sandringham in May 1986. Michael Oswald, on her left, is holding Time Charter.

Part Six ∽ A Thousand Winners

and we tore off after them. The driver was rather bemused when we went through the big gates of Clarence House. But we all saw the race on her television.'

In the world of racing the two royal owners are very different people. Lord Oaksey observes, 'There is a big difference between the public perception of the Queen and the Queen Mother. While they acknowledge the Queen's knowledge and expertise, they just love the Queen Mother. The relationship is far warmer between the Queen Mother and her trainers, her jockeys and just about everybody.'

Sadly the Queen may never fully cast off the shadow of the Dick Hern affair. Her duties as monarch and the almost compulsory remoteness of that role make it difficult to repair bridges with the racing community. It is obvious, however, that she shares her mother's enthusiasm for the sport. A busy schedule has restricted the amount of time she can devote to going racing but it would be wonderful if, in the future, she could follow her mother's example by presenting the trophy for some of the top races in the calendar. Perhaps Stewart Andrew and other owners could be just as thrilled to receive a trophy from the Queen as they are when they receive one from the Queen Mother.

Racing is clearly a more serious occupation for the Queen, who has always taken pains to run her interests as a business, than it is for Queen Elizabeth. Sir Michael Oswald does not think it would be thought appropriate for her to start 'splashing out like a Middle Eastern potentate'. There are hopeful signs that a better stamp of stallion is now being used for the royal brood mares but in world terms the Queen cannot compete with the Arab interests. She might have 15 foals in a year at the Royal Studs where the major Arab owners would have a couple of hundred. Sir Michael observes, 'She is a minnow in a very big pond.'

The Queen is a superb horsewoman and perhaps has a greater affinity with the horses than she does with many of the people in racing. We are only given occasional glimpses of just how much the sport means to her. Her delight at the exploits of Highclere springs to mind. However, her support of racing should not be taken lightly. Henry Cecil concedes, 'There would be a great emptiness in racing without the Queen. She is the head of our racing'. In these commercially minded days, the sport does not necessarily need royal patronage to provide it with charisma and glamour. Frankie Dettori, John Francome, Richard Johnson, Sir Alex Ferguson and Alex Hammond take care of that

Queen Elizabeth acknowledges the crowd on her way to the parade ring at Royal Ascot in June 1996. Her lady in waiting, Lady Angela Oswald, is walking next to her.

side of things. But as Colin Mackenzie, senior racing correspondent of the *Daily Mail*, acknowledges, 'We are a sentimental nation and we like nothing better than to throw our hats in the air for a royal winner. Both the Queen and the Queen Mother are the best public relations racing has.'

The Queen and the Queen Mother, who have had more than 1000 winners between them since Monaveen more than 50 years ago, take a great deal of interest in each other's racing affairs. After a particularly lean season for Queen Elizabeth at Fairlawne one year, the Queen offered to pay Peter Cazalet's account. Her mother accepted gratefully and signed her name at the bottom of the bill. Before sending it off to Buckingham Palace she had an afterthought and wrote underneath the amount, 'Oh dear!'

In the words of Cath Walwyn, 'What are we going to do without her?'

Bibliography and Sources

PART ONE

Cathcart, Mrs Helen, *The Queen and the Turf*, Stanley Paul, 1959

Childs, Joe, *My Racing Reminiscences*, Hutchinson's Library of Sports and Pastimes, 1952

Day, J. Wentworth, *King George V as a Sportsman*, Cassell, 1935

FitzGerald, Arthur, *Royal Thoroughbreds: A History of the Royal Studs*, Sidgwick and Jackson, 1990

Lee, Sir Sidney, *King Edward VII: A Biography* (volumes 1 and 2), Macmillan, 1927

Magnus, Philip, *King Edward VII*, John Murray, 1964

Rose, Kenneth, *King George V*, Weidenfeld and Nicolson, 1983

Seth-Smith, Michael, *Bred for the Purple: A History of the Monarchy and the Turf*, Leslie Frewin, 1969

Smith, Horace, *A Horseman through Six Reigns*, Odhams Press, 1955

PART TWO

Chapman, Frank, *Two Families at Fairlawne: The Story of the Vanes and the Cazalets*, Published by the author at Martins Oast, Shipbourne, Kent, 1998

Curling, Bill, *Royal Champion*, Michael Joseph, 1980

Davies, Paul, *The Anthony Mildmay–Peter Cazalet Memorial Handicap Chase 1951–99, The Complete Record*, 1999

Donaldson, Frances, *Yours, Plum: The Letters of P.G. Wodehouse*, Hutchinson, 1990

FitzGerald, Arthur, *400 Races Won*, M.R. Designs (private publication), Newmarket, 1994

Francis, Dick, *The Sport of Queens*, Michael Joseph, 1957 (Fourth revised edition 1988)

Herbert, Ivor, *The Queen Mother's Horses*, Pelham Books, 1967

Mortimer, Roger, *Anthony Mildmay*, Macgibbon & Kee (published on behalf of the family), 1956

Seth-Smith, Michael; Willett, Peter; Mortimer, Roger and Lawrence, John, *The History of Steeplechasing*, Michael Joseph, 1966

PART THREE

Carr, Harry, *Queen's Jockey*, Stanley Paul, 1966

Curling, Bill, *All the Queen's Horses*, Chatto & Windus, 1978

Curling, Bill, *The Captain: A Biography of Captain Sir Cecil Boyd Rochfort – Royal Trainer*, Barrie & Jenkins, 1970

Hughes, John, *My Greatest Race*, Michael Joseph, 1979

Mortimer, Roger, *The Flat*, George Allen & Unwin, 1979

Mortimer, Roger; Onslow, Richard and Willett, Peter, *Biographical Encyclopaedia of British Flat Racing*, Macdonald and Jane's, 1978

Piggott, Lester, *Lester: The Autobiography of Lester Piggott*, Partridge Press, 1995

Smith, Eph, *Riding to Win*, Stanley Paul, 1968

PART FOUR

Fuller, Bryony, *Fulke Walwyn: A Pictorial Tribute*, Lambourn Publications, 1990

PART FIVE

Baerlein, Richard and Cattermole, Mike, *Joe Mercer: The Pictorial Biography*, Macdonald/Queen Anne Press, 1987

Carson, Willie and Scott, Brough, *Up Front: A Racing Autobiography*, Stanley Paul, 1993

FitzGerald, Arthur, *Thoroughbreds of the Crown: The History and Worldwide Influence of the Royal Studs*, Genesis Grand History Series (limited edition), 1999

Pope, Michael, *All Such Fun*, The Sporting Life, 1992

Seely, Michael, *Willie Carson: The Illustrated Biography*, Headline, 1991

Willett Peter, *Dick Hern: The Authorised Biography*, Hodder, 2000

PART SIX

Laird, Dorothy, *Royal Ascot*, Hodder and Stoughton, 1976

Magee, Sean, *The Channel Four Book of Racing*, Sidgwick & Jackson, 1989 (revised 1995)

Pickering, Martin, *Directory of the Turf*, Pacemaker Communications Ltd, 1990 & 1997

ADDITIONAL SOURCES

Archive of *The Sporting Life*, National Newspaper Library, Colindale, London

Raceform *Horses In Training*

Royal Champion, Carlton (formerly Central) Television: Producer, Gary Newbon, 1987

www.racingpost.co.uk

∼ Index

Page numbers in italics refer to illustrations

❧ Index of Racehorses *Page numbers in italics refer to illustrations*

Picture Credits

BBC Worldwide would like to thank the following for providing photographs and for permission to reproduce copyright material. While every effort has been made to trace and acknowledge all copyright holders, we would like to apologize should there have been any errors or omission.

Camera Press pages 120T, 168

Cazalet Family 40/1T, 48, 60, 63, 64, 71, 81, 83, 86, 143

Gerry Cranham 12/13T, 13B2, 14, 16, 17, 85, 88/9T, 113, 120B, 123B1, 126, 131, 139, 145, 154, 156, 157, 159, 161, 164, 170, 173, 188, 189T, 191, 197, 198, 208M, 210, 217, 220, 226, 228T, 230, 235

Bernard Gourier 183

David Hastings 122M, 136, 163B3, 189B, 199T, 201, 224

Hulton Getty 12M, 18, 21, 24T, 27, 32, 34, 45, 55, 56B, 72, 96, 102, 105, 127, 186

Les Hurley 229

Trevor Jones Thoroughbred Photography 6/7, 24B, 204, 206, 215, 221, 225

Le Manoir Aux Quat' Saisons 213

Mirror Syndication 56T, 58, 88M, 103, 109, 162/3T

Laurie Morton 233

PA Photos 37, 39, 42, 44, 53, 87, 90, 94, 101, 110, 171, 177, 181, 199B

Bernard Parkin 11, 52, 67, 74, 78, 134B, 140, 148, 160, 202, 208/9T, 212

George Selwyn 122/3T, 124, 134T, 151, 175, 194, 195, 218, 222, 228B

Sport & General 34, 40M, 88B1, 115, 118, 146, 162M, 179, 192

Acknowledgements

This book has been a pleasure to write because of the generous help I have received from many people connected with racing. They have been happy to give up their time and share their stories of this great sport and its royal patrons.

Those I would like to especially mention are: Ian Balding, Raymond Blanc, Willie Carson, Edward Cazalet, Henry Cecil, Julie Cecil, Darkie Deacon, Andrew Franklin, Nicky Henderson, Dick Hern, Bruce Hobbs, John Kavanagh, Colin Mackenzie, Joe Mercer, Kevin Mooney, David Mould, Gary Newbon, Lord Oaksey, Sir Michael Oswald, Charles Radclyffe, Bill Smith and Cath Walwyn.

Thanks are also due to George Ennor who displayed great patience and expertise checking a mountain of racing facts and figures.

At BBC Worldwide Ben Dunn and Rachel Copus have given me great support. Susannah Parker did sterling work finding so many excellent pictures. I am also grateful to Zoë Lawrence for her help with the manuscript.